I0100652

THE
ANTI
ELITIST
CONSTITUTION

THE BI-PARTISAN ACTION PLAN TO UNIFY A DIVIDED NATION AND AVERT A SECOND CIVIL WAR

DAVID BARULICH

Published by Best Seller Publishing*, St. Augustine, FL
Best Seller Publishing* is a registered trademark.
Printed in the United States of America.
ISBN: 979-8-9912876-1-6

For more information, please write:
Best Seller Publishing, Inc.
53 Marine Street
St. Augustine, FL 32084
Or call 1 (626) 765-9750
Visit us online at: www.BestSellerPublishing.org
To contact the author, please write to davidbarulich@gmail.com

DEDICATION

To Daniel and Nadia, in honor of their service in the Marine Corps and the Army of the United States.

To my grandparents and mother — immigrants from the "Old Country" who always reminded me how lucky we are to be Americans.

To my father, who always preferred fostering peace and harmony over winning an argument.

AMERICAN PARTISANS' HYMN
(sung to the tune Bella Ciao)

We love our country
The greatest nation
It's so dear, raise a cheer, how we love it here
We venture onward
Into the future
To make it better once again

We love our freedom
It gives us power
To fight the fear, that is near, off the path we veer
Our constitution
Won't be defeated
Ameri-CANS will take a stand

In other nations
Not all lives matter
They sow the seeds for the creeds doing evil deeds
But this great nation
The people fight for
Their neighbors' peace and harmony

We are all equal
We must be grateful
So take a side, make a stride, please don't sob and cry
In this great nation
The future beckons
The Parti-SAN Ameri-CAN

TABLE OF CONTENTS

PART I

More Than Hope for a Change: Drafting and Ratifying a New Constitution

PREFACE

You can visit www.antielitistconstitution.com for the references to all numbered citations [#] throughout the book.

DEFINITIONS

The *1787 Constitution* was the document produced by the Constitutional Convention on September 17, 1787. It was sent to all thirteen States for ratification. It replaced the Articles of Confederation, America's first constitution, operative from February 2, 1781, to March 3, 1789.

The *1789 Constitution* was the 1787 Constitution, plus the Bill of Rights. Congress approved twelve amendments on September 25, 1789. Ten of those twelve amendments, the Bill of Rights, were ratified on December 15, 1791.

The *Principal Text* is the 1787 Constitution and twenty-seven amendments ratified from 1789 through 1992.

The *Auxiliary Text* comprises the canon of Supreme Court opinions that interpret the Principal Text and are cited most frequently by Supreme Court Justices to support their opinions. Others use the term *Unwritten Constitution*.

The *Elitist Constitution* comprises the Principal Text, the Auxiliary Text, history, structure, purpose, norms, and customs.

The *Elites* are the Justices of the Supreme Court, the Judges of the Federal and State Judiciaries, lawyers in the Justice Department and State Governments tasked with litigating Constitutional cases, litigators of

Constitutional law in private practice, professors of Constitutional law and politics, and the bureaucrats in federal and state agencies that draft and enforce regulations. Most are unelected persons whose opinions shape the Auxiliary Text's content and the Elitist Constitution's application to federal and state cases and controversies.

The Elites referenced in this book *are not* the billionaires, annual conference attendees in Davos, Switzerland, Council on Foreign Relations members, media company owners, writers, and video personalities.

Submissionists view political conflicts as moral struggles, attributing their opponents' disagreements to evil intentions and bad faith. They fight enemies and traitors, not loyal opposition. Their end game is unconditional surrender, like the surrender of the South to the North, which ended the Civil War in 1865.

Persuasionists view political conflicts as opportunities to compose well-reasoned arguments based on evidence to convince people to change their opinions. When Persuasionists fail to change opinions, they see this as an opportunity to improve their arguments. They do not treat their opponents like traitors or enemies. They seek solutions built on a foundation of shared values and compromise. The 1787 Constitutional Convention in Philadelphia was a meeting of Persuasionists.

Progressive refers to the left side of America's political spectrum. They tend to be Democrats or Socialists and support expanding the government's economic role.

Liberal refers to the left center, and *Neo-Conservative* refers to the right center of the political spectrum.

Conservative refers to the right side of the political spectrum who favor reducing the government's role in the economy, who tend to be Republicans and Libertarians (with apologies to Libertarians who reject being categorized as Conservatives).

Conservative Nationalists don't fit into this continuum of government intervention. They want to increase the government's role in enforcing religious values and regulating the economy to benefit Citizens most impacted by foreign competition and technological changes.

BACKGROUND INFORMATION

The book references the Declaration of Independence, the US Constitution, the Federalist Papers, and important Supreme Court cases. Without this background, you can still grasp the essential arguments about why the Constitution needs to be rewritten, but you will miss many of the steps in how the Constitution evolved.

The Declaration of Reformation in Chapter Two is modeled after the Declaration of Independence, so familiarity with it is essential.

An excellent primer on the foundations for our Constitutional conflicts is the video debate between Randy Barnett and Michael Dorf, entitled: *Has the US Constitution Lost Its Meaning? [1]*

For a more in-depth look at the protagonists in the debates over the Constitution, the following essays, articles, websites, and books from the Progressive and the Conservative sides of the political spectrum are the primary sources for the enumeration of grievances found in Chapter Two.

PROGRESSIVE CRITIQUES

Professor Sanford Levinson led a symposium of Progressive academics to draft a Progressive Constitution. [2]

Professor Levinson's essay *The Constitution Needs a Reboot* enumerates many flaws in the US Constitution from a Progressive perspective.[3]

The following writers continue these Progressive critiques:

Basav Sen *We Need a New Constitution* [4]

Dan Balz, *American democracy is cracking. These ideas could help repair it* [5]

The People's Parity Project [6]

David Leonhardt *A Crisis Coming': The Twin Threats to American Democracy* [7]

Mark Tushnet *An Open Letter to the Biden Administration on Popular Constitutionalism* [8]

Steven Levitsky Daniel Ziblatt *How American Democracy Fell So behind the rest of the World* [9] and *Tyranny of the Minority* [10]

The New Republic Rebuilding the Constitution [11]

Jill Lepore *Avoiding Constitutional Extinction* [12]

Terry Moe and William Howe *Our Outdated Constitution* [13]

George William Van Cleve *Making A New American Constitution* [14]

Sandy Levinson and Jack Balkin *Is the Constitution The Problem?* [15]

Al Carroll *How Would You Change The Constitution?* [16]

Mitchell Berman *Originalism Is Bunk* [17]

Thomas Colby *The Sacrifice of the New Originalism* [18]

Larry Sabato 23 *Proposals to Revitalize the US Constitution* [19]

Madibe Dennie *Originalism Is Going to Get Women Killed* [20]

Jedediah Purdy *The Left's Guide to Reclaiming the Constitution* [21]

Jamelle Bouelle *The Real Threat to Freedom Is Coming From the States* [22]

Ryan Doerfler and Samuel Moyn *The Constitution Is Broken And Should Not Be Reclaimed* [23]

Joseph Fishkin and William Forbath *Anti-Oligarchy Constitution* [24]

Ken Levy *Why The Late Justice Scalia Was Wrong* [25]

Edwin Chemerinsky's *Even the Founders Didn't Believe in Originalism* [26]

Corey Robin *Republicans Are Moving Rapidly to Cement Minority Rule. Blame the Constitution* [27]

Ezra Klein: *The crisis isn't too much polarization. It's too little democracy* [28]

CONSERVATIVE CRITIQUES

Randy Barnett *Bill of Federalism* [29]

Randy Barnett *Restoring the Lost Constitution* [30]

The Convention of the States [31]

William Voegeli *The Right Now* [32]

Sarah Isgur *It's Time To Amend the Constitution* [33]

John Daniel Davidson *We Need To Stop Calling Ourselves Conservatives. We are counter-revolutionaries* [34]

Jeff Anderson *"Our Democracy," Not Our Constitution* [35]

Glenn Ellmers *"Conservatism" Is No Longer Enough* [36]

Steven Gardbaum *New Deal Constitutionalism and the Unshackling Of the States* [37]

Charles Kesler *Crisis of the Two Constitutions* [38]

Larry Arnn *House Divided* [39]

Charles Kesler *America's Constitutional Crisis* [40]

John McGinnis and Mike Rappaport *Where Have All the Amendments Gone?* [41]

David Barulich
May 3, 2024
Pasadena, California

INTRODUCTION

We Are the Problem and the Solution

It's time to stop blaming "The Elites" and "The System." Instead, Moderate Middle Americans must grab the reigns of people's power endowed by the Framers to change our Elitist Constitution and create an Anti-Elitist Constitution.

The Elites are not *the problem*. The Elites respond to the challenges demanded by voters. We, the voters and Citizens, are *the problem* because we demand results that our system, built on our Constitution, cannot deliver. H.L. Mencken's aphorism, "Democracy is the theory that the common people know what they want, and deserve to get it good and hard," explains how we got into this mess.

It's crucial to understand that anti-elitism is not the same as Populism. Populism is a movement where the people are led by a charismatic figure, often swayed by emotional messages. In contrast, the Anti-Elitist Constitution is a movement driven by the people, not a single charismatic leader. Leaders will emerge, but their role is to organize a consensus for Persuasion.

Our movement is not about waiting for change to come from the top. It's about the people actively encouraging our elected representatives to fight for a new constitution. This movement is bottom-up, not top-down. It places the burden and responsibility of making changes on the people. The petition on www.antielitistconstitution.com is the first concrete step a reader can take to nudge our country in the right direction.

THE EXHAUSTED VOTER

The June 14, 2024, New York *Times* article, *In Pivotal West Michigan, Voters Are Exhausted and Underwhelmed,* [1] captures the mood of people clamoring for something — anything but Joe Biden and Donald Trump. The article concludes with Michele DeVoe Lussky's vow that, despite voting for Biden in 2020, she won't support either candidate in 2024. She is only one of several people profiled who shared the same frustration.

Are you an exhausted voter, No Labels fan, Never Trumper, Stop The Steal devotee, Ranked Choice Voting proselytizer, or someone else wondering how American politics became so rotten? Do you listen to Bill Maher and Joe Rogan commiserate with their guests on podcasts and television about the political shock troops treating their opponents as enemies, using language laced with venomous hatred?

You've come to the right place if you are disillusioned with American politics. The Anti-Elitist Constitution is not just a critique of the system but an antidote to the poison coursing through the veins of America's political system.

Let's take a closer look at the symptoms of our ailing political system: recurring government shutdowns, perpetual budget deficits, the January 6 Capitol invasion, a politicized Supreme Court, the disappearance of centrist members of Congress, the rise of coarse rhetoric, politically targeted investigations, a gridlocked Congress, special interests lobbying elected officials and bureaucrats, and the influence of dark money groups on pliable candidates. These are all signs of a nation veering off course, following a defective roadmap – our Constitution.

AN OLD IDEA MADE NEW AGAIN

Blaming the Constitution is an old American sport. In his 1885 treatise, *Congressional Government*, Woodrow Wilson complained about our separation of powers and a weak executive. He admired the British Parliamentary system's fusion of Executive and Legislative powers, enhancing political accountability.

The Old Idea was that constitutional reform could only occur by building a supermajority consensus. Since Woodrow Wilson, Herbert Croly, and Charles Beard, American intellectuals have discovered that irreverent critiques of the Framers and their handiwork are the modern fashion, easily performed from the armchair at a desk in a tenured university office or with a sinecure at an opinion journal. Getting out of the office to build a supermajority consensus to effect fundamental constitutional changes is much more taxing, so the Old Idea fell out of fashion.

The Preface contains a long list of books and essays blaming the Constitution for many problems while only a few offer concrete proposals to fix them. These recommendations are hyper-partisan, ideological proposals that could not ever get a majority vote in Congress, far short of the two-thirds majority necessary for submission to the State Legislatures for ratification by three-fourths of the states! Sara Isgur's proposal to amend Article 5 of the Constitution is the lone exception [9].

Each proposal pridefully rebukes the supermajority consensus required for adoption, neglecting this salient feature of constitutionalism in favor of preening. The 1787 Constitution was born after several contentious compromises, accommodating slave-holding and free states, rural and mercantile interests, and large and small states, so why should improving our Constitution in 2024 be any different?

Assuming the goal is improving the Constitution through peaceful means and regular order.

However, none of the authors of these proposals and critiques listed in the Preface intended to win Congress's supermajority support. These ideologues' blueprints strive to cement partisan policies beyond the reach of majority rule. All of them are dead on arrival.

Ideally, conservative and progressive Constitutional law and Political Science professors should have co-authored a version of the Anti-Elitist Constitution, which a prestigious university press should have published with detailed footnotes and an extensive index. However, that book was not written, so read on to discover why you are reading this book, written by an outsider instead.

Unfortunately, the incentives in academia, opinion magazines, and newspapers don't reward comity, consensus, and detailed, constructive proposals. Ideologues reading *The Atlantic, The Claremont Review of*

Books, the New York *Times*, the Washington *Post*, and the *Wall Street Journal* want excitement. They demand conflict. They prefer intellectual popcorn from the microwave instead of nutritious, full-course meals cooked on the stovetop and the oven.

You can read more paralysis by analysis and dead-on-arrival proposals in these "prestigious" journals of thought. Or, in Part Two of this book, you can dive into a detailed, feasible, bipartisan blueprint for the exhausted, Moderate Middle American voter to ignite the passion for constructive political action.

The Anti-Elitist Constitution revives the Old Idea of crafting a constitutional consensus. In Part Two, the author performs the mediator's role, writing the first draft of a new constitution to appease Conservative and Progressive partisans while building a structure that remedies the shortcomings of the Elitist Constitution. He constructed painstakingly a detailed document that could jump-start the work of a Blue-Ribbon Advisory panel of esteemed leaders and thinkers to draft a new constitution that could assemble two-thirds of Congressional support as James Madison's *Virginia Plan* did for the 1787 Philadelphia Convention.

BOOK OUTLINE

The book is divided into two parts. Part One contains the Preface, Introduction, and six chapters. The Preface includes essential definitions of terms used throughout the book.

Chapter One portrays January 6, 2021, as our generation's Apollo 13 moment. What began as a tragedy of our own making could end with a heroic rescue. January 6, 2021, could inspire Americans to unite in a noble mission to avert civil war by repairing their Constitution.

Chapter Two presents *The Declaration of Reformation*, a list of forty-one critical political problems and grievances. While it mimics the language of The Declaration of Independence, it is a rant and exhortation by American Citizens aimed at their fellow American Citizens, not King George III of Great Britain.

Chapter Three traces the history behind transforming the original 1787 Constitution into today's Elitist Constitution.

Chapter Four proposes a novel method for drafting and ratifying a new Constitution within the parameters of Article V of our Elitist Constitution. This chapter demonstrates that the only way to redress the forty-one grievances enumerated in Chapter Two is through negotiations, compromise, and tradeoffs. It presents the Grand Bargain outline that forms the basis for reaching a bi-partisan consensus for drafting an Anti-Elitist Constitution.

Chapter Five summarizes the core political tenets expressed by the Anti-Elitist Constitution.

Chapter Six catalogs portions of the Anti-Elitist Constitution motivated by economists' methods for structuring solutions, highlighting innovations to correct the flaws of our Elitist Constitution.

Part Two contains:

- The text of the first draft of an Anti-Elitist Constitution.
- A detailed exegesis of the Preamble and the text.
- Twenty-three articles comprised of two hundred thirty Sections and 36,360 words.

The exegesis explains the rationale for every Article and Section and how these sections pertain to the problems enumerated in The Declaration of Reformation and the terms of The Grand Bargain.

The website www.antielitistconstitution.com contains the end notes for the Preface, as well as Parts One and Two of the book.

Chapter One

America, We've Had a Problem

APOLLO 13: OVERCOMING ADVERSITY

On April 14, 1970 at 3:08:35 Greenwich Mean Time, 55 hours, 55 minutes, and 35 seconds after liftoff, Jim Lovell, the commander of Apollo 13, radioed this fateful message:

"Ah, Houston, we've had a problem." [1]

The "problem" was an explosion and rupture of oxygen tank number 2 in the service module of Apollo 13. The blast ruptured a line in oxygen tank number 1, causing it to lose oxygen rapidly. At the time, neither astronaut Jim Lovell nor Mission Control in Houston knew this was the problem.

Eighty-seven hours later, the Command Module splashed down in the Pacific Ocean 142 hours, 54 minutes, and 56 seconds after launch. The crew of Apollo 13 safely returned to Earth.

During those eighty-seven hours, the three astronauts and the Mission Control personnel devised solutions to unique and unexpected problems — problems they never expected or imagined would arise.

The entire world was captivated by the unfolding drama. Despite assassinations, Vietnam War protests, and race riots, the American public was riveted to their televisions, waiting for news about the fate of their astronauts. The astronauts and Mission Control united Americans in their support for a common purpose and their relief and pride when those astronauts returned safely to Earth. This rescue mission was a moment of national unity and pride, a testament to the strength of the American spirit.

Preparing for the movie *Apollo 13* [2], the scriptwriters interviewed Jerry Bostick, a Flight Controller on the Apollo 13 mission, to get a sense of what the people in Mission Control were like during these 87 hours. One of their questions was, 'Weren't there times when everybody, or at least a few people, just panicked?' Jerry answered, 'No, when bad things happened, we just calmly laid out all the options, and failure was not one of them.' This calmness and confidence in adversity made the Mission Control personnel heroes.

Those eighty-seven hours were the last time America exhibited pride, confidence, optimism, and swagger that it could conquer any challenge thrown in its path, and those eighty-seven hours Made America Great because Americans behaved as if failure was not an option for consideration.

JANUARY 6, 2021: OUR APOLLO 13 CHALLENGE?

Washington, D.C., January 6, 2021 — a day that will live in infamy. At 2:12 pm EST, the first rioters invaded the Capitol Building. At the same time, Senators and House Members assembled to certify the Electoral Vote count for President won by Joseph Biden. 5 hours and 48 minutes later, the US Capitol Police determined that the rioters had left and that the building was secure. On January 7, 3:32 am, Joseph Biden was officially certified to have won the presidential election.

Rather than despair, Americans should interpret January 6, 2021, as this generation's own Apollo 13 moment. January 6 should motivate us to demonstrate our best qualities as problem solvers facing seemingly impossible challenges. Today, America needs a committed group of Patriots, like the Apollo 13 Astronauts and the Mission Control staff in Houston, willing to adopt the mantra, "Failure Is Not An Option," to fix the flaws that failed to prevent January 6, 2021.

Because Trump's election in 2016 shattered the elite consensus about norms and customs, the plain text of an improved Constitution must deliver clear instructions and guidance to resolve disputes over Presidential elections and many other controversial matters enumerated in Chapter Two. January 6, 2021, exposed a leak in the oxygen tank of our government rocket Ship of State. That "leak" was caused by our Elitist Constitution and its reliance upon norms and customs followed by our elite governing classes.

When these norms are questioned, an Elitist Constitution cannot perform its mission because it depends upon the elite's adherence to unwritten norms to function. Once that consensus disappears, drafting a new Constitution is the only way to build a new consensus. We must restore the consensus to support our constitutional order to avert a looming Civil War at this moment in America's history. Ignoring these flaws ensures the recurrence of problematic, disputed Presidential election results during the 1876, 1960, 2000, 2004, and 2020 elections.

THE JANUARY 6, 2021, STRESS TEST FAILURE

America's system for electing its President embedded in its Elitist Constitution is an embarrassment for the United States. We have a faith-based system instead of an evidence-based system governing our elections.

Critics accuse Donald Trump of attempting a coup, going outside the law to overturn an election result. An alternative interpretation is that Trump exploited the weaknesses inherent in the Constitution's rules for presidential elections. January 6, 2021, was the stress test that fractured a fragile system, unable to withstand trampling upon the norms and customs that held it together.

> It all starts with the Constitution's Article II, Section 1:
>
> "Each State shall appoint in such Manner as the Legislature thereof may direct, a Number of Electors, equal to the whole Number of Senators and Representatives to which the State may be entitled in the Congress…"

> It continues with the 12th Amendment:
>
> "The Electors shall meet in their respective states, and vote by ballot for President and Vice President…and they shall make distinct lists of all persons voted for as President, and of

> all persons voted for as Vice-President, and of the number of votes for each, which lists they shall sign and certify, and transmit sealed to the seat of the government of the United States, directed to the President of the Senate; — The President of the Senate shall, in the presence of the Senate and House of Representatives, open all the certificates and the votes shall then be counted; — The person having the greatest number of votes for President shall be the President, if such number be a majority of the whole number of Electors, appointed…"

If no one received a majority of Electoral Votes, the House of Representatives would choose the President, where each State Delegation may cast one vote for one of the top three Electoral Vote recipients,

Who is absent from these procedures? None of this text mentions the voters or the State Secretaries certifying election returns, county registrars, State Supreme Court Justices, or other participants in the drama that unfolded between November 4, 2020, and January 6, 2021. The Framers of the Constitution established the chain of authority to originate with each State's Legislature, who then appoint Electors who then vote and submit their choices to the President of the Senate (the sitting Vice-President), who then opens the ballots to reveal the result. Obviously, the Constitution left out a lot of steps required to determine who will be the next President. The Framers in 1787 relied upon State Legislators, Governors, and Members of Congress to sort out these details of running elections for Federal offices.

Starting shortly after 1789, states began to allow their citizens to vote for President, and they used these results to guide the appointment of Electors. In 1832, South Carolina was the only State that had elected its electors without guidance from the voters. By 1880, every State had chosen its Electors based on the election results of its voters. Therefore, relying upon the voters has been a custom but not a written requirement in the text of the Constitution.

Likewise, when George Washington retired after two terms in office, he established a custom that no President serve more than two terms. That custom was ignored by Franklin Roosevelt in 1940 when he won a third term in office. It took the ratification of the 22nd Amendment to put this customary two-term limitation into writing.

The Supreme Court has had nine seats since 1869, but Franklin Roosevelt tried and failed to pack the Court with additional Justices. Frustrated by the Conservative rulings of the 2024 Supreme Court, Progressives likewise advocate for packing the Court in violation of unwritten norms.

Donald Trump followed this long tradition of violating norms, exploiting openings in the Constitution's text. His lawyers advised him that the Constitution's text gives State Legislatures the power to appoint Electors, neglecting to emphasize the phrase:

"Each State *shall appoint in such Manner as the Legislature thereof may direct….*"

Before the election, if the Legislature enacted laws delegating their powers to appoint Electors to their voters, most legal experts believe that the Legislators would have to abide by those laws and not arbitrarily revoke the "certified" verdict of the voters. However, if the Secretary of State or the State Supreme Court flouted these same laws [3], many Legislators and Trump's legal team believed this was the pretext for contesting a State's certified, official slate of Electors.

Trump hoped that Republican majorities in the Arizona, Georgia, Pennsylvania, Michigan, and Wisconsin Legislatures would reject the decisions of their Secretaries of State who certified Biden's victories. Trump's team hoped to create enough doubt about mail-in ballot fraud to give these Legislators the pretext to justify certifying a different slate of Electors.

Numerous writers have spilled too much ink about how close this nation came to a coup, but the outcome was never in doubt. The reason was that the political self-interest of every Republican State Legislator prevented them from reversing the verdicts of their State Election Officials.

Most of these Legislators knew they would be voted out of office at the next election if they brazenly overturned the norm and custom of following their voters' decisions. They could spin all they wanted about fraud, but without the smoking gun, never produced by Trump's team, they would never walk that plank into political oblivion.

The last remaining tool at Trump's disposal was to intervene in counting the Electoral Votes by the Vice President. Because the Electors voted on December 14, 2020, when they convened in their States to cast their votes, there was no suspense about who won. The Vice President performs a mere ministerial formality on January 6, 2021, when he counts these ballots. The only remaining suspense was if a member from the House and another from the Senate objected. Then, their objection could be debated [4]:

> "While the tellers announce the results, Members may object to the returns from any individual state as they are announced. Objections to individual state returns must be made in writing by at least one Member each of the Senate and House of Representatives. If an objection meets these requirements, the joint session recesses, and the two houses separate and debate the question in their respective chambers for a maximum of two hours. The two houses then vote separately to accept or reject the objection. They then reassemble in joint session, and announce the results of their respective votes. An objection to a state's electoral vote must be approved by both houses in order for any contested votes to be excluded."

The objection by the House and Senate members was the slim reed upon which Trump's hopes rested. However, the invasion of the Capitol and disruption of the proceedings incinerated any possibility that such an objection would prevail.

Nevertheless, the enthusiasm of the *Stop The Steal* [5] partisans has not diminished since 2020 because they continue to assert that many States continue to register non-citizens to vote, and these States count the votes of non-citizens, the deceased, and people who don't live in their district or their State.

Democrats are alarmed by the number of Republican State officials who deny that President Biden won the 2020 Election. Many of these officials occupy Governor's or Secretary of State offices that would have authority over the management of the 2024 Presidential Elections.

However, in 2020, these Democrats assured America there was no evidence of widespread electoral fraud. Even if ballots in Atlanta, Georgia, Detroit, Michigan, or Madison, Wisconsin, were counted by an overwhelmingly Democrat workforce in urban precincts who hated Donald Trump, you could rest assured this partisan workforce in these Swing States would correctly tabulate all the votes. In other words, "Trust but don't verify."

These contradictory narratives about the 2020 election reveal the shocking truth that America has a faith-based system of elections. Supporters of the faith-based system cannot independently verify the claims of election officials responsible for certifying results. Likewise, skeptics of this faith-based system lack the evidence to prove these election officials committed fraud or errors sufficient to overturn the results.

An analogy would be if the IRS could only order an audit of a taxpayer if the IRS already possessed evidence that the taxpayer needed to pay more taxes. But how would the IRS get the evidence to prove this suspicion without first doing an audit? The opponents of evidence-based voter registration and election systems use identical circular reasoning to swat away their critics with a "heads I win, tails you lose" argument. Without video footage or a confession by an insider who manipulated the ballots or vote counting, there is no way that an independent party could prove fraud or misconduct.

Therefore, Donald Trump has no way to prove that someone stole the election, and Joseph Biden has no way to confirm that the election was clean. Both sides must defer to the high priests, the elites who operate our elections and ballot counting, and place their faith in their pronouncements. This faith-based system is the fundamental truth that participants in this debate have yet to grasp. America's electoral controversies will continue until America builds an evidence-based system of elections.

Both sides of this debate refuse to engage in any constructive and practical recommendations [6] to eliminate the flaws that created doubts and fears about our elections.

For any evidence-based system, the burden of proof should be upon the managers of the voter registration, election operations, and ballot counting to produce an audit trail that could prove the following:

1. No mail-in ballots were opened to compromise the anonymity of the voters before delivery to the vote-counting facility
2. No counterfeit votes were manufactured and dumped into the pool of ballots
3. No non-citizens, under-age, deceased, or incarcerated persons' votes were counted

4. No one voted twice in an election
5. No ballots were destroyed or uncounted
6. No one coerced or bribed someone to vote for candidates on a mail-in ballot, and no one inspected that ballot before sealing the envelope and mailing it.
7. No one completed someone else's mail-in ballot and sent it in without their knowledge or consent.

Americans will cease fighting over Presidential elections after installing an evidence-based electoral system. Americans have grown too comfortable relying upon the elites, the courts, and partisan election officers to run our election system. If anyone still had doubts after the 2000 Presidential Election, then January 6, 2021, ended our smug confidence that a faith-based system was a dependable, noncontroversial method for a first-world nation to elect its President.

AMERICA'S ELITIST CONSTITUTION IS A BIG PROBLEM

These flaws in our federal election system are just the tip of the iceberg of the numerous deficiencies in the Elitist Constitution.

The recurring "shutdowns" of the Federal Government are more evidence for replacing our Constitution. As of April 2024, twenty-one shutdowns have occurred in the past fifty years [7].

The relentless growth of Government Debt due to Federal expenditures that have exceeded Federal tax revenues by increasing amounts since 2008 is another argument for blaming the Constitution.

The most compelling evidence for the case to replace America's Constitution would be the unending parade of controversies decided by stable, recurring ideological coalitions of Supreme Court Justices. There are larger protests outside the Supreme Court than occur outside the Capitol Building housing the Congress, our legislative branch tasked with making political decisions! There is something very wrong with this picture.

Political Pundits love to blame Presidents, Senators, and Representatives as incompetent or malevolent actors in a sprawling morality play of good versus evil. These pundits similarly describe Supreme Court Justices as partisan imposters masquerading as impartial tribunals. This cast of colorful characters frames compelling narratives in an easy-to-understand contest between justice and injustice.

However, this storyline has only one finale – the defeat and submission of the forces of evil to the forces of good, and it doesn't portend a peaceful ending.

The advocates for an Anti-Elitist Constitution tell a different story. They compare the federal government's performance with that of the States and democracies in Western Europe, and they believe that these comparisons yield clues that the source of the federal government's problems is its foundation—the Constitution. This story is like Apollo 13, where a team of characters is battling against circumstances created by their past mistakes. Will this cast of characters unite to rescue their team members, or will they devote their energies to winning the blame game?

These advocates envision a different storyline with a different finale—political opponents suspending their partisan combat long enough to peaceably convene writing a new rule book for playing a superior version of American politics. Because the elites' unwritten norms and customs have ceased working, it is time for political leaders to sit down and put things in writing so we don't repeat the same failure episodes.

These advocates must appeal to Moderate Middle Americans, the middle three-fifths of the political spectrum. They must rely on Persuasion and compromise to overcome their opponents' Submission tactics.

ARE WE REPEATING 1787 OR 1861?

In 1787 there was a universal sentiment among prominent political leaders that America's first Constitution, The Articles of Confederation, had to be fixed. These leaders had a unique bond forged through the Revolutionary War. Although each represented the parochial interests of their States and professions, they had a shared experience building a new nation, and these elites would not tolerate failure as an option after all the sacrifices they had made to attain independence from Great Britain.

Today, there is far less cohesion among the political factions that comprise America's ruling class among its elites and elected officials. Since the passing of the World War II generation, no shared experiences have united America's ruling class in the same way that the Revolutionary War and the Second World War did. The racial protests and riots of 2020 and the Capitol Invasion on January 6, 2021, have aroused foreboding of fundamental problems outside the realm of politics as usual. This foreboding has shaken Americans' confidence in the superiority and stability of their political system, and it has aroused the fear that we could lose everything we have taken for granted.

We should not let this crisis go to waste. This fear can unite the Moderate Middle Americans, who occupy the middle three-fifths of the political spectrum, to seize this 1787 Moment in Modern American History and recommit to those values and principles that have atrophied due to neglect. Drafting a new Anti-Elitist Constitution to replace our Elitist Constitution is the best exercise to renew the American Body Politic and avert the disintegration of a nation.

Getting into a room with political adversaries to build consensus is palliative politics. The psychological twist is that instead of scapegoating each other for their problems, these adversaries can blame their troubles on the rule book, the playing field conditions, or the incompetent umpires in politics. These are the beneficial effects of writing a new constitution.

This first draft of the Anti-Elitist Constitution could ignite a new passion for political reform, no longer confined by the cramped dimensions of our current Elitist Constitution. Like Madison's *Virginia Plan* [8] — this first draft of an Anti-Elitist Constitution would stimulate innovative proposals and constructive debates to replace our current Elitist Constitution.

The alternative to the 1787 Constitutional Convention is the 1861-1865 Civil War. In 1861, Americans had run out of ideas for compromise. There was no way to make accommodations for a growing nation that was half slave and half free, no way to maintain a political balance in the Congress between the slave states and the free states, and no grounds for Persuasion. Preserving the Union by force was one option. The other was a peaceful Secession.

Is America in an 1861 moment with irreconcilable political demands, or is America in a 1787 moment where Persuasion and compromise can create popular solutions that improve the conditions for the vast majority of the nation?

CONCLUSION

January 6, 2021, is like the Apollo 13 mission. It began as a tragedy but could end with a heroic rescue. January 6, 2021, could inspire Americans to unite in a noble mission to avert civil war by repairing their Constitution.

In place of this despair, there are remedies. Reminiscing about the Apollo 13 rescue, Americans can unite for a joint endeavor, and they should feel tremendous pride and optimism embarking upon this task. We don't promote national healing solely on compromise or conciliation but ambition. When Americans set their sights on achieving seemingly impossible goals, their differences become less relevant. These differences are not erased or ignored; they become less critical in pursuing a joint project. Americans will only regain their sense of solidarity with a shared sense of purpose.

Ben Franklin wrote, "Well done is better than well said." Following his counsel, this book is more than a hope for a change. Instead of the usual platitudes, analyses, and intellectual paralysis, it offers a tangible, detailed, and feasible bi-partisan proposal that can repair the fissures in America's political foundation, exposed during the violent protests of 2020 and culminating in the riot and invasion of the Capitol on January 6, 2021.

To repair these fissures in America's political foundation, Americans should begin working to draft a new Anti-Elitist Constitution that replaces America's current Elitist Constitution.

Chapter 2

The Declaration of Reformation

When, in the course of human events, it becomes necessary for this Nation's Citizens to repair the Political Bands that have connected them, they should declare the causes that have weakened these ties that have bound them together.

We hold this truth to be self-evident: that a free Citizenry endowed with representative Government must be ever vigilant to bequeath this legacy to their posterity. However, suppose this power to replace representatives does not alter the course of a government and is itself the cause of animosity among its Citizens. In that case, the value of that legacy is diminished, and the efficacy of endowing Citizens with self-government is in doubt. We have a Republic only if we can keep it.

Whenever any form of Government causes friction and conflict between its citizens, it is the right of the citizenry to alter or abolish it and institute a new government, laying the foundations for this new Government upon the lessons learned from their history.

Prudence, indeed, will dictate that Governments long established should not be changed for light and transient Causes, and accordingly, all Experience has shown we are more likely to suffer with the devil that we know rather than risk an encounter with a devil that we do not. But when the Citizens have finally surmised that their habit of blaming their problems on their representatives or each other has not remedied their recurring ailments, they realize that it is madness to repeat the same actions while expecting a different result.

Citizens must admit that they do not deserve to be governed as free people unless and until they exercise their power to alter their Constitution by collaborating and compromising with their fellow Citizens.

To prove this, let facts be submitted to a candid public of our shortcomings and the flaws in our Constitution:

1. Even though Congress has powers of Appropriation (Article 1, Section 9, clause 7 of the Constitution) and to borrow money on the credit of the United States (Article 1, Section 8, clause 2), it has failed to pass bills on a timely basis to prevent the shutdown of Government services.
2. Most of the budget is on autopilot, beyond the power of the current Congress to effect significant modifications to match revenues with expenses. Elections to transfer power have little effect on the course of the budget. Laws enacted in the past leave Congress very little discretion for changing current expenditures.
3. The Electorate rewards candidates for Congress and the Presidency who make binding promises for current expenditures that impose a large portion of the burden of paying for the present enjoyment of Government benefits upon our posterity, saddled with an ever-expanding public debt. Now is the first time that the public debt has exceeded the annual gross domestic output of the United States in peacetime, and it is projected to soar even higher.
4. Congress has delegated most of its law-making powers to the Executive and Judicial Branches by enacting vague and imprecise laws. This device evades accountability for interpreting and implementing these laws' vague and imprecise goals.
5. The descendants of American slaves and the Indigenous Tribes have suffered and continue to endure indignities and injustices at the hands of the Governments of this Nation and by their fellow Citizens.
6. Political discourse has coarsened. Partisans treat their competitors as enemies and traitors rather than as loyal opposition. This behavior turns every election and power transfer into a crisis filled with mistrust and fear that the victors will use their power to thwart the losers from winning a future election.

7. Partisans seek to use the law to categorize persons according to their immutable characteristics and to divide them into groups based on race, sex, sexual preferences, and other immutable traits rather than propound a unifying identity as Americans, persuadable by reason and evidence to decide matters as individuals.
8. The Supreme Court has become the most crucial policy-making branch of Government, exceeding its judicial role and undermining its authority and respect as an impartial arbiter of national controversies.
9. For several decades, the Stability of the Justices' Voting Coalitions on the Supreme Court in controversial cases undermined the notion that dispassionate legal reasoning formed the basis of their opinions. The Court acts like an unelected legislative body.
10. Some Members of Congress propose expanding the number of Supreme Court justices to alter the Court's ideological balance and eviscerate its role as a nonpartisan body. This Court-Packing scheme would violate over 150 years of precedence with Court Membership at nine Justices.
11. Many religious believers who advocate for the heterosexual marriage of only two persons, the separation of sexes in specific public spaces, and who oppose licentious sexual mores, abortion, and exposure of young children to sexual material face discrimination in Government institutions and legal prosecution and private discrimination for acts consistent with their moral beliefs.
12. Overcoming the high hurdles to amending the Constitution has encouraged the development of judicial doctrines that rationalize violations of the plain text whenever urgent and critical social phenomena demand policies absent in the plain text. This barrier has fostered the growth of an auxiliary Constitution, beyond the original text, that is understandable only to elite specialists interpreting the majority opinions in landmark decisions by the Supreme Court. That auxiliary Constitution is subject to the whims of changing majorities on the Court.

13. The doctrine of Substantive Due Process empowers Judges to discover a Constitutional right to vagrancy [1] so that people can live on public streets, urinate, defecate, traffic in drugs, use drugs, rob and harass pedestrians, and then these judges deny legislatures at all levels, the authority to rid their communities of this blight and danger.
14. Minority groups fear that their rights of privacy, marriage, non-discrimination, and others proclaimed in Supreme Court decisions could be reversed by a future Court, and they seek permanent protections in the text of the Constitution.
15. An incredulous Electorate cannot trust that ballot counting, registration, and authentication of eligible voters are executed without partisan prejudice because partisan officials manage elections in several States.
16. States and local governments operate electoral systems without essential safeguards to permit outside parties to hold election officials accountable. These officials must determine whether someone destroyed ballots, counted ineligible ballots, or counted ineligible voters' ballots. The lack of uniform electoral practices for national elections undermines any confidence in using popular vote counts to elect the President.
17. Because they move residences more frequently, lower-income voters are less likely to maintain records like birth certificates or possess a passport. Those States that impose onerous registration and voter identification requirements to secure partisan advantages make registration of lower-income voters more complex, and they are less likely to participate in elections.
18. Partisan Legislators manage the redistricting process, and they design districts that result in a grossly disproportionate number of representatives winning elections from the majority party relative to the number of votes cast for the minority party.
19. The Electoral College has bestowed a partisan advantage by repeatedly awarding the Presidency to candidates who have received fewer popular votes from the Electorate than their opponents.

20. Presidents have abused the Pardon Power to reward donors and siblings, enhance the electoral success of political allies, and reward persons for their testimony in criminal trials. The Constitution lacks an unequivocal textual prohibition of a President having the power to pardon himself.
21. The Senate gives disproportionate powers and a partisan advantage to the Electorates of small States to impede legislation favored by the majority of the population.
22. The Senate impairs the ability of the Executive and Judicial branches to function effectively whenever it stalls or refuses to even hold hearings for Presidential nominees to the Cabinet, Armed Forces, Department Staff, Supreme Court, and lower courts. The Senate's use of the filibuster has imposed minority rule and blocked significant legislative initiatives after elections for Members of Congress have transferred power.
23. Presidents have continued waging wars abroad without receiving regular and periodic consent from Congress.
24. The Justice Department cannot conduct independent investigations into the civil and criminal violations of the law by Members of the Executive Branch, the President, related family members, or political allies.
25. Elected and Appointed office holders in Government, members of the bureaucracy, their spouses, children, and families fail to disclose financial conflicts of interest that corrupt the law-making process, bringing shame to the Government.
26. Corporations and wealthy individuals, foreign and domestic, can donate money to political action committees, organized as nonprofit corporations receiving tax breaks, to exercise influence over elections and legislation without disclosure of the sources of this dark money.
27. Commercial enterprises, labor unions, and the wealthiest individuals fund lobbying of elected members and support candidates who more effectively promote their shareholders' and members' self-interests than the vast majority of unorganized individual voters. These practices are evidence that money can buy influence in politics.

28. The tax code is complex and full of provisions inserted in response to lobbying efforts that cater to special interest groups. This system enables wealthy taxpayers to engage expensive consultants to exploit loopholes unavailable to ordinary taxpayers and undermines the belief in the tax code's fairness.
29. Unelected bureaucrats exercise legislative, executive, prosecutorial, and judicial powers in their administrative capacity when enforcing the regulations they draft. Their Star Chamber proceedings dispense with Grand Juries and Jury Trials. They violate the traditions of common law and the protections in the Bill of Rights.
30. Bureaucrats are supposed to regulate special interest groups; instead, these interest groups have captured these unelected bureaucrats. Instead of working for the public interest, these bureaucrats treat these interest groups as their primary clients.
31. Urban centers suffer from killings by gangs using guns, but cities and States are thwarted by the 2nd Amendment to enact laws to regulate their sale, transfer, and use. Other parts of the Country are adamant about not relinquishing their rights to own and bear guns for self-defense.
32. State and local elected representatives rely upon Federal Block Grants to support a fifth of their program budgets. These Grants centralize power at the Federal Level and diminish the role of States as autonomous governments. These grants also confuse voters' ability to assign unqualified responsibility to their Federal, State, or local representatives.
33. The abuse of Asylum and Refugee Treaties has served as an excuse for masses of illegal immigrants seeking economic relief to enter this Country. This abuse imposes enormous burdens upon legal residents near the border, who are taxed for additional welfare services while also lowering the wages of legal residents who compete with these illegal immigrants in the labor market.
34. The President's refusal to faithfully enforce existing laws to stem the flow of illegal immigrants leads to the suspicion that Immigration and Citizenship policies are exploited as a tool for increasing partisan political power by apportionment and eventually naturalizing these migrants as Citizens who will primarily vote in support of his political party.

35. Over twenty million people reside in the United States without legal status. To obtain employment, they often fabricate Social Security and other identity documents or steal the identity information of legal residents. These illegal residents live in a legal purgatory that Congress has failed to fix.
36. Granting statehood to Puerto Rico and Washington, D.C., would secure a long-term, partisan advantage in the Senate. This is especially egregious because only half the residents of Puerto Rico speak English, and this territory receives extensive welfare support and tax advantages far exceeding those of the States. Congress could return portions of the District of Columbia to Virginia and Maryland instead of creating a new state that would merely be a dependent ward of the Federal Government.
37. Rather than protecting consumers from physical injury, fraud, and excessive pricing, Legislators enact onerous professional licensing regulations to restrict the entry of competent competitors, thereby preserving the monopoly position of entrenched commercial and labor interest groups.
38. Political extremists have employed violence, heckling, sabotage, disclosure of private information, and threats against the employers or customers of their opponents to suppress the dissemination of alternative views and violate their right to free speech. These actions have been permitted and often endorsed by institutions receiving taxpayer support.
39. Federal law grants social media companies an unfair advantage to shield them from damages arising from libel or other torts committed by their users on the Internet, exempting them from treatment as publishers of their users' content. However, these companies behave like publishers when they apply secret standards that deny or restrict service and compensation to users based upon a bias against their legally expressed political, cultural, and scientific content that other users oppose: the owners of these Social Media Companies and the Federal Government.
40. Governments and corporations' use of warrantless surveillance to capture data about their users on the Internet has enabled an unprecedented invasion of citizens' privacy. The Chinese Communist Party's implementation of social credit

scoring using information gathered from these surveillance methods is a chilling warning of our Country's future.

41. Financial Censorship to stifle political dissent is an alarming practice in a free society. Credit card and other digital payment companies discriminate in allowing vendors to access their payment networks based on political beliefs, even though their financial operations rely upon access to the Federally Regulated banking system. Canada froze the bank accounts [2] of political protestors and suspended their vehicle insurance, a portent of possible abuses for this Country.

Two hundred thirty-seven years ago, the Founders of this Nation endeavored to make a more perfect Union of States by replacing its Articles of Confederation with a new Constitution. Today, we summon our generation to reprise this act by repairing and strengthening our political union and making our descendants proud to be called Americans.

We, the Citizens, who are committed to remedies for these enumerated defects, appeal to our fellow Citizens, Elected Representatives, scholars, and opinion shapers who want to improve the quality and comity of discourse in our Nation's political affairs to declare their commitment to bequeathing a legacy of effective representative Government to our posterity. We urge them to defy the skeptics, pessimists, and others who profit by trafficking in fear, doubt, and dissension. We urge them to resist these naysayers who promote and exploit a political stalemate by issuing a continuous fusillade of destructive critiques of their opponents, Government, Constitution, and American Society.

We implore them to join the builders seeking solutions instead of naysayers assigning blame. We beseech them to trust their fellow Americans who possess sufficient wisdom, an ability to respect their opponents, compromise, and remedy our political disorder.

We, therefore, Publish and Declare that we have the duty and the power to remedy the defects of our Constitution by drafting a new Constitution for these United States of America, and thereby persevere in strengthening the ties that bind us together as one Nation.

Chapter 3

The Rise and Stall of the Elitist Constitution

THE BIRTH OF THE LIVING CONSTITUTION

In 1791, Alexander Hamilton proposed the establishment of the First Bank of the United States. This proposal was a pivotal moment in the history of the US Constitution. Even though Hamilton, James Madison, and other Framers in Philadelphia debated and rejected language that would have permitted the establishment of a national bank four years earlier, Hamilton argued that it was "necessary and proper" to establish this bank. You might say that Hamilton was the first person to enroll in the School of the *Living Constitution* [1].

Expressing an elitist perspective, Chief Justice John Marshall believed that "The framers of the Constitution contemplated there would be some degree of legislation by the judiciary." By 1819, in *McCulloch v Maryland*, Chief Justice Marshall, writing the unanimous opinion, settled the question of the constitutionality of a National Bank. It was indeed "necessary and proper." Even President James Madison abandoned his prior objections and supported the national bank.

This Chapter covers the long journey from how the 1787 Constitution, full of assurances of a Federal Government limited in its scope of power promised by authors of *The Federalist Papers*, evolved into the Elitist

Constitution of the Twenty-First Century that permits Social Security, Medicare, Medicaid, The Affordable Care Act, Housing and Urban Development, and a myriad of other federal programs, even exceeding the worst fears of the Anti-Federalists.

This Chapter also explains why Enumerated Powers in the 1787 Constitution failed to establish a durable Federalism that could effectively divide powers between the Federal and State governments and why this failure spawned the Elitist Constitution.

All Thirteen States eventually ratified the 1789 Constitution, which contained the Bill of Rights. However, this Constitution had a severe flaw that ultimately transformed into the Elitist Constitution: Enumerated Powers contained in Article 1, Section 8, and the Tenth Amendment.

A prescient Alexander Hamilton wrote in Federalist 25:

> "Wise politicians will be cautious about fettering the government with restrictions that cannot be observed because they know that every breach of the fundamental laws, though dictated by necessity, impairs that sacred reverence which ought to be maintained in the breast of rulers towards the constitution of a country, and forms a precedent for other breaches where the same plea of necessity does not exist at all or is less urgent and palpable."

Article 1, Section 8, and the Tenth Amendment fettered the government with restrictions that would "not be faithfully observed." Because Article 5 made amending the text too difficult, there was an irresistible urge to defy these textual constraints. This evasion of the Enumerated Powers metastasized into an Elitist Constitution — an expanding, porous net, partially enveloping but never enclosing the expanding powers exercised by the federal government. These Enumerated Powers were more honored in the breach than the observance.

Article 1, Section 8, and the Tenth Amendment were the wrong tools for establishing the Federalist Union of States envisioned by the Framers, and this failure has brought the United States to the brink of a twenty-first-century Civil War.

THE "ENUMERATED POWERS" SALES PITCH

Recounting the episode of the National Bank demonstrates that the 1787 Constitution, comprised of only 4,543 words, could not unambiguously resolve every potential dispute. Therefore, it was natural that Justices of the Supreme Court would be comfortable legislating from the bench and filling in the blanks. Considering that the 1787 Constitution had to establish a coherent structure for a new national government while also garnering supermajority support from a fractious collection of delegates with a variety of commercial and political interests and concerns, then it is a marvel that it worked as well as it did for as long as it has. Broad language facilitated its adoption, but this language created ambiguities that would later foment uncertainty.

Alexander Hamilton and James Madison wrote several essays in *The Federalist Papers* to assuage the fears of the Anti-Federalists [2]. The Anti-Federalists opposed the 1787 Constitution because it granted too much power to the federal government. The Framers of the Constitution were balancing two objectives: giving the federal government sufficient power to remedy the defects of the Articles of Confederation without granting too much power and risking a recurrence of the same abuses for which they had fought a war against Great Britain to escape.

The most crucial portion of the 1787 Constitution tasked with this balancing act is Article 1, Section 8. Herein were the eighteen enumerated powers of the federal government. In Federalist 45, Madison wrote:

> "The powers delegated by the proposed Constitution to the federal government are few and defined. Those which are to remain in the State governments are numerous and indefinite. The former will be exercised principally on external objects, as war, peace, negotiation, and foreign commerce….The powers reserved to the several States will extend to all the objects which, in the ordinary course of affairs, concern the lives, liberties, and properties of the people, and the internal order, improvement, and prosperity of the State."

In Federalist 32, Alexander Hamilton wrote:

> "But as the plan of the convention aims only at a partial union or consolidation, the State governments would clearly retain all the rights of sovereignty which they before had, and which were not, by the act, Exclusively delegated to the United States."

In Federalist 41, Madison chides the Anti-Federalists who predicted that the federal government would exploit the terms *general welfare, interstate commerce, and necessary and proper* in Article 1, Section 8 to negate the limitations of the eighteen enumerated powers. He wrote:

> "Had no other enumeration or definition of the powers of the Congress been found in the Constitution, than the general expressions just cited, the authors of the objection might have had some color for it."

He continues:

> "But what color can the objection have, when a specification of the objects alluded to [*the eighteen enumerated powers*] by these general terms [*general Welfare, interstate commerce, necessary and proper*] immediately follows, and is not even separated by a longer pause than a semicolon?" (Italics added)

He further ridicules his opponents' "paranoia" when writing:

> "Nothing is more natural nor common than first to use a general phrase [*The Congress shall have Power To ...provide for the common Defense and general Welfare of the United States*], and then to explain and qualify it by a recital of the particulars [*the eighteen enumerated powers*]." (Italics added)

To further assuage the Anti-Federalists, the Tenth Amendment was included with the Bill of Rights as a belt-and-suspenders guarantee that there should be no ambiguity about the enumeration of powers restricting the federal government:

> "The powers not delegated to the United States by the Constitution, nor prohibited by it to the States, are reserved to the States respectively, or to the people."

History has proven that the anti-Federalists were prescient, not paranoid. They correctly predicted that the 1789 Constitution would not constrain federal power. Even though most Americans are satisfied with the federal government's expanded role in the twenty-first century, they should understand how flouting these Enumerated Powers led to the problems created by the Elitist Constitution.

INSINCERITY OR NECESSITY

For the adherents of the Originalist/Textualist school of Constitutional thought [3], *The Federalist Papers* were solemn promises made by Hamilton and Madison to the Anti-Federalists, indicating the widespread *original understanding* [4] that the Federal Government's powers should be limited and enumerated.

Others interpret *The Federalist Papers* merely as a series of sales pitches published from 1787 to 1788 to persuade New Yorkers to support ratification. Only when the federal government was up and running would people know how the Constitution's clauses would survive contact with the real world. Therefore, readers should interpret these sales pitches as hopeful, best-guess predictions, not promises.

Hamilton and Madison could not know that the enumerated federal powers contained in Article 1, Section 8, and the Tenth Amendment would be ineffective in establishing a solid foundation for a division of powers between the national and State governments. They did not foresee this because while drafting the Constitution, they solely applied legal instead of economic ways of resolving these challenges. Their chief error was believing that incentives for *Members* of Congress seeking re-election were aligned with *the institution* of Congress jealously guarding against encroachment on its powers by the other branches.

This critique is not a policy judgment condemning the enlarged role of the federal government in establishing Social Security, Medicare, Agricultural Supports, Rural Electrification, Housing Subsidies, K-12

Education subsidies, and a myriad of other social programs, straying far beyond the 1787 Framers' vision of the role of the federal government. Instead, starting with the First Bank of the United States, the urge (or *necessity*, as some would claim) for the federal government to go beyond the plain text of the Enumerated Powers was irresistible. This irresistible urge weakened the commitment of all three branches of the federal government to enforce and defend the plain reading of the words and the Framers' central challenge – How do we fix the defects of the Articles of Confederation while thwarting the ability of the federal government to become tyrannical?

After ratification, when fear of tyranny receded from memory, the main challenge was: How do we nurture practical federal government actions to facilitate interstate commerce for a growing nation? After the Civil War, an additional challenge was: What can the Federal Government do to prevent the States from oppressing individual rights?

Absent any amendments to the Constitution that, thanks to Article 5, were too onerous to ratify, pragmatic Justices of the Supreme Court, like John Marshall, tolerated incremental encroachments upon the plain text of the Constitution that necessitated "legislation by the judiciary." With sufficient legal legerdemain, any proposal deemed *necessary and proper, interstate commerce*, or for the *general welfare* could percolate through the permeable barrier of the Enumerated Powers.

WHAT IS ELITIST ABOUT OUR CONSTITUTION, AND WHY IT IS A PROBLEM

The American Constitution of the Twenty-First Century is an *Elitist Constitution* comprised of two parts. The first is the text of the 1787 Constitution with 27 amendments, containing 7,591 words. The Principal Text is readily accessible to every American, fitting inside a pocketbook.

The second is the text of dozens of past Supreme Court opinions comprised of hundreds of thousands of words that are the foundation for citations in future Supreme Court decisions. (You can find a comprehensive list of most cases on pages 653-664 in *The Classical Liberal Constitution*, Richard A. Epstein). These cases are the *Auxiliary Text* studied, taught, and interpreted by specialists in Constitutional Law – the elites. There are several versions of this Auxiliary Text, and there are substantive disagreements among these elites about the proper conclusions to draw from those opinions and which ones to include in this canon.

Most of the Auxiliary Text represents efforts by the Supreme Court to resolve controversies whenever the Principal Text was inadequate for clearly adjudicating controversies. However, a large portion of this Auxiliary Text is devoted to rationalizing the expansion of federal powers by contradicting the interpretations of Article 1, Section 8 written by Hamilton and Madison in *The Federalist Papers*.

Over two centuries, majorities in the legal profession and the Supreme Court cobbled together doctrines through the Auxiliary Text that paved the way for government policies that would not survive a layman's interpretation of the Principal Text. Armed with convenient and sophisticated interpretations of the *necessary and proper, interstate commerce*, and *general welfare* clauses, these elites punched through the Constitutional barricades impeding their agenda – barricades erected by a conservative interpretation of the Principal Text and its recurring theme of limited, enumerated federal powers contained in Article 1, Section 8 and in the Tenth amendment.

According to these elites, pragmatic jurists and elected officials could not respond to exigencies like the *Great Depression*, World Wars, Industrial Monopolies, Old Age Poverty, and the *War On Poverty* unless they ignored outmoded constraints of the Principal Text and circuitous procedures required for amendments to the Constitution.

Over time, the power of this elite Living Constitution consensus has diminished. An opposing faction obstructed the pathway of using judicial shortcuts to avoid the political consensus required for constitutional amendments. The rise of this opposing faction weakened the consensus on applying the Auxiliary Text to Constitutional controversies.

This new faction of elites competing with the pragmatists in the Living Constitution elite has spread throughout law schools and State and Federal Courts. This new opposing faction, affiliated with *The Federalist Society*, advocates an Originalist/Textualist method of interpretation. They have intense disagreements with the old faction of elites adhering to the doctrine of the Living Constitution. Instead, these Originalists advocate an Auxiliary Constitution with interpretations that reduce National power, expand State power, and hew more closely with the views expressed by Hamilton and Madison in *The Federalist Papers*.

THE END OF THE ELITE CONSENSUS

The legitimacy of the Elitist Constitution relies upon a consensus interpretation of the Auxiliary Constitution to maintain the façade of an apolitical, neutral, and dispassionate Judiciary. This consensus was strong from 1953 until 1981 during the terms of Chief Justices Earl Warren and Warren Burger Courts. However, starting in 1986, this battle of elites between the schools of Originalists versus the Living Constitutionalists gained momentum during the Rehnquist Court and continues to the present under the Roberts Court. These battles brought shame [6] to the Judiciary from the Left. Then, the Left began to question the legitimacy of the Elitist Constitution once they lost their monopoly consensus on the Auxiliary Text.

While the Judiciary is an essential aspect of the Elitist Constitution, an even more significant source of elitism is the Administrative State, comprised of unelected bureaucrats who write regulations, levy fines, prosecute defendants, and judge cases. With Civil Service protections, most of these bureaucrats have enormous power because they are insulated from electoral influence and have little to no accountability.

Finally, the process of amending our Elitist Constitution has no direct connection to the voters. Under Article 5 of the 1787 Constitution, the Congress and the State Legislatures (or State Conventions) have a say, but never the voters. The elections for Representatives and Senators are the voters' only point of direct contact with the Federal Government. Even the Electoral College mediated the vote for the President because the Framers were very afraid of a demagogue winning the Presidency through a direct, popular vote by the people.

THE CASE OF AKHIL AMAR v RICHARD EPSTEIN

On March 4, 2024, the Supreme Court [6] ruled that the State of Colorado could not bar Donald Trump from appearing on the State ballot by applying Section 3 of the 14th Amendment. The most disturbing aspect of this case is the divergent opinions among legal scholars who support and oppose the Supreme Court's unanimous ruling.

Akhil Reed Amar [7] of Yale Law School and Richard Epstein [8] of New York University's Law School are prominent law professors. Both incredibly brilliant scholars write well-reasoned, nonpartisan analyses about major Constitutional controversies.

Richard Epstein's *The Classical Liberal Constitution* [9] is the best exposition of a logically coherent explanation of the Constitution closely related to the Textualist/Originalist schools of thought.

Akhil Amar has written and studied more history about our Constitution than anyone else and regards himself as an Originalist. One of his many books, *America's Unwritten Constitution* [10], is the best exposition of an *Auxiliary Constitution.*

While Amar's views generally fall on the Left side of the political spectrum, criticizing most of the Roberts Court's Supreme Court decisions, he makes decisions based upon consistent, reasoned standards that belie partisan stereotypes. For example, he opposed the exclusionary rule. He believes that the Second Amendment protects an individual's Right to self-defense but with allowance for government limitations on the kinds of weapons and the places they can use them. This opinion is at odds with most of his colleagues on the Left.

Richard Epstein's views generally fall on the Right side of the political spectrum, but he is also not partisan. He criticized the 2008 *District of Columbia v Heller* [11] Supreme Court decision that "private citizens have the right under the Second Amendment to possess an ordinary type of weapon and use it for lawful, historically established situations such as self-defense in a home, even when there is no relationship to a local militia." With his textualist approach and historical perspective, he believed that the Second Amendment did not cover residents of the District of Columbia and that the amendment only restricted the Federal government, not the States. Most of his colleagues on the Right did not welcome this opinion.

Therefore, their divergent opinions regarding the *Trump v Anderson* [6] case are distressing. Professor Amar recorded two podcasts, Part 1 [12] and Part 2 [13], critiquing the lead counsel's presentation of Colorado's case and explaining why he believes the Court made a massive error in finding for Trump. He also filed an Amicus Brief. [14]

You can listen to Richard Epstein in two podcasts explaining why he believes that it is evident that the Court should stop Colorado from excluding Trump from the ballot: Podcast 1 [15] and Podcast 2 [16].

When two intelligent, fair-minded professors disagree so vehemently, the Elitist Constitution is culpable for failing to create a meeting of such fine minds. Each scholar called balls and strikes using two different dimensions of the judicial strike zone. Therefore, it is the fault of the Elitist Constitution if these dimensions are not clearly defined so that these two intelligent, principled scholars can agree.

Chief Justice Robert famously remarked, "I will remember that it's my job to call balls and strikes and not to pitch or bat." However, when constitutional scholars and justices of the Court disagree about the dimensions of the judicial "strike zone," [17] maybe it is time to blame our Elitist Constitution for why judges act more like players than umpires. The Justices are not consciously malicious and insincere when they say they are acting like umpires because the Elitist Constitution does not even provide a fixed strike zone to decide whether Justices are acting more like players than umpires.

A new constitution should enable these two principled and brilliant scholars to converge on the same opinion most of the time on future cases brought before a Supreme Court by precisely defining a new strike zone for Constitutional Law.

ANTI-ELITIST CONSTITUTION v THE ELITIST CONSTITUTION

An ideal Anti-Elitist Constitution is a document that ordinary people could understand without relying upon elitist intermediaries like Professors and Judges. Justices on the Supreme Court could resolve most controversies solely relying upon the text without recourse to precedent in prior decisions to support a court judgment. The first decades after the ratification of the Anti-Elitist Constitution would likely see a change in the types of cases brought before the federal courts because the reduction in ambiguity with the expanded text would reduce the odds of litigants bringing matters of Constitutional Ambiguity to trial.

The Principal Text of an Anti-Elitist Constitution more precisely defines the dimensions of the judicial strike zone. There is little room for an auxiliary component because 36,360 words go a long way toward eliminating ambiguity and confusion. In other words, the dimensions of the strike zone are well-defined to make it far easier for Justices to behave like umpires instead of players. Like a good contract, a good Constitution creates a meeting of the minds, leaving few areas of disagreement.

If an unforeseen future controversy arises, creating the temptation for legislation by the Judiciary, then an Anti-Elitist Constitution must be flexible enough to be promptly and readily amended. This first draft of the Anti-Elitist Constitution in Part Two instructs the Chief Justice (Article 9, Section 11) to prepare an annual report sent to Congress that makes recommendations for legislation and amendments whenever the Judiciary believes that the text of the Anti-Elitist Constitution does not provide sufficient, unambiguous guidance for resolving causes of action in controversies tried in federal courts. This provision should minimize the temptation for judges to legislate from the bench.

An Anti-Elitist Constitution is comprehensive, and its plain text is comprehendible by most voters. It does not require an elite priesthood of intermediaries to illuminate its true meaning. This Anti-Elitist Constitution is almost five times longer than the Principal Text of the Elitist Constitution. Still, it is much shorter than the Auxiliary Text contained in the foundational Supreme Court opinions of the Elitist Constitution, and you don't need a law degree to understand how it works. By comparison, the German Constitution contains 27,379 words. The Indian Constitution contains over 100,000 words. The South African Constitution, so admired by Justice Ruth Bader Ginsburg [18], has over 43,000 words!

An Anti-Elitist Constitution should quell nearly all controversies about the structure of the Federal Government and the powers exercised by each of its branches. Nevertheless, ambiguous cases and contentious controversies regarding individual rights will persist even with an Anti-Elitist Constitution. Resolving conflicts between religious liberty, freedom of association, and nondiscrimination will likely continue because these rights, by definition, are in conflict and can never be absolute without violating another right. An Anti-Elitist Constitution would substantially reduce but wouldn't eliminate legislation by the Judiciary. The voters would decide other intractable and persistent controversies like gun control and abortion with plebiscites organized under provisions of the Anti-Elitist Constitution.

CONCLUSION

Two flaws of the 1787 Constitution led to its transformation into an Elitist Constitution. The first flaw was the Enumerated Powers imposed upon the Federal Government. The federal government routinely exceeded these Enumerated Powers, starting with the First National Bank. The second flaw was the rules for amending the Constitution in Article 5 because it imposed a high barrier for additions to the list of Enumerated Powers. In response to pressure from Congress and the President, the Judiciary facilitated evasions of the Enumerated Powers contained in the Principal Text of the Constitution. These evasions necessitated the Judiciary's development of the Auxiliary Text to facilitate this expansion of Federal powers. This expansion in Federal powers accelerated during President Roosevelt's New Deal, leading to the rapid growth of Administrative Agencies exercising legislative, executive, and judicial powers in a manner outside the structure of three independent branches of government described in the Principal Text.

The demise of Enumerated Powers diminished the importance of State governments. Voters primarily look to the Federal Government to solve local problems like education, homelessness, healthcare, or crime today because the bulk of tax revenue and media attention are devoted to the Federal Government. Nationalizing these local problems increased the number of political conflicts between elected representatives, making it more challenging to negotiate compromises for national issues.

This Elitist Constitution worked smoothly only as long as adherents of the Living Constitution School of Legal Thought dominated the judiciary and law schools. However, a rising elite from the Right challenged the dominance of the elites in elected office, the Judiciary, and academia, who did not question the continued expansion of the Federal Government. Beginning with the 1980 election of Ronald Reagan and Republican majorities in Congress, the growing influence of the Originalist legal philosophy exposed disagreements about how to interpret the Auxiliary Text to settle controversies before the Court. These challenges from the Right impaired the smooth application of the Elitist Constitution. Contentious debates over abortion, gun control, gay marriage, and the power of the bureaucracy eventually undermined the Progressive Left's respect for the Supreme Court and the Constitution. This reaction by the Left deepened cleavages between opposing factions throughout the government and the nation. The rise of Originalism has spurred a response from the Progressive Left to revive the dormant, acerbic Wilsonian and Progressive critiques of the Constitution from the late nineteenth and early twentieth centuries.

Unfortunately, the Elitist Constitution cannot redress the serious grievances enumerated in Chapter Two of The Declaration of Reformation. Only a new Anti-Elitist Constitution specifically built to redress these grievances and incorporate the lessons learned over the past two hundred thirty-seven years can stop the descent of America's political conversation into a violent phase.

SOLICITATION OF BOOK REVIEWS

Thank you so much for making it this far!

Your time is valuable, and I greatly appreciate that you brought my words into your life. As a small independent publisher, it means a lot, and I hope my words have enriched your perspective.

If you have 75 seconds, reading your honest feedback on Amazon will mean the world to me. Your review does wonders for the book, and candid feedback assists me in improving the second edition.

To leave your feedback:

1. Go to https://www.amazon.com/
2. Type The Anti-Elitist Constitution in the search field and hit ENTER

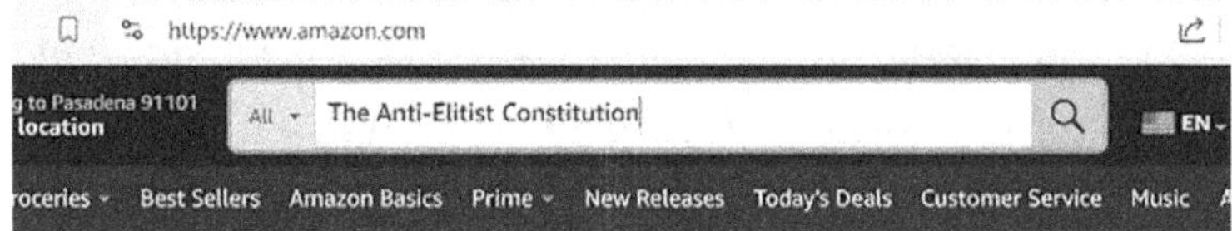

3. This will take you to a page with the picture of the book and the title. Hover your cursor over the title and click on the hyperlink that takes you to the book page
4. Scroll down until you see Book Reviews. Click on the Write a customer review button.

5. Please give other readers your honest perspective of the quality of the arguments and the book's readability, even if you did not agree with everything.

THANK YOU!

Chapter 4

THE PATHWAY TO RATIFICATION

If "War is nothing but a continuation of politics with the admixture of other means" (*On War* [1], Carl von Clausewitz), then a constitution is a treaty to prevent war during the conduct of politics.

Chapter Two's Declaration of Reformation is an indictment alleging that America's current Elitist Constitution is a tattered and worn peace treaty that fails to fulfill its primary responsibility to maintain domestic political peace.

However, for most experts, drafting a replacement for our Elitist Constitution seems too far-fetched and impractical. Their eyes roll, and they wave their hands to stop this pie-in-the-sky dreaming. They reason that if we cannot even get simple amendments to the Constitution approved by two-thirds of Congress, let alone ratified by three-fourths of the States, how could we ever organize a Constitutional Convention to draft an entirely new document? Why waste time entertaining such an outlandish proposal?

FEASIBLE PATH FOR A NEW CONSTITUTION

It is far easier in Congress to pass an Omnibus Spending Bill [2] than an Appropriation Bill for a worthy project (rebuilding a fallen bridge) or even a single Department like the Department of Defense because various factions in Congress have the leverage to acquire appropriations dearest to them by refusing to approve those appropriations dearest to those in other factions. The horse trading to cobble an Omnibus Spending Bill, encompassing all spending programs simultaneously, enables numerous conflicting factions to cooperate when everyone gains something in the trades.

Likewise, drafting and ratifying an Anti-Elitist Constitution is feasible because there is enormous potential for gains from trade by the Left, Right, and Center. Enacting legislation or ratifying a few amendments could not create a durable, enforceable political peace treaty. Only the Anti-Elitist Constitution could resolve the grievances enumerated in The Declaration of Reformation to each faction's satisfaction.

None of the prior proposals for rewriting the Constitution envisioned bargaining and compromise to achieve a consensus on the new document's text. Those proposals encoded partisan and ideological tenets and prescribed policies beyond the grasp of legislative majorities. Critics should distinguish these prior Submissionist proposals from a Persuasionist alternative based on compromise and consensus.

Another argument asserts that the Constitutional Conventional envisioned in Article 5 of the Elitist Constitution is not feasible or likely. Unlike the 1787 Convention in Philadelphia, where each State Delegation cast one vote, a modern Constitutional Convention would likely require that the voting strength of a state delegation, or the number of delegates from a State, be proportional to the number of Members in the House. Otherwise, a petition to Congress for a Convention of States would die on arrival.

A more likely scenario is for Congress to appoint a bipartisan, Blue-Ribbon Panel of Advisors who would assist a Joint Subcommittee of Members from the House and Senate to draft this new Constitution. If two-thirds of Congress approves of their work product, it would be up to three-fourths (thirty-eight) of the fifty States to ratify this new Constitution. This Blue-Ribbon Panel of Advisors would replace the role played by a Constitutional Convention and avoid the inevitable confusion about establishing and running a Constitutional Convention.

Below are recommended members for a bi-partisan Blue-Ribbon Advisory Panel of Persuasionists, bringing experience and expertise:

Co-chairs:

Mike Johnson (or current Speaker of The House)
Chuck Schumer (or current Senate Majority Leader)

Panel Members:

George W. Bush, ex-President
Barack Obama, ex-President
Hakeem Jefferies, House Minority Leader
Mitch McConnell, Senate Minority Leader
Gretchen Whitmer, Governor of Michigan
Ron DeSantis, Governor of Florida
Akhil Amar, Professor of Constitutional Law, Yale University Law School
Richard Epstein, Professor of Law, New York University Law School
Deidre McCloskey, Economist, author, Cato Institute
Paul Krugman, Nobel Prize-winning Economist, opinion writer, New York Times
Maya MacGuineas, President of the Committee for a Responsible Federal Budget

CAN'T WE ALL GET ALONG?

In 2018, the group *More In Common* released a study on political polarization in America- *Hidden Tribes* [3]. In it, they found that there is an undercurrent of voters who are exhausted by the polarization exhibited in media coverage of political affairs. A large majority of Americans have more in common than what divides them. They believe that compromise is essential for solving many problems plaguing the nation.

These *Moderate Middle Americans*, the roughly three-fifths in the center of America's political spectrum, are the "Exhausted Majority" who, in the words of Rodney King, plead, "Can we all get along?"

One fifty-four-year-old Moderate Tribe Member from this report worried about how people are selfish without any concerns about their fellow Americans. She did not know how to raise the consciousness of these people to band together to solve our common challenges.

One way to raise others' consciousness is to draft and eventually ratify a new Constitution for the United States—the Anti-Elitist Constitution. The Moderate Middle Americans must be leading the charge.

Suppose the middle three-fifths of the political spectrum believe they could engineer a Grand Bargain to exit from the Clown Carousel of recurring, intractable failures with our political process. In that case, there is more than hope for change. There is the Anti-Elitist Constitution, which is more than hope. It is an action plan for change.

BEYOND POLITICS AS USUAL

Visualize the political spectrum as a bell curve, with the Median Voter representing the highest point of the curve near the mid-point. Envision a horizontal axis measuring the percentage of national production consumed by government expenditures – the lower percentages representing the Right side and the higher percentages representing the Left side of the political spectrum. Envision the vertical axis as the number of Americans favoring a specific percentage of government involvement. There are cultural and moral issues (gun control, abortion, gay marriage) that we cannot measure in a two-dimensional political plane focused on economics. Let's put that aside to keep this visual aid in two rather than three or more dimensions.

In the two-party system of the United States, the standard strategy for winning majority rule is a process of coalition building to the median voter's left or right. Go too far to one side of the horizontal axis, and you will lose a mass of voters to the other side. This battle over the Median Voter is why pure ideological political programs seldom thrive in societies with a Bell Curve distribution of voters participating in a democratic system of government. Governing coalitions produce "messy" policy prescriptions that get poor grades from most academicians in political philosophy departments and law schools.

However, under our current Elitist Constitution, the two-party system fails to deliver compelling results. The voters no longer see a relationship between the cause (winning an election) and the effect (enacting policies) the winning coalition promised. Instead, year after year, this practice of politics-as-usual has yielded gridlock and stagnation that only empowers the loudest voices who promise a new strategy that can clear the debris obstructing the pathways of political power required to excise the obstacles to change.

For ongoing political governance, the two-party system chasing the Median Voter can be a stable way to run the government. However, ratifying a new constitution will require a different political calculus. The Median Voter will be in the middle of three-fifths of the political spectrum, mainly populated by the Persuasionists. Therefore, the centrist coalition drafting a new constitution will be temporary for as long as it takes to finish the job. After ratification, the normal partisan battles over the Median Voter will resume.

ALTERNATIVES TO THE ANTI-ELITIST CONSTITUTION

But why is this new Anti-Elitist Constitution the most sensible proposal for alleviating the angst gripping our nation in 2024? Why not form a centrist third party [4], adopt ranked choice voting [5], or a myriad of other panaceas like proportional representation [6] instead of our current structure with geographic districts? Wouldn't these alternatives be more feasible than holding a Constitutional Convention or convincing two-thirds of Congress to draft a new Anti-Elitist Constitution for ratification by three-fourths of the States?

The main reason to reject a centrist third party or proportional representation is that they treat the symptoms instead of the cause of political dysfunction.

Centrist political coalitions can never endure and thrive because they are constantly engaged in an unstable, multi-front war on the political spectrum's left and right sides with several different antagonists. A Superpower like the United States cannot operate like Germany or Israel. It takes months to form a coalition government under a proportional voting system where minority members of a governing coalition can extort concessions disproportional to their numbers. Also, in homogenous societies where party differences represent ideological factions, not ethno-religious cleavages, they typically have success adopting proportional representation. In non-homogenous societies like the United States, proportional representation would likely break into racial, religious, and regional political parties and exacerbate divisions rather than alleviate them as occurs in a two-party system.

Ranked-choice voting undermines political parties and strengthens the cult of personalities. Its fundamental flaw is confusing the attributes of a single officeholder with the effectiveness of the legislative process that the officeholder inhabits as a single gear in a larger machine. Ranked-Choice-Voting elevates the candidate's personal charm and idiosyncratic, milquetoast policy prescriptions above the skills required to form the majority coalitions necessary for passing bills. Instead of cultivating the character traits for compromise and collaboration across many individuals, ranked-choice voting will select individuals who campaign on charisma and personal popularity. These individuals can thrive in the political ecosystem of the Internet age, where personalities can emerge outside of social institutions. Those social institutions used to winnow candidates lacking essential character traits like leadership and team building. All of that is aside from the opaque machinations of the ranked-choice algorithm and the potential for elevating fringe candidates. In the 2022 election for Alaska's House seat, the most moderate candidate, Nick Begich, who received the most first-round votes, lost to the Progressive, Mary Peltola, after several algorithm iterations [7].

The two-party system is integral to America's tradition and the most stable structure. The two major parties engage on a narrow battlefront in the middle of the political spectrum, where combatants strive to occupy the territory populated by the Median Voter. If the two-party system is not working, it is because it rests upon a defective foundation: the Elitist Constitution. Blame the Constitution, not the two-party system.

The Anti-Elitist Constitution would restore the effectiveness of this two-party system and the connection between elections and policy changes that our two-party system used to deliver. The advocates for Ranked-Choice Voting, centrist third parties, and proportional representation would be more productive if they collaborated as partners in drafting a new constitution rather than diving into the swamp of partisan politics.

CONVERT FISSILE PARTISAN ENERGY INTO POLITICAL FUSION

Chapter Two's Declaration of Reformation is a compact and thorough enumeration of the essential grievances stoking the flames, heating the simmering cauldron of American politics. Numerous essays [8] and op-eds [9] have warned [11] of looming civil unrest motivated by many of these grievances. Concerns about civil war are part of the zeitgeist.

Many people talked and wrote about these grievances, and their writings were the source material for compiling the list of forty-one grievances in The Declaration of Reformation. A few of these critics even have opinions about redressing these grievances. However, opinion writers, podcasters, comedians, and academics are making money stoking the flames that heat the cauldron, promoting animosity among their readers and listeners against their opposition. Their business model thrives on exacerbating conflict and enmity to attract eyeballs and dollars. Their profits would diminish at the onset of an outbreak of comity. Their prescriptions for reform are Submissionist policies dependent upon the unconditional surrender of their "evil opposition." While these writers provide essential information about grievances afflicting our polity, they don't offer realistic solutions. Why don't they reach across the aisle to build a coalition big enough to make significant changes?

In contrast, The Declaration of Reformation holds every American Citizen accountable for fixing these problems and recommends replacing our current Constitution with a new one. The difference between a Declaration of *Reformation* and a Declaration of *Grievances* is that the emphasis is on action instead of wallowing in anger and resentment.

Such a daunting task as ratifying a new Constitution is the most sensible path because it requires the approval of three-fourths of the States. That cannot happen unless the middle three-fifths of the political spectrum can engineer collaboration and compromises like the Framers did in Philadelphia in the summer of 1787. Suppose we want to avert the Civil War. In that case, a supermajority of Americans who believe in the goodness of their fellow citizens will have to collaborate for a common goal rather than compete to beat the other side.

We need a process where the Progressive and the Conservative activists are compelled to make trades and compromises to redress their grievances, enumerated in The Declaration of Reformation. Drafting a new constitution could improve the standing of these activists compared to their present predicament, practicing politics as usual. The horse-trading required to negotiate a first draft of the new Constitution converts the divisive partisan fissile energy into a cohesive partisan fusion energy, if only for the brief period required to compose the final draft of the Anti-Elitist Constitution.

An apt sports analogy would be a meeting between Boston Red Sox and New York Yankees fans to change baseball's rules. Both sides agree to adopt a pitch clock, increase the size of the bases, and allow for video replays to appeal for reversing calls by the umpires. They also agree to maintain the grass and base paths to high standards to minimize odd bounces. All these changes make the game more enjoyable for the fans and ensure that teams win on the skill of their play rather than outside factors like umpires and bad bounces off rocky base paths or outfielders tripping over gopher holes. During the rule's meetings, the fans shed their animosity for each other to work for their common interest. After the meetings, they resumed their traditional enmity, and this enmity is what makes the games between these bitter rivals so enjoyable for their fans. In sports, like politics, conflict is necessary for the vitality of its practice. Our Constitution and game rules should not suppress conflicts.

The Anti-Elitist Constitution won't stop political conflict. Indeed, attempts to suppress conflicts by promoting centrist third parties and ranked-choice voting will only increase the alienation of voters who don't get recognition and respect for their grievances. The Anti-Elitist Constitution permits the federal and State governments to convert political conflicts into productive, peaceful, and tolerable policies.

PERSUASIONISTS v SUBMISSIONISTS

Victors impose a Submissionist Treaty in a war upon the vanquished under terms of unconditional surrender. An example of a Submissionist domestic political treaty is when the Union imposed the 13th, 14th, and 15th Amendments, The Reconstruction Acts, and the military occupation upon a defeated Confederacy after the Civil War. The Union could unilaterally impose terms without any input from the Confederacy. Persuasion could not work when the gulf between the two sides was vast. Violence was the only way to preserve the Union if the Northern States believed that the benefit of forcing the Southern States to remain exceeded the cost of war.

The 1787 Constitution is an example of a Persuasionist Treaty. The delegates at the Philadelphia Convention negotiated a replacement for the Articles of Confederation. This domestic political treaty between the thirteen States incorporated numerous compromises, including a Bill of Rights, to gain the unanimous support of all thirteen States. Everyone was dissatisfied with specific features of the Constitution. Still, most agreed that it was superior to its predecessor and that these distasteful compromises were palatable in the quest for a stronger union. In the absence of military force, persuasion had to be deployed to draft, approve, and ratify this Constitution.

Are Americans in an 1861 Moment, on the brink of a violent civil war where each side uses violence to force the vanquished to surrender to the Submissionists' constitutional reforms? Or are Americans in a 1787 Moment where they can persuade and compromise to fix flaws in their Constitution as was done with the Articles of Confederation 237 years ago? The answer to this question will determine the path to effect lasting political reforms.

THE SUBMISSIONISTS IN OUR MIDST

During the past ten years, numerous Professors of Politics and Constitutional Law and opinion writers have written essays about amending or entirely replacing the Constitution. Dozens of these essays and proposals are sources for the list of grievances and flaws enumerated in *The Declaration of Reformation*. This Declaration is a punch list of items Americans must fix before the Constitution can be acceptable to these Partisan Critics.

Here's an example of a Submissionist gathering [11]. In November of 2022, the *Anti-Oligarchy* authors discussed their book at a Georgetown Law School conference [12] stacked with all the big names in the academia supporting a Constitutional reform movement and significant figures like

Maryland Representative Jamie Raskin and E. J. Dionne of *The Washington Post*. The event, which the American Constitution Society organized, a left-leaning counterpart to the Federalist Society founded in 2001, had an air of possibility, action, and invention, in sharp contrast to the glum "what-can-you-do" coverage that followed the *Dobbs* abortion rights defeat at the Supreme Court. Unlike other political forums, the participants were willing to criticize Supreme Court Justices by name directly.

Two archetypes best illustrate divergent proposals for constitutional reform. The Democracy Constitution Project represents the Liberal/Progressive Archetype [13] led by Professor Sandy Levinson in collaboration with other Progressive Law Professors. Randy Barnett's *Bill of Federalism* represents the Conservative/Libertarian Archetype. Label these as the *Sandy* and *Randy* Proposals.

Sandy's and Randy's proposals are Submissionist, and both are merely academic exercises—unrealistic Constitutional reforms that are dead on arrival at Congress's doors. Neither was drafted in consultation with their ideological adversaries, intending to build a coalition of supporters outside the narrow band of the opposing ends of the political spectrum that each occupies.

Nevertheless, their efforts were worthwhile because they provided most of the grievances in the Declaration. Although Constitutional Law Professors have important insights as consultants about the flaws of our Elitist Constitution, they are ill-suited to negotiating the text of a new document.

PERSUASIONIST COMPROMISE v COMMON GROUND CONSENSUS

There is one example of constitutional law professors who have differing ideologies and work together to draft amendments [14] to the Constitution. In 2021-2022, the National Constitution Center sponsored a group of Conservative [15], Libertarian [16], and Progressive [17] Law Professors to draft their own separate, ideal version of the US Constitution. Later, they collaborated to draft five amendments to the current Constitution that they jointly recommended to be submitted to Congress.

However, comparing their amendments to their model constitutions produced no examples of significant compromises. The proponents merely identified common ground that would not contradict the central provisions of their versions of an ideal constitution.

Because of the narrow scope of their endeavor, none of these five amendments grapple with the most essential grievances enumerated in The Declaration of Reformation.

In contrast, during the 1787 Constitutional Convention, the delegates were not merely searching for areas of agreement. Their most challenging task was figuring out whether the benefit of forming a more vital union was worth the price of accepting distasteful proposals: a National Government imposing taxes, a Senate giving small States disproportional power, accommodating Slavery, or the Supremacy of Federal Law and this new Federal Constitution over their own States. Delegates compromised with deeply cherished interests and beliefs in exchange for provisions that allowed opposing delegates to make similar tradeoffs necessary for creating a workable Constitution.

The Conservative, Libertarian, and Progressive project participants did not have the same skin in the game as the delegates to the 1787 Convention. These Professors merely preserved their academic reputations, while the delegates in 1787 had to preserve a Union of States. In these circumstances, the delegates had to engage in debates to persuade their adversaries to bargain away precious beliefs in exchange for the hope of a better future.

THE FIRST DRAFT OF A NEW CONSTITUTION

The first draft of the Anti-Elitist Constitution in Part Two of this book is only the beginning, not the end, of a meaningful conversation, debate, and negotiation. Its role is analogous to the *Virginia Plan* [18] presented to the Constitutional Convention on May 29, 1787. James Madison, the primary author of the *Virginia Plan*, proposed that the national government consist of three branches, with checks and balances, to prevent the abuse of power. Playing the role of editors and critics of a first draft enabled delegates to accomplish more in a shorter time than they would as a committee of authors tasked with writing a story starting with a blank slate, without characters or plot lines. Madison provided the outline of the characters (Legislative, Executive, Judicial) and the plot lines (checks and balances) so that the Convention could produce a finished document in four months that was approved by two-thirds of the delegates and, eventually, by adding a Bill of Rights, ratified by all thirteen States.

Contrast our 1787 Convention with the 2021-2022 Chilean Constitutional Convention [19], which lacked a consensus starting draft—a Chilean version of the Virginia Plan. Instead, 154 popularly elected Chilean delegates took twelve months to produce a constitution with 388 articles [20]. In a landslide vote on September 4, 2022, sixty-two percent of Chilean voters rejected this proposed radical, Submissionist Constitution.

The first draft of the Anti-Elitist Constitution in Part Two would be a good starting point for launching the conversation among the members of a Blue-Ribbon Advisory Panel like Madison's *Virginia Plan* did for the delegates at the Philadelphia Convention in 1787.

THE GRAND BARGAIN AND OTHER TRADES

Whenever a Progressive Submissionist asserts that the Electoral College is a stain on the Constitution, then they should answer a simple question, "What are you willing to offer as a concession to Conservatives in exchange for abolishing the Electoral College, moving to a popular vote, and receiving an advantage in Presidential Elections for at least the next twenty years?"

Usually, they are baffled by the question because they don't accept the premise that they should have to engage in any bargaining regarding matters of "justice and morality."

Their response: "Replacing the Electoral College with a Popular Vote for President is right. Only bigots and anti-democracy ideologues could oppose this anachronistic vestige created by white, male slave owners who did not invite women and blacks to participate in the Philadelphia Constitutional Convention in 1787."

The Submissionist mindset is a corrosive element causing current political strife. It has no role to play in The Grand Bargain. Drafting a new Constitution involves barter and compromises, not moral platitudes. The

Grand Bargain relies upon Persuasionist methods to mediate conflicts by proposing concessions from both sides to arrive at a global solution, improving almost everyone's position vis-a-vis the Elitist Constitution.

The Anti-Elitist Constitution incorporates the fears and hopes of both sides, and it anticipates the kinds of compromises that all factions could offer and accept. It makes pre-emptive concessions and claims, imagining Conservatives and Progressives ensconced in a hearing room trying to hammer out a treaty. The one constraint on this process is that this Constitution, or treaty, has to form a coherent organizational structure for an efficient government that does not repeat the mistakes of the Elitist Constitution. The Anti-Elitist Constitution provides the coherent organizational structure, skeleton, steel girders, and framework to support this political skyscraper's curtain walls and interior space.

LAYERS OF COMPROMISE FOR THE GRAND BARGAIN

The First Layer

The first and foundational layer of the Grand Bargain grants greater majoritarian control in exchange for dividing the taxing powers between the Federal and State governments into exclusive domains. It also imposes restraints on Federal Borrowing.

For Progressives:

- Eliminate the Enumerated powers of Congress.
- Abolish the Electoral College, state-controlled redistricting, and state-controlled voter registration for Federal Elections.
- States and their Political Subdivisions may not simultaneously hold elections for their office holders as elections for Federal office holders.
- Federal control over voter and ballot authentication for federal elections. The National Voter Registry automatically registers all eligible Citizen voters in their home precinct.
- Decrease the scope of the Senate's power and reduce its size to one seat per State.

- Require a majority vote of the Senators to meet a second test: the States represented in that majority must comprise a majority of the nation's Citizens for enacting a bill or approving a nominee.
- The Senate cannot originate any bills.
- Institute a first-round popular majority vote for President.
- No Presidential vetoes of budgets passed by the House. Appropriations for Defense, State, Justice, State, and Homeland Security Departments are continuing resolutions until Congress enacts a replacement budget, thereby preventing government shutdowns.

For Conservatives:

- Convert Social Security and Medicare Trust Funds into defined contributions using Special Obligation Debt for individual taxpayers, insulating these programs from political manipulation.
- Congress sets the debt limit, but the President has the discretion to decide whether to borrow within the limit set by Congress.
- The President has a line-item veto on the amount of deficit spending in the budget enacted by the House of Representatives.
- The maximum federal individual income tax rate on Citizens is 12.5%.
- Sales, consumption, value-added, corporate income, pollution, interstate road tolls, estate, and inheritance taxes are exclusive to the Federal government.
- States have no cap on individual income taxes.
- Wealth and property taxes are exclusive to the States.
- Mineral and hydrocarbon extraction taxes based on volume and weight are exclusive to the States.
- Whenever there is no first-round winner of the popular vote Second-round voting for the President is an instant runoff using Electoral Votes by the House District and one Electoral Vote for a Statewide winner.

Severing the leash of Enumerated Powers is a huge concession to Progressives because the Federal Government could do almost any spending program under the Anti-Elitist Constitution. This concession requires an equally large concession to assuage Conservatives' fears.

These reforms exemplify the economic way of thinking about Federalism. The economic way of thinking about fencing in the Federal Government is to follow the money rather than rely upon the failed, legalistic approach of Enumerated Powers used in the 1787 Constitution. The States and Federal governments will reach an equilibrium of power-sharing within the budget constraints imposed by the Anti-Elitist Constitution.

These reforms would restore Federalism by increasing the tax revenue that States could raise, leading to a transfer of many federal programs to the States. States would have to compete for residents by offering a quantity and quality of services commensurate with the price of residing in the State. Personal income and property taxes should be shielded from Federal encroachment so that there is a high correlation between those who enjoy the services delivered by a State and those who pay for them. Giving States these taxing powers strengthens the ability of voters to assign responsibility to their State or Federal officials separately.

Discarding Enumerated Powers in favor of taxation and borrowing constraints will restrain the Federal Government's ability to over-extend its domain of policy involvement. Eliminating Enumerated Powers would eliminate innumerable court cases from the federal docket regarding the structure and extent of federal powers. The Federal Welfare State would rest upon a solid constitutional foundation without employing the legerdemain of loose interpretations of the *necessary and proper or interstate commerce* clauses to support the constitutionality of the Welfare State.

Progressives could rest easy knowing that a future Supreme Court could not declare the Affordable Care Act, Social Security, Medicare, the Department of Education, the Federal Trade Commission, or Sugar Beet Subsidies unconstitutional violations of Article 1, Section 8 of the Elitist Constitution. Under the Anti-Elitist Constitution, there are only fiscal limitations on what the Federal Government can do. The Anti-Elitist Constitution relies upon economic incentives and budgetary constraints, rather than legal prohibitions, as a more reliable guarantor of an effective federalist structure.

This profound resetting of the domains to taxation between the Federal and State governments will generate opposition. Cities like Las Vegas thrive on sales tax revenue from gambling, hotels, and restaurants. Some cities cater to attracting businesses into their jurisdictions to generate sales tax revenue to supplement their property tax collections. The Anti-Elitist Constitution would force cities, counties, and States to raise the bulk of their tax revenue from personal income and property taxes instead of sales and corporate income taxes.

Anticipating these objections, the Anti-Elitist Constitution allows the federal government to share its sales tax revenues with States according to the origin of the sale. However, there are no guarantees that Congress will have sufficient surpluses to consider revenue sharing with the States.

The Second Layer

The second layer of the Grand Bargain divides the current Executive Branch powers between a popularly elected President and a Governor General elected by Members of the House. The Governor General would have control over domestic policy matters. In contrast, the President would have authority over foreign affairs, using force, prosecuting crimes, collecting taxes and fines, and borrowing. This second layer also disperses the powers of the Administrative Bureaucracy to the Executive, Legislative, and Judicial branches.

For Conservatives:

- Impose enumerated powers for a President that limits their domain of authority to *Departments* of War, Justice, State, Homeland Security, and the Treasury.
- Divide the powers of the Administrative Bureaucracy between the President, Congress, and the Judiciary.
- The President and Treasury Secretary have the power to borrow money. The House sets the debt limit. The debt limit resets to 102% of outstanding Public Debt at the end of each fiscal year.
- Three-fifths vote of Congress to admit new States.

For Progressives:

- Create a new Executive Branch under a Governor General whom the House of Representatives elects. The Governor General oversees the *Ministries* of Agriculture, Commerce, Education,

Environment, Energy, Health, Housing, Interior, Labor, Transportation, and Veterans Affairs.

- Create non-partisan Boards (Federal Reserve, Census, Elections, Research and Records) whose five members elect and oversee an Executive Director to run their agencies.
- The President gets fast-track authority to submit a budget for Defense, Justice, State, Treasury, and Homeland Security Departments to the House for a vote without amendments.

These changes to executive powers combine the advantages of the Parliamentary and Presidential systems. The President, elected by the entire nation, oversees matters requiring national cohesion. Foreign affairs, military readiness and deployment, law enforcement, borrowing management, and tax collection should not be matters with significant partisan differences. The President can submit a budget with fast-track authority to avoid most of the parochial bargaining by House members to preserve unneeded weapons programs, military bases, or underutilized office buildings.

The Governor General runs the part of the government charged with domestic policies rife with partisan differences. This parliamentary structure clearly shows which political party oversaw the adoption and execution of domestic spending programs and tax policies. Party ideology and economic interests guide decisions about domestic spending programs, so a party leader should manage these domestic affairs, leaving no doubt about their party's accountability for success and failure.

The Executive Directors run the parts of the federal government that need shielding from partisan influence.

Presidents need to possess the essential qualities demanded of a wartime leader. They must be able to rally the nation in foreign policy struggles against its adversaries, and they will be less effective in this role if domestic policy fights divert their attention and tarnish their leadership with partisan hostility. Assigning these partisan, domestic responsibilities to the Governor General boosts the prestige of the President and gives Congress more power, thereby ending the Imperial Presidency [21].

Dispersing the powers of the Administrative Bureaucracy to the Executive, Legislative, and Judicial branches retain the competence and experience of career Civil Servants while maintaining greater political and legal accountability for their actions.

The Third Layer

For Conservatives:

- The rules for assigning Birthright and Naturalized Citizenship and Refugee Status to migrants are fixed in the Constitution beyond meddling by Congress or Treaties.
- Persons who violate immigration laws have a lifetime ban for Citizenship but not residency.
- Amnesty and pardons for immigration violations are prohibited.
- State and Federal Government employees (with few exceptions) are not permitted to vote or make political contributions.
- Apportion House Districts by the number of Citizens instead of persons.
- Dual citizens may not vote or contribute to campaigns.
- Guarantee the Right to a secret ballot and describe the protocols for secure and verifiable elections.
- Fix the number of Supreme Court seats at nine.

For Progressives:

- Create two types of non-citizen permanent residents: US Nationals with US Passports and US Residents with foreign passports.
- Set rules for State Citizenship and Federal District and Territory residency.
- Create a Transient Citizenship status for those living abroad or leading a nomadic lifestyle who do not qualify for State Citizenship or Federal District and Territory Residency.
- Create a Federal House District with full-voting privileges to represent residents of Washington, D.C., Puerto Rico, and Guam, as well as Transient Citizens with no fixed residence.
- Political contributions to candidates and political parties can only come from natural persons who are Citizens.

- Dark Money and political action committees face discriminatory taxation rules.
- Self-financed candidates have contribution limitations.
- The four-day in-person voting period for Federal Elections is from Saturday through Tuesday.
- Guarantees for mail-in voting and automatic voter registration.
- Four-year terms for House Members.
- Expand House Membership by lowering the average district size to 400,000 Citizens.
- States may not levy income taxes on federal salaries paid to federal government employees.
- Term limits for Judiciary

Conservatives are alarmed by the unchecked migration of persons into the United States. These migrants could alter the political balance of power in two ways. First, apportionment counts these people and adds Congressional seats in States with Progressive representatives. Second, if Congress grants amnesty and a pathway to Citizenship, coupled with generous welfare support, these migrants would likely vote for Progressive candidates.

The Anti-Elitist Constitution places the definition of Citizenship, counting for apportionment, and admission of new States beyond partisan manipulation. It also forecloses Court Packing as an option to alter the ideological balance of the Supreme Court.

In exchange, the Progressives receive concessions on their efforts to expand voting rights to residents of US Territories and increase the size of the House of Representatives. They get the ban on corporate donations to candidates and parties, restrictions on self-financed campaigns, and curtailment of dark money in politics. They also get expanded Saturday through Tuesday voting hours and guarantees for mail-in ballots to make voting easier for their constituencies.

The Fourth Layer

While the first three layers pertain to structural aspects, the fourth layer is more wide-ranging. The best way to summarize this fourth layer is to divide the grievances in The Declaration of Reformation into Progressive, Conservative, and Bipartisan.

The following grievances emanating from Progressives are numbers 5, 8, 9, 14, 17, 18, 19, 21, 26, 27, 28, 31, and 35.

The following grievances emanating from Conservatives are numbers 2, 4, 7, 10, 11, 13, 15, 16, 29, 30, 32, 33, 34, 36, 37, 38, 39, and 41.

The following grievances are Bi-Partisan: 1, 3, 6, 12, 20, 22, 23, 24, 25, and 40.

The first three layers cover several of these grievances, and the remainder comprise this fourth layer. For example, grievance number 20 concerns the abuse of Presidential pardons. Republican and Democrat Presidents have abused this power, and Trump caused further umbrage by suggesting that he could pardon himself. This grievance is labeled Bipartisan, and its remedy is in Article 5, Section 3 of the Anti-Elitist Constitution in Part 2.

Article 19, Sections 5, 6, and 22 remedies the Left's grievance number 14. Article 19, Sections 2, 3, and 7 remedies the Right's grievance numbers 11 and 38. This pairing of offsetting protection is just one example of how concessions are exchanged and valued protections are codified throughout the Anti-Elitist Constitution to facilitate its drafting and eventual ratification. This spirit of compromise and exchange permeates the document.

CONCLUSION

If we ignore the conventional wisdom and failed past attempts to amend the Constitution, there is a realistic pathway for drafting a new one. This pathway models the Omnibus Spending Bills routinely passed by Congress. These spending bills succeed because they rely upon layers and layers of compromises with various factions and special interests.

Similarly, the Anti-Elitist Constitution relies upon The Grand Bargain between Conservatives and Progressives, the Left and the Right, anchored by the middle three-fifths of the electorate. Each side received concessions from the other to redress grievances in The Declaration of Reformation. Enshrining the remediation of these grievances into the Anti-Elitist Constitution establishes an enduring political peace treaty to avert the potential Civil War simmering under the surface.

Chapter 5

Philosophical Foundations of the Anti-Elitist Constitution

POWER IS POLITICAL CURRENCY

Imagine the Speaker of the House, Senate Majority Leader, and members of the Blue-Ribbon Advisory Panel locked away at Camp David during the Congressional winter recess for December. Their task is to produce a new Constitution to submit to the Joint Congressional Special Committee for their review and amendments.

Consider the outcome of their work, a product that would closely resemble the Anti-Elitist Constitution in Part Two. This first draft of a new Constitution, born from a unique collaborative effort, could reshape our political landscape.

The transcript of these imaginary proceedings would not list citations from John Locke, Montesquieu, John Rawls, or Aristotle. Instead, this transcript would cite Census maps and redistricting scenarios. You would read about the matrix of tax revenue data by municipality, county, State, and Federal, sorted by personal income, corporate income, sales, estate, and property tax. The transcript would contain citations from population studies that estimate the number of illegal immigrants by nation of origin. Other population studies would provide data by sex, race, and age cohort sorted by zip code.

The transcript would contain several proposals for settling controversies heard before the Supreme Court over the past seventy years: privacy, gay marriage, racial preferences, judicial deference to administrators' interpretations of statutes, taxation of wealth, redistricting, free speech, and dozens of other matters.

These imaginary discussions would be debates about how the text of a new Constitution would shift the balance of power between political parties and between the national, State, and local governments. Power, not philosophy, comprises the substance of these discussions.

What will Progressives be willing to offer in exchange for the popular vote for President and requiring that Senate majority votes must also represent a majority of the nation's population?

What will Conservatives offer in exchange for tightening rules granting refugee status and preventing a President or the Congress from granting amnesty and Citizenship to millions of illegal aliens?

Compromise and bargaining will secure the required three-fifths consensus guiding the deliberations of the Blue-Ribbon Advisory Panel at Camp David. Political power is the currency that balances the ledgers in these deliberations to measure these exchanges.

However, philosophical guardrails constrain acceptable options within these power negotiations. The most critical philosophical guardrails of the Anti-Elitist Constitution follow:

CITIZEN SOVEREIGNTY

In the Anti-Elitist Constitution, the Citizens comprising the Electorate are the Sovereign. The Citizens delegate all powers exercised by representatives of any level of authority, and a constitution that the Electorate ratifies is the instrument that regulates those powers. Layers of government (national, State, local) are malleable tools, not talismans or holy relics with inherent moral qualities. Because the Elitist Constitution never unambiguously adopted Citizen Sovereignty, the executive, legislative, and judicial elites vied for authority to interpret the Constitution and assume authority over policies throughout its history. The Anti-Elitist Constitution ends this ambiguity, putting the Electorate in charge.

BUILD ON THE CURRENT FEDERALIST STRUCTURE

Rather than re-imagining a unitary state organized on a decentralized basis, like France and England, the Anti-Elitist Constitution preserves the existing federalist structure with States and a National government. Unlike the Regions, Departments, and Municipalities of France, the States in the Anti-Elitist Constitution still possess legislative and judicial powers independent of the national government.

Advocates for a unitary state cite the example of the Civil War as evidence for curtailing the role of the States. However, the Civil War was a tragedy born of the bargain with the slave states to ratify the Constitution in 1787. It was not a demonstration of the moral superiority of the National versus the State level of government. It was a demonstration that flawed Constitutions can produce civil wars.

Others support a unitary government that elects a president for a limited term with total control and accountability for government operations, free from the constraints of a legislative branch or the interference of bureaucrats. The Anti-Elitist Constitution rejects this model as too radical and susceptible to tyrannical abuse and disruption of institutions with wholesale dismissals and replacements of competent civil servants with incompetent partisans. We want to preserve the human capital in our Civil Service and preserve its valuable contributions and storehouse of institutional knowledge and not allow Presidents to exploit them as a valet service to promulgate a partisan agenda.

WE CAN NOT INDULGE THE VICE OF BREVITY

The Anti-Elitist Constitution will be long enough to ensure a precise and unambiguous judicial strike zone.

The first draft of the Anti-Elitist Constitution exceeds 36,300 words, and that is a virtue, not a vice. Thorough text reduces the likelihood of exploiting ambiguity for political ends that violate the understanding at the time of adoption. In 1787, the Constitution's ambiguity and generalities were unavoidable and necessary to win ratification. However, with two hundred thirty-seven years of experience, the twenty-first-century rewrite of the Constitution will require detailed, written agreements to allay fears and secure a durable consensus for ratification.

GOVERNMENT POWER FOLLOWS THE MONEY

Writing about the House of Commons in the United Kingdom, Woodrow Wilson observed, “From the moment when its sole right to tax the nation was established by the Bill of Rights, and when its resolve settled the practice of granting none but annual supplies to the Crown, the House of Commons became the supreme power in the State....” [1]

The Anti-Elitist Constitution thoroughly prescribes limits and responsibilities for taxation, appropriations, expenditures, borrowing, and control of the money supply. The formation of the Federal Reserve in 1913, the removal of the gold standard in 1932, and the emergence of the dollar as a world reserve currency after World War 2 are fundamental transformations the Framers could not anticipate. Based on this experience, the Anti-Elitist Constitution devotes far more attention to fiscal affairs to ensure that government institutions cannot be employed to evade accountability to the voters’ representatives.

Rather than relying upon devices such as Enumerated Powers to regulate the scope of government activities, the Anti-Elitist Constitution regulates the domains of taxation between the national and State governments. Money is easier to measure, regulate, and adjudicate than the boundaries between a State and the National government’s exercise of interstate commerce powers.

FEDERAL TAX CODE FOCUS ON REVENUE, NOT DOLING OUT BENEFITS

Unlike the Federal government, under the Anti-Elitist Constitution, the States have no maximum personal income tax rate, so the States can charge progressive marginal tax rates to “soak the rich.” The competition between States is the only constraint upon a State Legislature’s desire to wage class warfare through taxation. With a maximum 12.5% personal income tax rate, the federal government has no room to wage class warfare, so it can focus on regulating and taxing commercial activities in the global economy characterized by an increasing interstate and international division of labor.

The Anti-Elitist Constitution forces the Federal government to make annual appropriations and expenditures to support favored factions with a transparent price tag rather than hiding these costs in the tax code where they can survive unnoticed for decades. These restraints channel the Federal government's energies to maximize revenue instead of contending with complicated deductions, deferrals, and credits that reduce its collections.

After ratification of the Anti-Elitist Constitution, tax lobbyists will have to decamp from Washington, D.C., and move to State Capitals. Eliminating tax credits, deductions, and deferrals will simplify the tax code and free Congress from the corrupting influence of corporate lobbyists offering donations in exchange for tax benefits.

MAKE IT EASIER FOR VOTERS TO HOLD REPRESENTATIVES ACCOUNTABLE

Woodrow Wilson [2] wrote that power and strict accountability for its use are the essential constituents of good government. Therefore, it is a radical defect in our federal system that it parcels out power with checks and balances between the branches and thereby confuses responsibility.

Americans usually vote for national, State, and local representatives on the same ballot. These voters typically need help to identify which level of government is responsible for specific matters affecting their lives, and they seldom have enough information to hold the responsible elected officials accountable. The voters elect a President, House Members, and Senators, and each of them often works at cross-purposes. Within this regime, voters cannot accurately assign blame or credit for what the government does. The Anti-Elitist Constitution assigns power and strict accountability to each branch of government to remedy these defects in the Elitist Constitution.

KEEP TAX DOLLARS LOCAL

Cities like Las Vegas, New York, Los Angeles, and Chicago obtain a large percentage of their tax revenue from sales taxes and corporate income tax revenue generated by persons who don't live in these cities. Federal block grants [3] to cities and States have a similar effect. These policies weaken the linkages between who pays for and benefits from a city's expenditures and exacerbate the Principal-Agent Problem [4]. Elected Officials (the agents) are less likely to be monitored by the Principals (their voters) when the voters' tax contributions are a small percentage of the budget for a city or State.

The Anti-Elitist Constitution requires that States primarily depend on personal income and property tax revenue to strengthen the bonds between Voters and their Representatives at the State and local levels.

USUALLY, MAJORITIES RULE

Majorities *do not create good governance*. Majorities *can only expel bad governors.*

The Anti-Elitist Constitution's view of Majority Rule is that it is the best method for a peaceful transference of power in a durable regime that relies upon individuals to govern themselves in most economic and social affairs. Majority Rule is a technique yielding good results in these limited circumstances. It is not a political sacrament. Majority Rule does not represent the chimeric *Will of The People*. Majority Rule merely expresses dissatisfaction and the authorization for peaceful regime change.

A majority vote cannot create organizations with rational, coherent plans to execute objectives by making tradeoffs based on constraints. A Majority can favor lower drug costs and higher wages for doctors and nurses. Still, a Majority vote cannot conjure up an organization that could deliver lower-cost, high-quality, and promptly provided healthcare services any more than a Majority vote could repeal the laws of physics.

After a peaceful regime change, the most essential value of majority rule is that it fosters compliance with tax collections and obedience to the laws. Tax collections are the oxygen supply for healthy governments.

Unlike Saudi Arabia or Russia, which can generate government revenue through state ownership of oil, gas, and mineral enterprises, the United States primarily relies upon internal revenue collections from its taxpayers. When voters have a voice in their governance, they are less likely to feel alienated from the police and the tax collectors.

SOMETIMES SUPERMAJORITIES ARE NECESSARY

Today, our elected representatives swear an oath to protect and defend the Constitution. Why don't they swear an oath to honor the majority wishes of their constituents or the entire nation? Wouldn't that be the proper oath, adhering to a doctrine of Majority Rule, honoring one person, one vote?

Why should amending Constitutions require supermajorities? Is it proper that many provisions within the Elitist and the Anti-Elitist Constitutions require supermajorities or other methods not conforming to "one person, one vote?"

You find the answer in the Preamble of the 1787 Constitution. It states that:

> "We the People of the United States, in Order to…secure the Blessings of Liberty *to ourselves and our Posterity….*"

The Preamble of the Anti-Elitist Constitution supports this sentiment when it states that:

> "[T]his Constitution shall be the covenant between *Us and Our Posterity* to govern those who govern Us."

The rationale for supermajorities is the ethos of responsibility to our posterity. Only political narcissists postulate that a majority vote of voters in the present possess a mystical, inviolate authority over all persons in a polity, even though such a majority could enact policies that would diminish the future well-being of our descendants and our future selves.

Requiring Citizenship for membership in the Electorate is another anti-majoritarian feature of our constitutional Republic. Considering that the policies of the United States Federal Government affect the lives of Canadians and Mexicans more than their governments in many cases, shouldn't these foreigners have a right to vote and participate in the same elections as Americans? On what grounds should they be excluded? Why exclude children and felons in prisons from the Electorate?

Is burdening people with laws enacted by majority rule more than eighty years ago, by primarily deceased persons, a proper application of majority rule? How frequently should Americans get to vote on whether Social Security and Medicare should remain in force? Should laws and our Constitution automatically expire in one, five, or ten years so that a future electorate could periodically refresh their majority consent?

Once you raise these questions, you realize that simple, extremist doctrines of majority rule have serious shortcomings that undermine their critiques of supermajority voting requirements or unequal weighting of voting strength, as is done in the Senate.

The American proponents of republican government, who drafted the 1787 Constitution, arose from the traditions of English common law with rights and liberties. They believed that majority rule by an electorate comprised of a large portion of the population to select representatives responsible for enacting governing policies is a superior method for transferring power. Compared to the right of the eldest son to inherit his father's throne or to a Politburo announcing their selection of the new Premier at a Congress of Peoples' Deputies, Americans settled upon a system of majority rule expressed in recurring elections of representatives, *constrained by a Constitution*.

However, adopting and altering the Constitution, the domestic peace treaty, and the rule book governing the conduct of political combat by majority rule required supermajorities because of their multigenerational impact on the nation's or State's long-term health. Recognizing that our descendants don't have a vote, we require supermajorities as a stand-in for their unheard voices.

In our Republic, customs and norms attenuate Popular Sovereignty. Customs and norms are products of centuries of practice, not rational design. Supermajorities slow down changes and dampen volatility to create the stability that every system requires to operate effectively without descent into chaotic disorder.

THE AMERICAN TRADITION v NON-DEMOCRATIC ALTERNATIVES

The best mechanism to execute a peaceful change of political power has vexed humans for thousands of years. Many durable dynasties transferred power to the first-born son of the monarch, but even in those societies, noblemen, clergy, and, later, parliaments shared power with the king.

More recently, political theorists (e.g., Communists and Fascists) have advocated for a Single Party with a monopoly on political and military power that selects a few promising young people for leadership training in governance practice. These recruits rise through the ranks, and over time, they assume broader powers as they gain experience as governors while they imbibe and proselytize the tenets necessary for commitment to the realm. Americans accept this practice for cultivating officers in our armed forces, so why not do the same for the government?

Neither of these traditions assigns any special authority to the majority rule *of the entire adult population* to eject the Party or Monarch from power. In their philosophical system, *The People* need to be led and improved by their betters in the same way that teachers and parents with more excellent knowledge and experience lead and train children, and officers lead their enlisted soldiers into battle.

These philosophical traditions believe that wise experts should be in charge because governing requires skills that must be cultivated and trained like any other profession. These thinkers advocate for leaders possessing the requisite knowledge, not the masses, vulnerable to populist rhetoric and corrupt ideas bereft of evidence. In societies where majority rule is likely to devolve into rule by ethnic, religious, or socioeconomic factions oppressing the out-groups, leading to the collapse of social cohesion, these non-democratic traditions could be more durable and practical than those governed by the Majority Rule of the adult population.

Note to political philosophers: *more durability and effectiveness do not equal more just*. The natural selection of political institutions over time and across many societies does not care about theology or philosophy.

Many critics of the Constitution's Framers believe they were elitist snobs fearful of the lower classes. Supposedly, those prejudices motivated the insertion of anti-majoritarian provisions like the Senate, Supreme Court, Article 5 for Amending the Constitution, the Presidential veto, and the Electoral College. However, all these measures are consistent with older, anti-majoritarian concepts from the English Common Law and political traditions, like the requirement of a unanimous jury for convictions in criminal trials.

The truth is that the Constitution's framers did not fall for the "rule by experts" arguments proffered by the Aristocrats of their day, nor would they have acceded to the twentieth-century doctrines claiming that the single-party monopolists ruled in the best interests of the masses as "Vanguards of the People."

The Framers didn't trust the "experts" or the "elites" to rule as altruistic angels. They believed that monarchs, noblemen, and Single Party Monopoly Members all succumb to the same temptations for self-interest and misrule as the masses whipped into a frenzy by a Populist Leader in a democracy. Their supermajority, anti-majoritarian impulses were rooted in the study of historical episodes of tyranny, not by a disdain for the lower classes.

"Each according to his ability and each according to his need" might sound like an acceptable principle for justice. However, constitutions derived from ideological precepts like this, rather than from experience and customs, usually produce misery and tyranny.

CONCLUSION

The assembly of negotiators for drafting the Anti-Elitist Constitution will primarily fight and compromise about power. However, these negotiations occur within a philosophical framework native to America.

The Anti-Elitist Constitution follows the intellectual traditions of the 1787 Constitution's Framers. It applies the lessons from two hundred thirty-seven years of tradition to remedy the flaws of the Elitist Constitution and improve the operation of our government. Applying these lessons is the surest path for securing a three-fifths supermajority of support among the public and their representatives, the necessary condition for ratifying a new Constitution.

CHAPTER 6

The First Draft of the Anti-Elitist Constitution: Selected Highlights

This Chapter features segments of the Anti-Elitist Constitution that incorporate the economic way of thinking, preferring incentives for good behavior over proscriptions against bad behavior. The Enumerated Powers of the Elitist Constitution is an example of a proscription against bad behavior that eroded over time, which is why Article 16 was written to replace it.

Citations of Article and Section numbers refer to segments of the first draft of the Anti-Elitist Constitution in Part Two.

SPECIAL OBLIGATION DEBT AND UNDER-FUNDED PROMISES

Article 16, a tribute to Alexander Hamilton's fiscal priorities, is a cornerstone of the Anti-Elitist Constitution. Its focus on Taxation, Appropriations, and Debt, a subject close to Hamilton's heart, underscores its significance. Section 15 of Article 16 is a pivotal part of the Constitution because it curbs escalating federal government debt attributed to the Social Security and Medicare programs.

The Social Security Trust Fund is an insidious fiscal device that upended Congress' control over the federal budget.

> "Section 201 of the Social Security Act (42 U.S.C. §401) requires the managing trustee of the Social Security trust funds (the Secretary of the Treasury) to invest Social Security tax revenues in special "nonmarketable" federal public-debt obligations called **special issues (i.e., securities available only to the trust funds, not to the general public). {emphasis added}**
>
> "The Social Security tax revenues that are exchanged for the U.S. government obligations go into the general fund of the U.S. Treasury, and they are indistinguishable from all other revenues in the general fund. Social Security benefits and administrative expenses are also paid from the general fund of the U.S. Treasury. When Social Security payments are made from the general fund, an equal amount of U.S. government obligations are redeemed from the Social Security trust funds." [1]

In simple accounting terms, this nonmarketable federal public debt (*Special Issues*) is simultaneously a federal government asset and a liability—on the same balance sheet! Read further to discover why the federal government engages in this accounting legerdemain.

The analogy for personal budgeting to the Social Security Trust Fund would be someone earning $100,000 this year writing, "I promise to spend ten percent of my salary on vacation next year and take my family to Disney World" on a sheet of paper. They frame that piece of paper with the masthead, *My Special Issue*. They don't save $10,000 in a bank or investment account. Instead, they spent the entire $100,000 salary this year on living expenses and made a *Special Issue*, a personal resolution, to pay $10,000 on a vacation out of their unknown earnings next year.

The federal government is more serious about its commitment to spending on these Special Issues because it claims that, under law, these *Special Issues* are "real" assets. This commitment to pay down the Trust Fund is equivalent to violating the law if you don't spend $10,000 on your vacation next year with money you haven't set aside in a bank account today! Quoting from the Congressional Research Paper:

> "There is no separate pool of cash set aside for Social Security purposes. However, that is not to say that the holdings of the Social Security trust funds are not "real" assets. The U.S. government obligations purchased by the trust funds are backed by the full faith and credit of the United States and guaranteed with respect to both principal and interest by the United States, as specified in Section 201(d) of the Social Security Act (42 U.S.C. §401(d))." [2]

Congress can change the rules about how much it owes Social Security recipients in the future to exceed the amount of "real" assets in the Trust Fund. Going back to our vacation-pledged individual, he could change his mind and decide to spend $12,000 instead of the $10,000 he promised himself earlier.

If you're beginning to think this is a stupid and confusing budgeting device, you're missing the point of why Franklin Roosevelt's New Deal Congress created Special Issues for the Trust Fund in 1935. The most important thing to realize is that Special Issues are federal debts intended to hamstring future Congresses to spend money to pay Social Security recipients the same way Congress is obligated to pay bondholders who purchased US Treasury Debt with cash in the market. Essentially, the Special Issue debt is a placeholder, an earmark, an "Entitlement" in the federal budget that locks Congress in to pay these Social Security benefits. The federal government can only retire Special Issue Debt by sending out Social Security Checks. That's right! You must spend money to pay off those debts.

In 1940, Six Years after the establishment of Social Security, the remaining life expectancy at age 65 for females was 14.7 years; for males, it was 12.7 years.

When Medicare was established in 1965, the remaining life expectancy at age 65 for females was 16.3 years; for males, it was 12.9 years.

However, in 2019, the remaining life expectancy [3] at age 65 for females was 20.7 years; for males, it was 18.1 years. That is more than a **40% increase in the remaining lifespan** for both sexes that taxpayers must cover beyond the original expectations when Congress enacted Medicare and Social Security.

This change in life expectancy's fiscal effect is mathematically equivalent to telling the owner of a US Treasury Bond with a $100,000 face value at maturity that the government changed its mind and now owes the bondholder $140,000 at maturity. Is it any wonder why Social Security is so popular, at least with Americans over age sixty-two?

To match the actuarial assumptions that prevailed when Social Security and Medicare were adopted, Congress must increase the eligibility age to at least seventy-two for full benefits. Today, sixty-seven is the full-benefits age for anyone born in 1960 or later – five years less than the program's original budgeting assumptions!

Theoretically, Congress could enact a law raising the full benefits age to seventy-two, and the deficit problems would disappear. In reality, any member of Congress casting this vote would touch the proverbial "third rail" [5] of American politics. For our vacation-pledged individual, the "third rail" of family politics is telling your spouse and four and six-year-old children that you're going to the Jersey Shore instead of Disneyworld due to unforeseen budget cutbacks.

Congress can never gain control of deficit spending and its ever-growing debt until Special Issues and Social Security and Medicare benefits can adjust to changes in life expectancy and tax revenue fluctuations. Article 16, Section 15 of the Anti-Elitist Constitution offers a clever solution to this "third rail" problem: convert Social Security from a defined benefit life annuity plan into Personal Treasury Accounts, an individual, defined contribution plan.

Instead of crediting every federal taxpayer's payroll tax to a generic Trust Fund pool, the government credits the payroll tax to an individually owned Personal Treasury Account (PTA). Over the taxpayer's working life, the federal government credits the cumulative amounts of payroll taxes paid plus the interest credited every year, indexed to the average twelve-month US Treasury interest rate multiplied by the PTA balance.

Congress will establish a minimum age at which taxpayers can withdraw money from their PTA and enact a maximum distribution formula [4] to ensure that the account owner won't outlive their account balance. (Today's minimum age for Social Security withdrawals is sixty-two.) The account owner's PTA balance is distributed to their heirs when they die. In contrast, Social Security's life annuity plan unfairly penalizes population subgroups with shorter average lifespans, where heirs receive nothing if the taxpayer dies after only receiving benefits for a few months.

Converting Social Security into a defined contribution plan aligns with the popular perception that Social Security recipients only get back what they pay in taxes. That perception is false under Social Security's defined benefit structure but valid under the PTA's defined contribution structure. PTA's eliminate the "third rail" problem because the statutory category of *full-benefits age* disappears. Everyone decides how long to work to increase their PTA balance and when and how much to withdraw from the account. Congress only regulates the payroll tax rate, maximum income subject to payroll tax, minimum distribution age, and maximum distribution rules. There are no "third rails" to worry about.

Mathematically, converting from the defined benefit life annuity structure of Social Security to the defined contribution structure of the PTA is equivalent to raising the full benefits age from sixty-seven to seventy-two. Politically, there is a world of difference between assuming responsibility for what you earned and saved and being a victim dependent upon the whims of politicians to decide how much you are entitled to receive. This is why the PTA is politically palatable while increasing Social Security's full benefits age to seventy-two is political Kryptonite.

During the conversion of Social Security to the PTA, an age cutoff will separate taxpayers who continue receiving Social Security's life annuity versus those receiving their cumulative payroll tax contributions plus interest within a PTA. A lower age cutoff will lower the overall savings from the conversion.

The PTA also exposes the fact that Social Security is a massive wealth transfer program masquerading as a retirement plan. Many retirees will eventually discover that their PTA account balance is insufficient for retirement at age sixty-seven. Either they will have to work longer, or the government will offer old-age welfare programs to ensure these retirees have sufficient food, shelter, and healthcare.

Voila! The PTA has solved the most vexing fiscal challenge of the past fifty years.

INCENTIVES FOR MODERATION

Presidents always strive to nominate the most ideologically extreme nominees for the federal courts, commissions, boards, and other offices that the Senate will tolerate. Presidents have no incentive to nominate technically excellent persons with broad, bipartisan support. The Anti-Elitist Constitution solves this problem in Article 23 with a simple rule called the *Tenure Percentage Vote*.

Suppose we have nine Supreme Court Justices. Justices with eighteen-year tenure must receive a two-thirds majority in the Senate. Justices with thirteen-year tenure require a five-ninths majority, and Justices with less than a five-ninths majority receive six-years tenure.

For example, split the nine Justices of the Supreme Court into three groups. Three justices each have eighteen, thirteen, and six-year terms. According to the Tenure Percentage Voting method described in Article 23, the total number of years in the denominator used for the calculation would be:

(3 x 18) + (3 x 13) + (3 x 6) = 121 years

121/2 = 60.5, so a coalition of Justices equal to 61 years of tenure is a simple majority. 121 x (⅔) = 80 2/3, so a coalition of Justices equal to 81 years is a two-thirds majority.

Three Justices with eighteen-year terms plus one Justice with a thirteen-year term equals 67 votes, a majority vote with only four Justices. This formula forces Presidents to consult with Senators of both parties before nominating a Justice. Neither the President nor the nominee would want the embarrassment of anything less than a thirteen-year tenure. The same applies to nominees for Boards.

COMPENSATION INDEX ADJUSTMENTS FOR INFLATION

The Seventh Amendment of the Constitution states: “In Suits at common law, where the value shall exceed **twenty dollars**, the right of a trial by jury shall be preserved….” The “twenty dollars” poses the vexing question: how should a constitution deal with inflation? Twenty dollars in 1789 has the equivalent purchasing power of $714 in 2024.

Section 23 contains the *Compensation Index*. It equals the sum of the pecuniary and non-pecuniary compensation of a Member of the House of Representatives during the previous fiscal year. The Compensation Index is used thirty-eight times in the Anti-Elitist Constitution to compute the compensation for elected and appointed office holders, government officers, campaign contribution limits, fines, and other monetary limits. Presumably, Congressional pay will adjust with inflation, although there is an annual maximum increase of 2.5%, ensuring that Congress has the proper incentives not to depreciate the dollar too rapidly.

SUPREME COURT AND JUDICIARY REFORMS

The Tenure Percentage Vote (see above) incentivizes Presidents to nominate non-ideological, technically respected jurists to the Supreme Court. Nevertheless, Article 9, Section 2 of the Anti-Elitist Constitution adds another wrinkle to thwart the practice of strategic retirements where Justices try to retire while the President and the Senate majority are members of their party, assuring their successor will possess the proper ideological bona fides.

Section 2 creates two Provisional and nine Permanent Seats on the High Court. The nine justices in the Permanent Seats decide a case. When a vacancy arises, the senior Judge in a Provisional Seat ascends to the Permanent Seat to serve their tenure and vote on cases. In instances of recusal or illness by a Permanent Justice, the Provisional Justice serves as a Temporary Justice with a four-year tenure for calculating the Tenure Vote Percentage.

Then, the President nominates someone to replace the Provisional Seat vacancy. This situation creates a lag between the President's appointment and that nominee's start of service as a Permanent Member of the Court.

After ratification, all Members of the Judiciary will participate in a random drawing. The Speaker sorts the judges into groups of nine. The Speaker will draw numbers one through nine, representing the remaining years of the Judge's tenure. In ten years, a new appointee will replace every Judge. These new appointments rid the Judiciary of the judges nominated in an ideologically tainted environment under the Elitist Constitution. New judges should have an open mind about the new Anti-Elitist Constitution and replace the old judges who worked under the Elitist Constitution. With the Tenure Voting Percentage applying to the inferior courts, the President has the incentive to nominate non-ideological, technically competent jurists to secure the longest tenure, and the courts will be replenished with these superior quality judges.

The President could nominate the termed-out judges to serve again, but most are not likely to receive a five-ninths majority in the Senate to secure a thirteen-year tenure, a minimum tenure for the President and the nominee to avoid embarrassment.

Section 3 sets the minimum age for a Supreme Court Justice at fifty and for an Inferior Court Judge or Adjudicator at thirty-five, assuring observers that these nominees have an adequate record for assessing a nominee's qualifications.

THE NEW AND IMPROVED SENATE

Article 7 of the Anti-Elitist Constitution contains the powers and responsibilities of the Senate. There is one Senator per State. For their first term, a Senator must be a member of their State Legislature. They are appointed for a four-year term by a majority vote of their colleagues. The Legislature can re-appoint them for a second, third, fourth, or fifth additional four-year term—twenty years maximum service. Once a Senator leaves the Senate, they would have to rejoin the Legislature before they could be re-appointed.

Senators are employees of their State and may not receive outside labor compensation. They receive no federal compensation. Each State decides how much it wants to pay its senators and staff. The federal government only provides office space and security.

Senate votes have a two-part test. The Committee of the Whole Senate requires a majority of Senators present for passage of a bill or approval of a nominee. However, the population of the States represented by the majority vote of Senators must exceed fifty percent.

The Senate cannot originate any bills. However, they can veto non-budget bills passed by less than a two-thirds majority in the House.

Ex-Presidents and Ex-Vice Presidents can serve as ex-officio members of the Senate, but their votes don't count toward the population test. Ex-officio status allows former Presidents and Vice Presidents to remain relevant and pass their wisdom along in a meaningful way.

With a seven-thirteenth supermajority (twenty-seven out of fifty Senators), the Senate can appoint a Special Prosecutor with the same powers as the Federal or State Attorney General. They operate independently of the Federal Government. The States voting in favor of the Special Prosecutor appointment bear the investigation costs and enforce financial discipline on the investigators.

Because their Legislature appoints them, Senators won't spend time fundraising for their re-election. The Senators will bury the filibuster alongside the woolly mammoth as a relic of a bygone age because the House can pass budgets or statutes without a Senate vote. Senators will review the qualifications of the President's nominees for judge, ambassador, Department Secretary, or other officers. They ratify treaties. They can study legislation passed by the House and decide if they should take action to veto the bill. They could be vigilant about ferreting corruption in the Executive and Judicial branches by appointing Special Prosecutors whenever the Attorney General plays politics with the law.

Because the current Senate must approve the Anti-Elitist Constitution by a two-thirds majority before sending it out to the States for ratification, Senators will demand changes to Section 7. These Senators enjoy their popular election by their State's voters for six years instead of four-year terms. A grandfather clause to exempt current Senators from being members of their State Legislature is likely a minimum requirement.

THE ADMINISTRATIVE BRANCH

Article 10 overhauls the federal bureaucracy. Before the Anti-Elitist Constitution, administrative agencies existed in an Elitist Constitutional netherworld not mentioned in Articles I, II, and III, but exercising powers from each one. Congress created these agencies, and the President oversees their operations. Like the judiciary, these bureaucrats can hold hearings to level fines and jail terms. They put their spin on vague statutes and issue regulations with the force of law.

The Supreme Court unanimously ruled in *Sackett v Environmental Protection Agency* [6] that the environmentalist zealots had overstepped their authority by classifying ponds on private property as wetlands subject to EPA regulations for the noble cause of hampering habitat destruction by any means available.

Article 10 splits these agency responsibilities into four parts. The first is that bureaucrats can recommend clarifying amendments to existing, vague statutes. The bureaucrats send recommendations to the President for review. If the President agrees, then he forwards the amendment to the House for consideration. If the House fails to pass the amendment before one hundred eighty days elapse, then the amendment dies. Otherwise, the recommendation to amend the statute is adopted. This process not only establishes democratic accountability for any new laws but also ensures that unelected bureaucrats no longer possess that power. Article 10 sends bureaucratic regulations into the dustbin of history, and it forces Congress to write more detailed legislation to guide the bureaucrats and the Adjudicators and Judges ruling on cases.

Second, if bureaucrats uncover law violations, they contact the Attorney General to assign a prosecutor to the case. Bureaucrats lose their power to charge people with violations.

Third, an Adjudicator who is a member of the Judicial branch will hear cases. Article 10 recognizes that most of these cases are unsuitable for a common law court hearing, so Adjudicators with industry knowledge plus proper judicial skills will conduct these trials.

Fourth, a jury comprised of an independent Panel of Experts not working for the State or Federal Governments will judge the facts of a case unless the defendant waives their right to a jury trial. For cases with high fines and prison time, the defendant can always appeal for a hearing in a common law court.

These reforms end the worst Star Chamber horror stories, where bureaucrats run amok. Article 10 restores the separation of powers, reinstating our system's much-needed checks and balances.

COMBINING THE PRESIDENTIAL AND PARLIAMENTARY SYSTEMS

The Cheesecake Factory menu offers more than 250 dishes made fresh from scratch daily and more than 40 legendary cheesecakes and desserts [7]. They are famous for their cheesecakes, not for their burgers, Chinese, Thai, and barbecue menu items.

The modern Presidency is far more challenging than operating a Cheesecake Factory restaurant. A president cannot be renowned as a great military strategist while mastering the intricacies of crop subsidies and high-speed rail. With dozens of departments, agencies, and policy priorities, Presidents cannot focus on narrow policy specialties without suffering political setbacks, neglecting matters outside their specialties.

To remedy the over-loaded Presidency, the Anti-Elitist Constitution split the Article II Executive Authority of the Elitist Constitution into three parts: the President (Article 5), the Governor General (Article 6), and the Executive Director of a Board (Articles 11, 12, 13, 14, and 15).

The President

Article 2, Section 16 describes the election of the President by a first-round majority popular vote. If no candidate receives a majority, the two candidates receiving the most votes go into an electoral vote runoff, where popular votes convert to electoral votes according to pluralities in House Districts and Statewide.

The President oversees all uses of force and foreign relations. The President appoints Secretaries in the Cabinet to run the Defense, Homeland Security, Justice, State, and Treasury Departments. The President also appoints Judges, Ambassadors, and commission officers of the armed forces with the advice and consent of the Senate.

The President has the power and discretion to issue or not issue debt to finance budget deficits. Suppose the President does not issue sufficient debt to close the gap between appropriations and revenues. In that case, the President can delete programs with a line-item veto until the gap is closed.

The President will focus on national security, foreign relations, and fiscal health. These policy matters are less partisan and require a broad consensus among voters and legislators. The President serves a maximum of three four-year terms in office.

The Governor General

Article 6 regulates the Governor General. The Governor General oversees Agriculture, Commerce, Education, Environment, Energy, Health, Housing, Interior, Labor, Transportation, and Veterans Affairs. A majority vote of the House of Representatives elects the Governor General for the House tenure until the following election. The Governor General appoints Ministers from Members of the House to run the Ministries. The Attorney General, under the President, must enforce any statutes under the Ministry. The Ministers would petition the Attorney General for any enforcement matters.

This parliamentary structure assigns total political accountability to the majority party for domestic programs, which are more partisan and divisive.

Executive Directors

Board Members appoint the Executive Directors to run these agencies, which oversee nonpartisan agencies. The President and the Governor General appoint Board Members, and their tenure and Tenure Vote Percentage varies according to the supermajority vote in the Senate. The Board of Directors can terminate the Executive Director at will.

CAMPAIGN CONTRIBUTIONS AND ELECTIONS

Article 4, Sections 1, 2, and 3 prohibit Corporations, Unions, Political Action Committees, foreigners, non-citizens, government employees, and dark money groups from donating to Political Parties or Candidates. Only Eligible Voters are allowed to make donations. Section 9 requires only Eligible Voters can make loans to Political Parties and candidates, not banks or other legal entities.

Section 4 imposes limits on self-financed campaign donations by the candidate or spouse.

Section 6 requires donors to send all contributions to the Elections Board to verify the donor's eligibility and ensure they have stayed within contribution limits. The Elections Board forwards the contributions to the Candidate or Political Party.

Article 4, Section 14 allows for anonymous donations at one-fourth of the maximum amount permitted for non-anonymous donations. The public, candidates, and political parties could not see who donated. However, the Elections Board would know the donor and screen their eligibility to donate. Eliminating corporate, union, and political action committee funding sources requires that individuals must donate to fill this gap. Most donors wish to remain anonymous to the candidate, political party, and the public, so the new constitution should honor that. Donor anonymity to the candidate and party keeps the donor off solicitation lists. Donor anonymity to the public prevents threats and intimidation from political opponents.

Section 10 ends the practice of donating to multiple candidates running for the same office as a political hedge. Section 12 ends the practice of accumulating a war chest to use in future elections. Candidates must zero out their campaign accounts by donating funds to their Party or returning pro rata amounts to the donors.

The Elections Board assumes responsibility for issuing financial disclosure reports for each candidate's campaign every week starting eighty-nine days before the Final Voting Date so that the last financial report falls on the Friday before the first day of in-person voting on Saturday.

Section 15 requires every candidate to make financial disclosure reports of income, assets, and liabilities.

Fifteen days before the Final Voting Date, Section 18 requires campaigns to give all the other campaigns forty-eight hours' notice of any advertisements before public release.

Article 12, Section 1 requires the Elections Board to create a National Voter Registry so that every Eligible Voter is automatically registered to vote in their home precinct.

Article 14, Section 3 requires a lifetime tax audit of every Supreme Court Justice, President, and Vice President within six months of assuming their office. The non-partisan Research and Records Board would conduct the audits, not the Treasury Department. Any citizen has the right to request a lifetime audit by the Research and Records Board. Presumably, donors will require prospective candidates to submit to an audit before starting a campaign so that they aren't surprised by adverse findings after someone has already assumed office.

FIXING THE KELO DECISION COMPROMISE

In 2005, the Supreme Court's ruling in Kelo v. City of New London [23] allowed the city to condemn someone's home and transfer the ownership of the property to a private developer for urban renewal. The city of New London argued that it was in the public interest to condemn land of low value so that a developer could increase the value of the land or generate jobs, and it prevailed over Kelo, the homeowner.

Article 19, Section 9 provides a compromise for this situation. Suppose the Government condemns property and transfers it to a non-government person. In that case, the only legitimate public purpose is that tax collections from the project must exceed twice the amount paid for the taking during the first twenty years after the taking. Taxes can derive from property, income, or sales taxes.

During these twenty years, the Government shall, in addition to the original compensation for the taking, make annual payments to the original and subsequent property owners the greater of one-twentieth of the incremental amount of yearly tax collections or one-half of the original amount paid for the taking, adjusted for inflation.

Section 9 requires the Government to exercise caution before expropriating property on behalf of a developer and prove that the benefits exceed the costs. The victim will make a tidy profit to soften the blow of losing their home or other property.

The Courts will appreciate precise guidance about how to rule in these situations.

THE RIGHTS OF JURORS

Anyone who has reported for jury duty will cheer the inclusion of Article 19, Section 11, in the final draft of a new Constitution. This might be the most important reason for someone to sign the Anti-Elitist Constitution petition.

Prospective jurors must report to the courthouse and take time away from work or childcare. You often sit in a large room with many other jurors biding their time, awaiting a call to a courtroom. When the judge calls you to a courtroom, you wait again until the judge asks you about any reasons why you cannot serve. Then, the judge might dismiss you, or the attorneys might ask questions and determine if they wish to reject or accept you on the Jury. If the judge orders you to serve as a juror, you are committed to serving days or weeks, depending on the trial.

Jurors are treated like this because they are low-paid, conscripted labor. They are the lowest rung on the totem pole in the courthouse, and no one respects the value of their time.

Section 11 changes this:

> "Jurors must be Citizens who have attained thirty years and not more than eighty years. Their convenience shall supersede those of the Judges, Staff of the Judicial Branch, plaintiffs, and defendants. To encourage the formation of the most representative jury pools, trials by Jury shall be scheduled at times that impose the least disruption to the ability of Jurors to earn compensation and to care for their dependents, or the Government shall provide sufficient compensation and support services to offset these disruptions."

Section 11 places jurors on the top rung of the totem pole. Judges, attorneys, and court staff must schedule later afternoon, evening, and weekend hearings to avoid paying much higher compensation for the usual weekday, 9:30 am to 4:00 pm. These weekday hours are the maximum inconvenience for most jurors. Wouldn't a Judiciary that valued its jurors provide plenty of electrical outlets, desk space, and a robust WiFi network so jurors with remote work options can get things done while waiting? The Judiciary is the least responsive branch to political grievances, so the Anti-Elitist Constitution establishes this Constitutional Right to force them to respect jurors.

BALANCED BUDGETS, DEBT FINANCING, LINE-ITEM VETOS

If Congress runs a surplus or a balanced budget, it has complete control over appropriations for spending. Congress has the power to authorize an increase in the debt limit, but only the President and the Secretary of the Treasury can go to the market and borrow money no higher than the debt limit.

Consider this scenario: Congress appropriates five trillion dollars in expenditures on federal programs, authorizes an additional two trillion dollars of borrowing, and projects tax revenues of three and one-half trillion dollars.

The projected budget deficit: $5 Trillion minus $3.5 Trillion equals $1.5 Trillion.

The President could go to the market and borrow $1.5 Trillion to fund the entire $5 Trillion appropriation. However, the President could deploy a line-item veto and delete up to $1.5 Trillion from the budget to balance the budget. Congress cannot force the President to borrow the money to fund its programs fully.

Once Congress decides to finance its budgets with borrowed funds, the President has all the leverage in budget negotiations.

First, the budgets for the Departments under the President must be approved by the House before the House can enact any budgets for the Ministries under the Governor General. That eliminates the ability of the House to threaten cuts in the President's Departments to gain leverage in negotiations.

Second, the previous fiscal year's budget for the Departments under the President is a continuing appropriation. Even if Congress disapproved the President's requests, money would flow to these departments. The continuing resolution for Department funding eliminates the threat of a government shutdown of the essential services rendered by the military, Homeland Security, Justice Department, Treasury, and State Department.

Third, the President can submit up to six budgets per year to the House, significantly influencing the budgeting process. The House may not vote on any other business before voting on the President's budget. Also, House members cannot offer any amendments before the vote. If the House rejects the President's budget, they can return it with amendments. If the President accepts the amendments, then it is enacted. Or the President can submit another budget and hope for a different outcome.

This power dynamic underscores the President's responsibility for the nation's debt. With the power to refuse to borrow money and exercise the line-item veto to cut programs out of the budget, Presidents cannot blame anyone else if government debt grew on their watch.

James Madison would have appreciated this counteracting of ambition versus ambition to achieve a political equilibrium between the branches. This flexible process is superior to the rigidity of balanced budget mandates.

GOVERNMENT EMPLOYEES AND AT-WILL STAFF

Article 20, Section 1 prohibits States from levying personal income taxes on federal government compensation paid to employees. Federal employees would still have to pay State property, wealth, and income taxes on income derived from other sources. This benefit is a consideration offered to federal employees in exchange for preventing government employees from political participation. This feature also increases the net, after-tax compensation of federal employees so Congress could appropriate less for the employee's gross compensation to spend less on salaries while still offering competitive net compensation.

Article 2, Section 4 prohibits voting in elections, and Article 4, Section 11 prohibits political donations or campaign volunteering. These prohibitions ensure that the Civil Service performs the non-partisan, technically competent role of trusted public servants under Presidents and Governor Generals, regardless of political party.

Preserving and protecting civil servants' human capital and experience serves the public interest. The corollary of this public interest is that civil servants have a conflict of interest in participating in a political process when the common good requires the termination of a program or workforce reductions. We cannot have the foxes guarding the hen house.

However, there is a countervailing problem. How can Presidents implement the policies they promised voters on the campaign trail? Civil

Servants (or the pejorative moniker, *Deep State*) are biased toward the status quo and will resist changes that affect their employment and tasks.

Article 5, Section 8 creates a category of At-Will Staff for Presidents. The aggregate compensation for At-Will staff cannot exceed five percent of the total labor compensation budget across all Departments under the President. At-Will Staff are not Principal or Inferior Officers requiring Senate approval. However, they are crucial in executing the President's directives, serving as transitory partisan participants in these bureaucracies without Civil Service protections. At-Will staff will serve as managers, overseeing Civil Servants. After the President's term finishes, the next President will likely dismiss all of them, underscoring the partisan nature of their responsibilities.

CONCLUSION

The Anti-Elitist Constitution in Part Two is roughly 36,360 words, and the exegesis is over 28,000 words. These chapter's highlights provide a small sampling of a myriad of unique and innovative reforms. Review Part Two's Table of Contents to see the breadth of topic coverage and then realize the heavy load carried by the Auxiliary Constitution all these years. Reading through all 230 Sections written in plain English is revelatory.

You'll need to read the entire document to appreciate the tradeoffs and compromises offered to fix the grievances in Chapter Two's Declaration of Reformation. If a Progressive reads Article 1 regarding immigration and citizenship, they will assume that the Anti-Elitist Constitution is biased against Progressive values. If a Conservative reads Article 4 regarding political parties and campaign donations, they will assume that the Anti-Elitist Constitution caved to the Progressives. The entire political agreement, domestic peace treaty, and rule book for playing politics work as a bundle, not when picking apart disagreeable Sections.

Article 19's Individual Bill of Rights is a testament to the inclusivity of the Anti-Elitist Constitution, offering protection for partisans of all persuasions. The Plebiscites for Abortion and Self-Defense in Article 22 further demonstrate the Constitution's commitment to resolving contentious issues through voter consensus post-ratification.

Ultimately, the weight assigned to different grievances is subjective. Many Conservatives will claim that surrendering Enumerated Powers is a fundamental retreat from non-negotiable core principles. Progressives will argue that transferring more tax revenue to the States irrevocably weakens the federal government, the main engine for adopting national policies like Universal Healthcare. However, eliminating Enumerated Powers in exchange for transferring tax revenues removes the ability of the Supreme Court to strike down Universal Healthcare as unconstitutional.

These objections underscore the need for the Moderate Middle American Persuasionists to take the lead in enacting these reforms and resisting the Submissionist's demands. Their role is pivotal to writing and ratifying a new Constitution.

SOLICITATION OF BOOK REVIEWS

Thank you so much for making it this far!

Your time is valuable, and I greatly appreciate that you brought my words into your life. As a small independent publisher, it means a lot, and I hope my words have enriched your perspective.

If you have 75 seconds, reading your honest feedback on Amazon will mean the world to me. Your review does wonders for the book, and candid feedback assists me in improving the second edition.

To leave your feedback:

1. Go to https://www.amazon.com/
2. Type The Anti-Elitist Constitution in the search field and hit ENTER

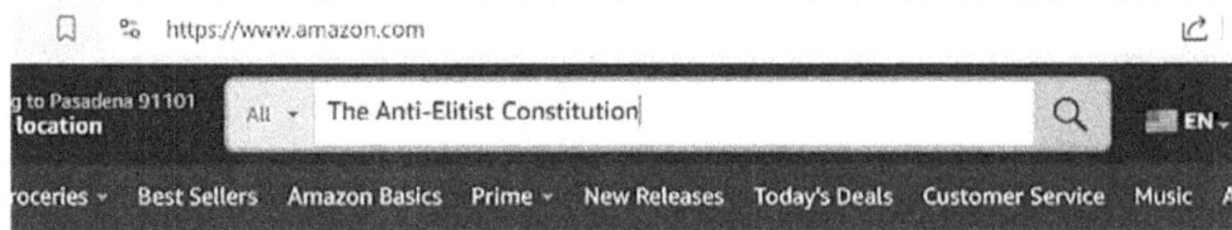

3. This will take you to a page with the picture of the book and the title. Hover your cursor over the title and click on the hyperlink that takes you to the book page
4. Scroll down until you see Book Reviews. Click on the Write a customer review button.

5. Please give other readers your honest perspective of the quality of the arguments and the book's readability, even if you did not agree with everything.

THANK YOU!

PART II

The Text and Exegesis of the Anti-Elitist Constitution

June 19, 2024

The First Draft of America's New Constitution

Table of Contents

The text of the Anti-Elitist Constitution is in Open Sans in a 10-point font.

The Exegesis is in Times New Roman in a 11-point font, indented.

PREAMBLE

We, the Citizens of the United States, agree that this Constitution shall be the covenant between Us and Our Posterity to govern those who govern Us. This Constitution shall bind Us together as a Nation by ensuring that Our Governments judge and rule Us by the content of Our character, not the color of Our skin, group affiliation, possessions, or kinship.

Therefore, We, the Citizens of this Nation and Our respective States, do ordain and establish this Constitution for the United States of America to secure the Blessings of Liberty to Ourselves and Our Posterity.

The Preamble establishes that Federal and State Governments are instruments of Citizen power accountable to the Citizens.

The covenant between Us and Our Posterity means that this document does not derive its legitimacy and purpose solely from those alive today. This phrase emphasizes the connection between the present and the future and that Citizens have obligations to their descendants.

A constitution is a document that governs not only the citizens but also the elected and appointed government officials. These officials, in turn, govern the very same voters who placed them into power. This circular logic is the essence of any Constitution for Representative Government.

The phrase *to govern those who govern Us* comes from Madison in Federalist 51:

"You must first enable the government to control the governed; and in the next place oblige it to control itself."

The power of the State and National Governments is derived entirely from their Citizens. Citizens are bound to obey the laws and can only change them by electing different representatives. However, it is important to note that the Constitution governs these representatives as the law above them.

Citizens do not engage in direct democracy to govern each other. Instead, they establish the rules that govern those they hold accountable through elections. This is akin to addressing the presiding officer during a debate instead of talking directly to your opponent. Representatives act as a mediating party between their voters. In this context, the Constitution symbolizes authority, much like a king is the head of state in a Constitutional Monarchy.

Our representatives take an oath to preserve, protect, and defend the Constitution. They don't take an oath to do whatever their constituents ask. This oath to a constitution violates the Majoritarian Theories of governance. Majoritarianism cannot abide by a constitution that restrains majority rule, so Majoritarianism inevitably devolves into tyranny by the many and the oppression of the few.

This Constitution shall bind Us as a Nation by ensuring that Our Governments judge and rule Us by the content of Our character, not the color of Our skin, group affiliation, possessions, or kinship.

This sentence expands Dr. Martin Luther King, Jr.'s wish by including other attributes that erode Individualism and promote group allegiances that can form the basis of bigotry and discrimination. The goal of this document is to bind individuals together as a nation.

The phrase *We, the Citizens of this Nation and Our respective States*, acknowledges Federalism and Individualism, recognizing disparate individuals from different corners of the Nation (i.e., States) coming together to establish a new government. National Citizenship is the common bond that unites disparate individuals.

However, this phrase also recognizes and protects differences between Citizens in different States. This phrase acknowledges that their differing governing philosophies are an essential characteristic protected by this document. Respect for these differences is necessary for uniting Citizens into a single Nation. Suppressing these differences would be the ruin of the national unity enterprise.

Contrast this Preamble with the Preamble of the 1787 Constitution:

We the People of the United States, in Order to form a more perfect Union, establish Justice, insure domestic Tranquility, provide for the common defence, promote the general Welfare, and secure the Blessings of Liberty to ourselves and our Posterity, do ordain and establish this Constitution for the United States of America.

The Anti-Elitist Constitution replaces *We the People* with *We the Citizens*. Immediately, it distinguishes Citizens from persons or people. In the 1787 Constitution, the term *We the People* is ambiguous. Does it refer to a collective will or individual people?

The voters who supported ratification of the 1789 Constitution were not identical to the People. In one sense, it was appropriate because enslaved Blacks and women could believe in the Preamble as potential beneficiaries of the Blessings of Liberty. *We the People* is grander and more inclusive than *We the Citizens*, but it is also less accurate because race and sex are not qualifications for Citizenship in the Anti-Elitist Constitution.

To form a more perfect Union is replaced by *shall bind Us together as a Nation*. The significant difference is that the 1787 Constitution refers to a more perfect *Union of States* emphasizing the importance of unity among State governments whose delegates ratified the Constitution. There is a substantial philosophical difference between the Anti-Elitist and the 1787 Constitution. For the Anti-Elitist Constitution, it would be more accurate to assign the name *The United* ***Citizens*** *of America rather than The United* ***States*** *of America* because it captures the essence of the sovereignty of the Citizens while the federal and state governments are merely their instruments for wielding power.

Article 1.

United States Citizenship, Residency and State Citizenship

Citizenship should not be manipulated for partisan goals because it defines who can participate in the political process. It should be a fixed foundation, the bedrock of the political process. The 1787 Constitution was vague about the matter until the 14th Amendment:

All persons born or naturalized in the United States, and subject to the jurisdiction thereof, are citizens of the United States and of the State wherein they reside.

There is a significant debate around the idea that place of birth should not automatically grant citizenship, particularly if the parents are not citizens, do not uphold American civic values, and enter the country illegally. The document aims to remove this strong incentive for illegal entry, with the hope of preventing parents from seeking citizenship for themselves through their children born on US soil.

The 1787 Constitution uses the terms *people, persons, and citizens*, and it's not always clear if they are interchangeable or refer to different groups of individuals or individuals collaborating. *People* is used in the 1st, 2nd, 4th, 9th, and 10th Amendments, *person* in the 5th, *owner* in the 3rd, and *accused* in the 6th.

Person, owner, and accused clearly mean individuals. *The People* refers to the collective, the customers of the public servants who rule at the people's sufferance. *The people* are distinct from the aristocracy, whose right to rule in the past was hereditary or tyrannical without the consent of the governed.

In the 1787 Constitution, *Citizen* appears in Article 1, Sections 2 (qualifications for electors and Members of the House), Section 3 (qualifications for Senators), Article 2, Section 1 (qualifications for President), Article 3, Sections 1 and 2. *Citizen* also appears in the 11th, 14th, 15th, 19th, 24th, and 26th Amendments. This document will be more precise in the usage of these words.

Section 1. Value of Citizenship and A Common Language

Citizenship and the amendment powers vested in a Citizen are both antecedents to this Constitution before its Ratification.

The Citizens are the sovereign above the Constitution. Whoever was a Citizen (Birthright or Naturalized) before the ratification of this document remains a Citizen, even if they would not qualify under its provisions. For example, Vice President Kamala Harris or Senator Ted Cruz would not be eligible as a Birthright Citizen under this document. However, their Birthright Citizenship pre-dates this document so that ratification would not change their status.

Upon Ratification, this Constitution not only establishes the requirements for new members of the Citizenry but also serves as a guide to preserve and bolster the institutions of this Nation for Our Posterity. Whether through Birthright or Naturalization, membership in the Citizenry fosters a unified sense of community and national purpose among diverse individuals in their individual quests for happiness and significance.

This paragraph describes the purpose of citizenship, which is to unify individuals under a standard set of values.

Citizens have a reasonable expectation that their fellow Citizens are proficient in using a single, common language for the conduct of conversation, commerce, and government to strengthen the fraternal bonds of this Nation. The language used to compose this Constitution shall be that single, shared, official language used in the proceedings of and in the text of the laws enforced by Government officials. No law may compel the Government to conduct its affairs in another language. No person who does not comprehend this official language, who is in the custody of the police or on trial, may be denied the services of a translator.

There was something that unified the colonists in their battle against England. In Federalist 2 [1], John Jay wrote:

"With equal pleasure, I have as often taken notice that Providence has been pleased to give this one connected country to one united people—a people descended from the same ancestors, speaking the same language, professing the same religion, attached to the same principles of government, very similar in their manners and customs, and who, by their joint counsels, arms, and efforts, fighting side by side throughout a long and bloody war, have nobly established general liberty and independence."

A Common Language is not just a convenience but a necessity for a unified country with a vibrant economy and effective military, legal, and political institutions. We must learn from the challenges faced by nations like Belgium, Canada, China, Spain, Russia, and others that incorporate different nationalities within their boundaries, where linguistic divisions have often led to social and political tensions. This section adopts the practice of most Western European nations that require linguistic fluency as a precondition for naturalized Citizenship, recognizing the role of language in fostering national unity.

Section 2. Limitations on Additional Immigration

The exclusion of persons from Citizenship and residency in the United States is necessary to balance protecting natural resources and wilderness habitats with accommodations for human habitation. Limiting exogenous population growth is essential for sustainable practices for agriculture, animal husbandry, mineral extraction, timber harvesting, and sustainable use of aquifers, rivers, lakes, and oceans. Laws regulating the entry into the country by non-Citizens and rules for permanent and temporary residency cannot degrade the ecological, economic, and civic well-being of current Citizens and their Posterity.

> This paragraph connects the nation's ecological health to the number of inhabitants. Endogenous reproduction shows signs of tapering off in the future, so the population could remain close to the current level if not even decline. Our immigration policy influences the ecological health and the economic and civic well-being of current Citizens. This paragraph does not consider racial or cultural factors. Citizenship has no value without the ability to exclude.

Pursuant to these goals, the number of additional refugees and other persons entering the United States for the fiscal year cannot exceed one-four hundredth of the existing population of Citizens living in the United States, according to the most recent census by the Census Board. With a three-fifths vote, Congress may enact legislation to suspend this limitation for twelve months.

> This Section thwarts the political manipulation of immigration for partisan advantage. With an estimated 300,000,000 Citizens in 2024, this Section permits an annual immigration of 750,000 persons, including Refugees.

Section 3. Sanctions for Illegal Entry

Any person who has violated the laws governing immigration, entry, or travel may not obtain Citizenship during their lifetime. No pardon or laws enacted to grant amnesty can exempt a person from this prohibition, nor may this violation be expunged from their record.

> This Section provides powerful deterrence against illegal immigration. It does not bar illegal immigrants from seeking legal residency, but they would have to exit the US and apply through the proper channels. The prohibition of pardons, amnesty, and expunging a record is necessary to prevent the exploitation of illegal immigrants for partisan advantage.

Section 4. Birthright Citizenship

The following persons are Birthright Citizens of the United States:

The biological descendant of a female and a male who were both Citizens of the United States on the date of birth of the descendant.

Birthright Citizenship is a necessary qualification for elected Government officials. Therefore, some effort is devoted to defining and differentiating it from Naturalized Citizenship. This document adopts *Jus Sanguinis* – the right of blood doctrine of Citizenship where the Child's birthright citizenship is not dependent upon where he was born, just the status of his parents. *Jus Solis* – right of the soil doctrine of Citizenship central to the 14th amendment is mostly discarded for birthright citizenship in this document, except for cases of surrogate births where it combines with *Jus Sanguinis*. This definition of Birthright Citizenship removes the incentive for persons to illegally enter the US to have their children become Birthright US Citizens. However, their children can become legal permanent residents or naturalized US Citizens.

The Citizenship of the female whose egg was fertilized shall determine the maternal line of Birthright Citizenship in cases where there is artificial insemination or a surrogate that carries a fertilized egg from another female. The Citizenship of the male who inseminated the egg shall determine the paternal line of Birthright Citizenship.

The descendant may receive Birthright Citizenship or Legal Permanent Residency from a single female or a single male applying such methods only when they are born in the Territory of the United States and when the female and male assume parental custody and financial responsibility for the descendant.

Medical technology challenges the standard understanding of the connection between parents and their children and how parents bestow Birthright Citizenship within the *Jus Sanguinis* doctrine for Citizenship. A male US Citizen could inseminate thousands of foreign females, and we wouldn't want to grant all their offspring US Citizenship.

> In cases where foreign surrogates are employed, then requiring that these children be born in US Territory facilitates the authentication that the female egg carried by the surrogate came from a US Citizen. The requirement for assuming parental custody and financial responsibility for the child eliminates trafficking in children with Birthright Citizenship. It is tempting to leave these matters to Congress, but including them in this document leaves no opportunity to manipulate Birthright Citizenship for partisan advantage.

Congress shall have the power to enforce this Section by appropriate legislation. This includes legislation for biological methods used to authenticate the maternal or paternal line and evidence of birth in the territory of the United States.

Section 5. Naturalized Citizenship

Entry, residency, or Naturalized Citizenship is a privilege, not a right. No Treaty shall abridge the authority of Congress to regulate this privilege. Congress shall establish uniform Rules for Naturalization as a Citizen of the United States that are subject to the following requirements:

> The first sentence establishes the value of Naturalized Citizenship as a privilege. The second sentence eliminates the possibility of using Treaty Agreements to evade the supremacy of Congress to regulate these matters.

The applicant provides evidence of legal entry into the United States and at least five years as a United States National or Resident. Excepting non-citizen, minor children born to or adopted by a Citizen with legal custody of the children, the applicant must provide evidence of a minimum of five consecutive years of payment of taxes to the Government and no tax payments in arrears and no convictions for any felonies.

> The five-year legal residency is the trial period when the Government evaluates the applicant's compliance with the laws and ability to survive without welfare support.

The applicant provides evidence they have not received cumulative financial assistance from the Government for a minimum of three consecutive years immediately before the date of the grant of Citizenship exceeding one-tenth of the Compensation Index.

> In 2024, if they received more than $17,500 in financial assistance during the prior three years, then they don't qualify. Only productive members of society qualify for Naturalized Citizenship.

The applicant demonstrates proficiency in understanding the language used to compose this Constitution, an understanding of the Civic Institutions of the United States, and the ability to fully participate in the civic and economic affairs of the nation using this language without reliance upon language translation.

> Many Western European countries require language fluency as a condition for Citizenship. It is unlikely that someone could fully participate in civic affairs like jury duty, following election campaigns, and voting unless they were fluent in reading and speaking English. This document does not prevent them from becoming legal permanent residents if they aren't fluent in English. It reserves Citizenship for those who can fully participate in commerce and civic affairs.

Section 6. American Nationals and Residents

Two classes of persons possess the rights of Legal Permanent Residency:

United States Nationals are not Citizens. They travel under a United States Passport and do not retain citizenship in another nation. They have the right to reside, work, travel, and own property in the United States.

> These categories are valuable classifications for DREAMERs and Refugees, so they are not stateless. These are people who don't have a passport or Citizenship in another country or who cannot return to their country but still wish to have the ability to work and reside in the US. These people can come out from under the shadows by achieving legal status without upsetting the partisan balance in government. This classification strengthens bi-partisan immigration policy efforts.

United States Residents are not Citizens. They travel under a foreign passport and retain citizenship in another nation. Contingent upon the relationship with their country of citizenship, the United States may revoke their right to reside, work, travel, and own property in the United States.

> Under this classification, illegal immigrants from Mexico and Central America could retain their passports and Citizenship in their country of origin. With US Residency, they obtain legal status and can emerge from under the shadows. They can work, but they cannot vote. This classification eliminates the potential partisan threat of illegal immigrants and makes their acceptance more likely.

Congress may enact laws to discriminate in treating members of these two classes. Congress shall enact laws to receive applications for and approve Legal Permanent Residency.

Section 7. Legal Temporary Residents and Refugees

Legal Temporary Residents are persons who obtained legal permission to enter the United States for travel, school, or work within the United States. Except for diplomatic missions, permission for Legal Temporary Residency shall not exceed eighty-four months for any person during any consecutive twenty-year period.

> This Section covers people on work, school, or travel visas. This paragraph imposes maximum time periods to ensure this loophole cannot be exploited to bypass the requirements for Legal Permanent Residency.

If an individual bypasses the standard procedures for admission as a Legal Temporary Resident and instead seeks asylum as a legal means to enter the United States under a Treaty or Statute, they will be classified as a Refugee. Prior to admission and acceptance of Refugee status, the applicant must consent to irrevocably forfeiting the ability to obtain United States Citizenship for themselves, their spouse, and their children during their lifetimes. Furthermore, admitted Refugees may be subject to confinement and restrictions upon travel within the United States.

> After removing the oppression motivating their exit, Refugees should eventually return to their country of origin. Foreclosing the option of obtaining Citizenship for himself, his spouse, parents, or children deters those abusing Refugee laws for economic motivations. However, the path to legal permanent residency is not blocked.

The President has the authority to transfer Refugees to another country that will not subject them to persecution or involuntary repatriation to their country of origin.

> Refugee Treaties are a big loophole used by illegal immigration supporters. This Section deftly handles the problem because a Treaty cannot supersede the Constitution. The US can outsource its Refugee care to other nations, and this is a further deterrent to abuse of Refugee applications experienced since 2021. Refugees are supposed to return to their country of origin after the crisis causing their migration to end. It is not a substitute pathway to apply for permanent residency.

Legal Temporary Residents, Refugees, and illegal residents are the Federal Government's financial responsibility. States, Citizens, and Legal Residents are entitled to reimbursement for documented expenditures.

> This relieves the fiscal burden endured by the border States from lax enforcement. However, unless the authorities can document the expenditures and identify the responsible parties, then they won't get reimbursed. You cannot be a sanctuary city and get reimbursed.

Section 8. Transferring Legal Residency to Descendants

The biological descendant of a Citizen, on its date of birth, and a non-citizen shall be a United States National, provided there is proof that the descendant was born within the Territory of the United States.

A biological descendant of a male and female who were both Legal Permanent Residents on the date of birth shall be a United States National who may apply for Naturalization as a Citizen when they attain thirteen years old.

This section describes various Citizenship and Residency status combinations to determine how their descendants will be classified. The first case deals with a US Citizen who has a child with a non-Citizen. A non-citizen could be a legal permanent resident, an illegal resident, or a foreigner traveling and working in the US or living abroad. In each case, that child would be a US National if born on US Soil. Presumably, this would be most common with a female US Citizen giving birth on US soil, while the offspring of male Citizens with women overseas would not obtain this classification. The parents of US Residents with foreign Citizenship may give their own child foreign Citizenship. Nevertheless, as a US National, this child could apply to become a Naturalized Citizen as early as age 13.

A natural person who has not attained thirteen years and is adopted by a Citizen shall acquire the rights of a United States National.

A biological descendant from a male and female who were a Legal Temporary Resident, a Refugee, or an Illegal Resident on the date of birth shall be a United States National, provided there is proof that the descendant was born within the Territory of the United States. That person is ineligible to become a Naturalized Citizen during their lifetime unless they leave the United States for at least one hundred twenty consecutive months before applying for Citizenship.

This paragraph considers adoption when assigning persons to a class of residency. If a Citizen adopts a child before age 13, they automatically become US Nationals. Their adoptive parents must apply for legal permanent residency on the adoptee's behalf if they are older than 13.

This child will not be stateless, but they won't be anchor babies used to ease the way for their parents to obtain Citizenship or Legal Permanent Residency. This paragraph motivates parents to take their children when they leave the United States. This child could later apply to become a US citizen in the same queue as others. This section applies to the DREAMERS who were born in the US. Although these DREAMERS did not illegally cross into the US, this 10-year exit requirement to apply for Citizenship removes a significant incentive for future persons to attempt illegal entry to benefit their future children.

Section 9. Transparency of Queue and Presidential Discretion

The Government shall publicly disclose the queue of applicants for temporary and permanent residency and naturalization. Separate from this queue of applicants, the President may offer expedited processing every fiscal year to no more than five thousand persons specifically in exchange for the conduct of warfare, espionage, or testimony in prosecuting criminal suspects. These persons may remain anonymous if the Speaker certifies the President's compliance with this Section. Congress may temporarily increase this limitation by a three-fifths vote each fiscal year, which expires at the end of the fiscal year.

A transparent queue deters bribery of officials. Presidential discretion for exceptions to this rule recognizes that particular skills and emergency needs may arise that require anonymity. This transparency also exposes discrimination in favor of nationality due to a crisis of the month, unfairly punishing those applicants who went through the process in an orderly manner.

Section 10. State Citizenship; Federal District or Territory Residency

The Citizen of a State must be a Citizen of the United States. The Government will register a Citizen of the United States as a resident of a Federal District or Territory or as a Transient Citizen with voting rights in the Federal House District unless they are registered as a Citizen of a State. A Citizen reports a single primary residence to the Census Board to determine their State Citizenship for eligibility to vote exclusively in elections held by their State and in Federal elections.

States cannot give State Citizenship to persons who are not US Citizens. This Section ensures that State politicians cannot exploit non-citizens for partisan advantages. Also, homeless persons without a home address, those who travel the country in RVs, or those who live abroad without a fixed home address in the USA are designated as Transient Citizens.

No State may abridge the right of Citizens and legal residents of the United States to enter their State or to travel within or outside the State unless these persons are charged with or convicted of a criminal offense.

Section 11. Surrendering Citizenship

If a Territory or State of the United States becomes an independent nation, then the residents and Citizens of this new Nation who were Citizens or Legal Residents of the United States on the date of independence forfeit their Citizenship and Legal Residency in the United States.

A person may voluntarily renounce their Citizenship by a written declaration witnessed by an official of the Federal Government and a Citizen not employed by the Government whom that person designates. The Government shall revoke the Citizenship of any person who committed fraud in their application for naturalization. Otherwise, the Government may not unilaterally rescind the Citizenship of a Citizen.

The US Government cannot unilaterally revoke someone's US Citizenship, except when fraud occurs. This Section does not protect the right to possess a US Passport, so that's the harshest sanction the Federal Government could mete out. This Section defines the method for voluntarily surrendering Citizenship. The Government could offer to drop or reduce criminal charges in exchange for surrendering their Citizenship and accepting expulsion to another country that would take them.

This Section also contemplates the possibility that US Territories like Puerto Rico or Guam might seek independence. With independence comes the surrender of US Citizenship and residency privileges.

Article 2.

ELECTIONS

Citizenship and Elections are essential Foundations of Representative Government. Therefore, both are defined in detail at the beginning of this document, unlike the 1787 Constitution that left States in charge of running federal elections. This Article governs how both Federal and State elections will operate.

Section 1. Sovereign Power and Eligibility of Voters

The Electorate, comprised of Eligible Voters, is the Sovereign; this Constitution and State Constitutions are instruments for exercising this sovereign power. The power to establish and amend these Constitutions is vested with Eligible Voters. Eligible Voters delegate the powers exercised by Elected Representatives under these Constitutions.

The hierarchy of power puts Eligible Voters at the top, with control over the Constitution and Elected Representatives. Unlike the UK, where Parliament is the Sovereign, the US Electorate is the Sovereign. This sovereign power is exercised through federal and state constitutions. This emphasizes that the federal government is a mere instrument, alongside the states but below the voters.

Every Citizen of the United States shall be an Eligible Voter for Government Elections if they attained the age of eighteen years, are not in prison, and are not a Citizen of another country. The text of this Constitution shall be displayed in front of the Speaker in the House of Representatives whenever the Committee of the Whole House is in session, and it shall be removed during recess.

Even persons who have served their time in prison or haven't paid fines and taxes cannot have their right to vote abridged as they did in Florida. The only other restrictions included later relate to employment by the government and mental illness. Dual nationals are prohibited from voting. We say, pick a side and stick with them. No fence-straddling.

Like the Mace in the United Kingdom's House of Commons, this document symbolizes the sovereign's power. House Members will constantly be reminded that they are subject to rule under this document.

Eligible Voters have the right to participate in Elections. To have their ballot counted, Eligible Voters must comply with regulations required of all other Eligible Voters to operate a secure electoral system. This electoral system ensures that for each office on the ballot, only Eligible Voters may cast one vote for one candidate for a single office in a single election.

Notice that there isn't a right for every vote to be counted. Instead, there is a right to cast a ballot, but it is only counted when the voter complies with the regulations. The reputation of the electoral system is more important than a single voter. Voters are responsible for maintaining the reputation of the system.

Section 2. Right to a Secret Ballot

Eligible Voters have the right to cast a single secret ballot with a list of offices and candidates for each office and a write-in option. The Eligible Voter must select voting options on an unmarked ballot. To facilitate automated counting and enhance secrecy, the ballot instrument used for counting may omit listing the names of candidates next to the marking made by the voter.

The Secret Ballot was an essential innovation in the 19th Century that significantly reduced vote-buying, intimidation, and fraud. This Section gives Secret Ballots protected status. Punch card ballots do not have the names of candidates following the punch mark, so they enhance secrecy. These are allowed and encouraged. Government officials could more easily violate voting privacy when the candidates' names are adjacent to the voter's marked selection.

The vote-casting procedures and the ballot's color, shape, and material composition shall not disclose which candidates the voter chose.

The Soviet Union used to have two separate ballot boxes. One box was for votes cast for Communist Party candidates, and the second box was for *None of the Above*. This allowed poll workers to identify the dissidents.

A common practice in some countries is having slate ballots with different colors and boxes depending upon the political party you support. While technically a secret vote after entering the ballot box, these methods allow anyone to observe how someone voted, so it is not genuinely secret. This paragraph prohibits these and other methods that could compromise secrecy.

An Eligible Voter is guaranteed the right to cast a Secret Ballot to protect a voter from inducement, coercion, and punishment. Any method for delivery of ballots and in-person voting of ballots that could connect the identity of the Eligible Voter to their ballot at any point in time after selecting the voting option and transferring the ballot to the custody of an Election Official shall be a violation of this fundamental right to secrecy.

The Secret Ballot is the default assumption for the voting method. It has primacy. This paragraph emphasizes the importance of secrecy in preserving voters' independence and making decisions about the persons holding power without fear that the government could retaliate against them.

Section 3. Procedures for Non-Secret Ballots

When an Eligible Voter does not wish to vote in the presence of an Election Official who would authenticate their eligibility to vote, that Eligible Voter has the right to request a ballot that is not secret. For each election, Eligible Voters must make a separate request for a non-secret ballot. Non-secret ballots must be inserted within an envelope imprinted with information that links the envelope to the identity of the Eligible Voter who marked it. Voter identification shall not be on any ballot.

This paragraph acknowledges that Mail-In Ballots are a convenience demanded by many Voters, emphasizing their crucial role in the election process. There are two main reasons why the government cannot send mail-in ballots without a request. The first reason is that voters could have mailed their ballot, forgotten, and then voted in person. This underscores the importance of each voter's responsibility. First, count all the Secret Ballots and compile the list of people who voted. Then use that list to exclude counting Mail-In Ballots of persons who already voted in person.

The second reason is that if voters automatically receive Mail-In Ballots, then everyone knows you have that option. Influencers could threaten a voter if the voter doesn't permit an influencer to inspect a voter's selections before the influencers seal the envelope and mails it. This Section permits a voter to claim that they never asked for a Mail-In Ballot, and the influencer is unlikely to know enough to confirm if this is true.

Mail-in ballots are not secret, so they are labeled as Non-Secret Ballots. However, there are ways to obscure the identity of the person voting with a Mail-In Ballot to most persons handling the envelopes containing the ballots. Instead of requiring a voter's signature and printed name, you could have a pre-printed Q-R Code or Bar Code on the ballot envelope. Machines linked to the Voter Registration database could read this code at the vote-counting center. If the code doesn't match someone in the database, then the envelope containing the ballot is rejected. As a backup, you could request that the voter print their birthday and last 4-digits of their SSN, in case the code reader malfunctioned. This backup ensures that poll workers don't see the identity, but the few higher-level managers with access to the database could figure it out.

The Government may not deliver non-secret ballots to voters who did not request to use one. The Government must provide a valid, Non-Secret Ballot and identifying envelope.

> You must make a new request every election to receive a Mail-In Ballot. Forcing someone to make this request each election eliminates mailing out ballots to persons who have died or moved.

To prevent duplicate and fraudulent voting, the Government may not begin counting non-secret ballots before compiling the identities of eligible voters who cast a secret ballot, excluding non-secret ballots from those who have already cast secret ballots.

No Eligible Voter may allow another person to inspect selections, nor may they make a copy of those selections on their secret or non-secret ballot. A violation shall be punishable by suspending voting privileges for no less than six years from the date of conviction. The Elections Board shall make exceptions when someone physically coerces a voter and the voter identifies the assailant. The Elections Board shall identify Eligible Voters with a physical handicap that impairs their competence to make an independent vote.

> When voters take photographs of their ballots, they compromise the secret ballot system for others. This prohibition prevents vote manipulators from having the evidence they require to authenticate bribes or threats made to voters. Making these displays illegal protects the other voters who wish to keep their selections secret and not be subject to this intimidation. Prescribing harsh sanctions will provide a meaningful deterrent.

Any person who coerces selections or offers bribes in exchange for selections on the ballot of an Eligible Voter shall be fined no less than the Compensation Index, be imprisoned for no less than five hundred days, and suspended from voting for no less than six years from the date of conviction.

Section 4. Prohibition of Government Employees Voting

Excepting Elected Government Officials, any person who was an employee of the Government of the United States at any time during the period between six months before the Final Voting Date and the Final Voting Date is ineligible to vote in that election. Citizens serving in the military reserves, not on active duty, who are not also Government employees, and Citizens drafted into military or other involuntary servitude by the Government shall be exempt from this prohibition.

> Voluntarily employed government workers are servants of the citizenry and have a conflict of interest in decisions about taxation and spending. Managers cannot exploit government employees for political purposes, offering them protection. However, involuntary government servitude in a military draft cannot be used as a tool to suppress the voices who might disagree with the policies forcing their service. We carve out an exception for persons in the military reserves because that is not a full-time government job. The six-month window prevents terminating Federal employment just before an election and then rehiring to evade the spirit of this prohibition.

Section 5. Protections Against Electoral Fraud

Citizens of the United States have a fundamental right to an election process that ensures that an Eligible Voter casts no more than one ballot in a single Election and that only Eligible Voters may cast one ballot. The Government shall record the chain of custody for every secret ballot to identify the Precinct of Origin and the Official from the Elections Board who authenticated the voter who cast a ballot. The Elections Board shall adopt procedures to verify the identity of an Eligible Voter before they cast their ballot. Persons found guilty of electoral fraud shall be barred from any employment by the Government and shall serve no less than five hundred days in prison.

> This paragraph requires that elections operate with security protocols and audit trails that can identify individuals committing electoral fraud. The Elections Board must implement a voter identification system to prevent fraudulent misrepresentation of the voter's identity. Voter sign-in lists can have a birth date and last four digits of SSN visible to the poll worker so that they can query the voter to authenticate their identity instead of asking for a picture ID.

The Elections Board shall adopt procedures for processing Non-Secret Ballots that ensure an Eligible Voter casts no more than one ballot in a single Election, and only Eligible Voters may cast one ballot. The Elections Board shall record the chain of custody for every Non-Secret ballot to identify the Officials from the Elections Board who handled the ballot to count its votes.

Section 6. Deadline for Registering for a Precinct and Privacy

After the thirty-fifth day before the Final Voting Date, the Elections Board shall not register Eligible Voters to a precinct list for any Federal Election. Eligible Voters for a District must have been registered residents of that District for no fewer than sixty days before the thirty-five-day deadline. The Elections Board will announce the total number of Eligible Voters and their names for each precinct on the thirtieth day before the Final Voting Date. Eligible Voters who move out of a District after the thirty-fifth day before the Voting Date may not vote for candidates in their new District, but they are still eligible to vote for candidates in the District of their prior Final residence.

> This 35-day cutoff gives the Registrar enough time to compile a list of voters to begin the 30-day Early Voting Period. At some point, the list must be frozen simultaneously for all precincts. Otherwise, one person could vote in the same election in two or more precincts. The Elections Board won't exclude a voter who moved from casting a ballot for candidates in their old home district. This 35-day cutoff and 60-day minimum residency requirement also

thwart schemes where voters could be bused in from safe Districts outside the District for election day or a brief time to pad the vote totals for a party or candidate in a closely contested District.

Section 7. Reconciling The Number of Voters To Ballots Cast

The Elections Board shall count and publish the number of Eligible Voters who cast a secret ballot before commencing the count of Eligible Voters who cast a non-secret ballot. The Elections Board shall compare the names of persons casting Non-Secret Ballots to the list of persons who cast a Secret Ballot, and the Board will withdraw invalid, duplicate ballots. The Board shall count the remaining ballots by precinct and record and announce the results. The counting of votes for candidates contained on the ballots may not commence before the announcement of the total number of Eligible Voters who cast a ballot. Once the Board initiates tabulation of votes on the ballots, the Board may not include additional ballots to determine the outcome of the election unless fifty Members of the House of Representatives or five Senators petition the Supreme Court to halt the commencement of the tabulation for no more than three days if they present material evidence of excluded or fake ballots.

Election officials must fix the number of eligible ballots before counting them to have a system that prevents and detects fraud. The current system counts ballots as other ballots arriving, sometimes weeks after the voting date. Any method that does not announce the total number of ballots before beginning the count allows corrupt officials to gauge how many fake ballots to dump into the system based on the preliminary tallies showing the gap between candidates. After announcing the total number of ballots, election officials cannot add or subtract ballots to corrupt the count. This system does not permit an election night call of the winner because it might take a few days before announcing the total number of ballots.

Suppose all voters visiting a precinct sign into the registration booklet, which is how the precinct measures the number of persons who cast a ballot. If the number of ballots counted exceeds the number of sign-ins, someone stuffed the ballot boxes with counterfeit ballots, or someone who didn't appear on the registration list was allowed to cast a ballot. If the number of voters counted exceeds the number of ballots counted, then some ballots were destroyed, or some of the persons who signed in, didn't cast a ballot. Bringing things down to the precinct level allows us to identify the perpetrators of the fraud more efficiently and to contain the problem at the lowest level possible.

The Elections Board shall propose statutes to govern the conduct of new elections in these disputed precincts and to add the new ballots to the count of total votes cast. If the Board discovers a material discrepancy between votes counted for all candidates for a single office from the announced number of voters who cast ballots that could change which Candidate received the most votes, then the Board shall withdraw the votes in those precincts from the total count and order a new election in those precincts starting the following Saturday and finishing the following Tuesday. The Elections Board shall add these new votes to the adjusted vote total to determine the Candidate that has received the most votes.

This paragraph anticipates that fraud or errors could occur in several precincts. If there is a material number of discrepancies that could change the outcome, then this Section prescribes the remedy – re-running the voting in those precincts with the discrepancies. Presumably, extra care and oversight will occur in those districts to eliminate the material discrepancies during the first round of voting. Under the 1787 Constitution, every state and every county registrar within a state oversaw the detection of differences and provided a remedy. The Anti-Elitist Constitution doesn't permit partisan election officials to have discretion in counting ballots and detecting fraud.

Section 8. Oversight of Ballot Count

Elections Board Employees shall not count the number of Eligible Voters who cast a ballot, nor shall they count the votes for candidates contained on the ballots cast from the precincts where they administered the voting. Every candidate on a ballot can designate an observer in every place where the Elections Board counts ballots with the candidate's name and counts the number of Eligible Voters who cast a ballot. The Elections Board must apply equal treatment for all Observers and provide no less than twenty-four hours notification to ensure Observers have adequate time to appear before the commencement of counting. All Observer objections shall be recorded and reviewed by the Elections Board. Observers can take audio and video recordings of the Elections Board staff while they handle the ballots.

Poll workers aren't allowed to count the voters' ballots from their precinct to prevent tampering with the audit trail, which is basic common sense.

Because later Sections of this document will limit the maximum number of candidates on a ballot to six, having six observers at counting stations will not present any practical difficulties. This paragraph requires election officials not to prevent observers from recording the counting of ballots by video to ensure transparency of the process. This Article eliminates the faith-based elections of the current regime, where voter registrars could inhibit the inspection of vote counting using complaints that observers are interfering with the efficient operation of the vote count. Write-in candidates are excluded to prevent overcrowding of observers at vote-counting sites.

Section 9. Storage of Ballots, Audits, Recounts

The Elections Board shall provide ballots made of a durable physical medium that preserves selections by voters. The Board shall observe recounts and audits of ballots and voter registrations requested by Candidates. The Board shall store ballots no less than three hundred days after the Final Voting Date. Every unaffiliated Candidate and every Political Party with a candidate on a ballot can designate an Observer in every place where ballots with the Candidate's name are recounted. Any candidate on a ballot has the right to deposit reasonable costs into an escrow account sufficient to pay for a recount or to audit the chain of custody of all the ballots cast in their area of representation. The escrow shall refund this deposit if the recount reverses the announced results.

Section 10. Ordinary Voting Period for Secret and Non-Secret Ballots

The Final Voting Date shall be the Tuesday following the first Monday of November in every even-numbered calendar year. The Ordinary Voting Period for Federal Offices shall be the Saturday, Sunday, and Monday preceding the Final Voting Date and the Final Voting Date on Tuesday. The Elections Board shall not count Non-Secret Ballots post-marked earlier than the preceding Tuesday of the Final Voting Date. The Board shall not count Non-Secret Ballots post-marked after the Final Voting Date. Only Elections Board staff may collect ballots from Eligible Voters before the preceding Tuesday of the Final Voting Date.

> More voters can participate, especially those with family care and work obligations, by spreading voting out over four days, including the weekend. For many, voting in person on Tuesdays is inconvenient. It also lessens the waiting times for voting. You could have greater spacing between people waiting in line during a pandemic. Voters will not send Mail-In Ballots sooner than a week before the Final Voting date, lessening the chance of people voting too early and missing late-breaking campaign information. This paragraph makes ballot harvesting more difficult because harvesters cannot legally collect ballots sooner than one week before the Final Voting Date, compressing the time to collect ballots.

Section 11. Special Accommodations for Disabled Voters

The Extraordinary Voting Period for Eligible Voters who are physically disabled or who are under police protection and unable to visit a voting precinct shall be no more than thirty days before the Final Voting Date. The Elections Board shall propose statutes to Congress for the classification of persons qualified for Extraordinary Voting privileges and the procedures for the manner, time, and place of visits by Elections Board Employees.

An Election Board Employee shall deliver the voting instruments and collect them directly from the voter after authenticating the voter's eligibility during the Extraordinary Voting Period.

> This paragraph eliminates the need for ballot harvesting by persons not employed by the government. A 30-day window is open for poll workers to visit disabled voters in their residences to pick up their ballots if they don't opt to mail them.

The Elections Board shall provide Special Ballot instruments to blind voters or voters suffering motor-ability ailments that prevent using the Standard Ballot. If the Elections Board Employee believes that an Eligible Voter is mentally impaired and unable to make an independent selection, that voter will be reported to the Elections Board for review, possible removal from the Eligible Voter Registration, and adjudication in the event of a dispute over this finding.

> The elderly in nursing homes, incapable of voting, won't have to rely on private parties filling out their ballots. Doing this over 30 days should be plenty of time to handle valid requests. The Elections Board must propose statutes to determine valid requests for personal visits by Elections Officers to prevent abuse of this service by persons able to vote during the regular 4-day period of in-person voting at the precinct.

Section 12. Exclusive Federal Voting Period

Except for special elections to fill vacancies in the House of Representatives, no State or its political subdivisions may sponsor an election sixty days before or after the final voting date of a biennial federal election.

This Section eliminates the cluttered and confusing ballots that differ across the country. The Federal Election will stand above the clutter and protect the State elections so that the media's focus on the Federal Elections won't drown them out. State election campaigns won't overlap Federal ones with the 60-day window.

Section 13. Biennial Federal Elections

Elections for Federal Offices shall be held every two years on even-numbered years. The Electorate shall vote for the Presidential Slate every four years. The Electorate shall vote for Members of the House of Representatives every four years.

Members of the House will have 4-year terms instead of the current 2-year terms, which make it difficult for Members to get acclimated to their work while constantly engaged in running a continuous campaign. Having the House Members run separately from the President permits voters to focus more effectively on the different roles of the Executive and Legislative branches instead of confusing their roles and responsibilities.

The Electorate shall vote for Members of the House of Representatives for an initial term of two years on the date of the first Election for President following the Ratification of this Constitution. After that, Members shall serve a term of four years.

Section 14. Limiting Number of Candidates on Federal Ballot

Except for Plebiscites by Article 18, Section 5, the Federal Election ballot shall not contain any candidate, question, or proposition other than the names of Candidates for the House of Representatives or the Presidential Slate. No more than six different candidates or Slates may appear on a ballot for a single office, plus the option for a write-in candidate.

A maximum of 6 candidates further simplifies the ballot presentation. Only names of candidates for office may appear. Voter initiatives or other questions alongside the candidates cannot clutter the ballot.

Section 15. Disqualifying Dual Citizens from Voting and Holding Office

Any Citizen who does not relinquish their passport or other documents attesting to citizenship in another country and renounce that citizenship is ineligible to vote in Government Elections or to be an Elected Official or Principal Officer of the United States. Persons who violate this Section shall be subject to a minimum fine equal to the Compensation Index.

> Dual loyalties taint the undivided commitment to the United States. This restriction applies to Federal and State elections.

Section 16. Selection of President by Majority or Electoral Votes

The Presidential Slate shall be elected as follows:

The votes shall be counted in each House District and for each Federal District and Territory.

> It opens voting for presidents to citizens of the federal territories (Puerto Rico, Guam, Virgin Islands, and Northern Mariana Islands).

The Presidential Slate, receiving a majority of the popular votes from the States, Federal Districts, and Territories, wins the election.

> Later sections discuss the Slate in more detail. The mandatory Slate includes the President and Vice President. Candidates can add five names to the Slate who would assume Cabinet positions after the election and bypass Senate Confirmation hearings.

The winning Slate must achieve a majority. If no Presidential Slate wins a majority, the following process is followed:

The Elections Board publishes the rankings of the Presidential Slates. The two Presidential Slates receiving the most popular votes nationwide shall have their Electoral Votes Tabulated according to the following process:

The Electoral Votes for each State equal the number of Representatives plus one Senator.

The Elections Board shall tabulate the popular vote for the two Presidential Slates by House District and the entire State. The Slate with the most popular votes in the State receives one Electoral Vote. The Slate with the most votes in a single House District receives one Electoral Vote.

If the number of electoral votes is tied, the Presidential Slate receiving the most votes from the Federal House District wins.

> This process eliminates the need for an Electoral College, even in cases where no one wins a majority of the popular votes or when more than two major parties split the vote. This process eliminates the need for a run-off election, as in France, two weeks after the first election. Using Electoral Votes will favor a candidate with more broad-based support across the nation rather than concentrated regional support. Because the total number of House seats will increase to over 750 and the Senate will decrease to 50, Electoral Votes will no longer be tilted heavily in favor of small States, as is the case with the 1787 Constitution.

Section 17. The Presidential Slate and Line of Succession

The Presidential Slate includes the President, Vice President, and a maximum of five additional appointees for Secretaries of State, War, Domestic Security, Treasury, and Attorney General. Names for Cabinet Posts appearing on the Slate are appointed, not elected office holders. If the President and Vice President are elected, these appointees fill their positions without the possibility of removal by the Senate, except by impeachment. They would be in line to succeed the Vice President and President in the case of vacancies in those offices before or after the Final Voting Date. A majority vote of the Senate must approve any other Official appointed by the President in the Line of Succession for the Office of President. The President may only terminate a Secretary in the Line of Succession after the Secretary has served for three-hundred sixty-five days.

This Section encourages the President and Vice President to disclose their management team to the voters before the Election. The incentive to add persons to a Slate is that these appointees can assume their posts without approval from the Senate, and the President can begin his administration on Day 1 without being at the mercy of the Senate's calendar. Also, this clarifies the line of Succession should the President and/or Vice President die before the Election Date or before the inauguration.

The inclusion of a 365-day minimum service requirement for the President's appointees on the Slate is not a mere formality but a crucial protection. This measure ensures that the President cannot involuntarily dismiss them until they have served at least 365 days in office. This safeguard against the potential misuse of the Slate, preventing the inclusion of individuals as mere window-dressing to entice voter support, only to be discarded soon after inauguration.

The 1787 Constitution omitted procedures for what to do because the Framers assumed that the Electoral College would handle this problem. However, under the Elitist Constitution, where voters make the selections instead of the Electoral College, these situations create a problem. Congress can pass laws to deal with situations where the candidate dies before election day, after election day, and before Inauguration Day. However, it makes more sense to define Succession within the Constitution.

Section 18. Eligibility and Selection of House Members

The Electorate, who are Citizens registered in the House District, choose the candidate receiving the most votes to represent their District as a Member of the House of Representatives. A Member of the House or the Senate, their spouse, and minor children retain Citizenship in their State during their term in the House of Representatives or the Senate.

This Section retains the current first-past-the-post method and geographical districts for specific candidates in contrast to the system of proportional representation, which involves voting for a political party and filling seats using lists of candidates, as is done in several European nations. This first-past-the-post method encourages forming an electoral system with two major parties so that bargaining and coalition building are done before an election, not afterward, as in many European nations and Israel.

The first innovation is increasing the House term from 2 to 4 years. The second is creating a House District with its Members representing Citizens not residing in the States or persons with no permanent address. This Member will be the only one representing more than 400,000 Citizens. However, most of these residents in federal districts and federal territories will be government employees and, hence, will not be eligible voters. Creating this district ensures that all US Citizens have representation in the House, and it solves the problem of handling transients with no permanent address. Every eligible Citizen will be registered to vote, and if they are homeless or transient, they can vote for candidates for the Federal House District.

Section 19. Special Elections for House District Vacancies

The Elections Board shall hold a special election in a House District within sixty days after a Vacancy occurs whenever more than two-hundred fifty days remain before the next election. Otherwise, the seat shall remain vacant. All persons who qualified for the ballot as an Unaffiliated Candidate for the previous election for that District shall be eligible for this special election. All Political Parties that sponsored Candidates in the prior election who qualified for the ballot for that District may nominate a Candidate for this special election. The Electorate shall have a write-in option.

Section 20. Voting in the Federal House District

All Citizens who are Eligible Voters in a Federal Territory and a Federal District can participate in the Election of the Presidential Slate.

> US citizens who are residents of territories will now have the right to vote for president, the same rights as those currently enjoyed by the residents of the District of Columbia.

Section 21. Date for Inauguration for President and Seating of House

The winning candidates for the Presidential Slate and the House of Representatives certified by the Elections Board shall be sworn into office on the first Tuesday of December following the Final Voting Date.

> This Section shortens the lame-duck session to one month. This timeline eliminates the games some states play in counting and certifying their election results. Now, the votes will be counted by the National Elections Board rather than hundreds of different county registrars.

Section 22. Rules for Succession to the Presidency

When a Presidential Slate qualifies to appear on the ballot, the Presidential candidate may designate a Line of Succession in cases that the candidates for President or Vice President vacate the ballot due to death or resignation before the Inauguration Date. If the candidate for President vacates the ballot, the candidate for Vice President assumes the position of President, and the nominee for Secretary designated by the former candidate for President shall assume the position of Vice President. The new candidate for President can designate a new Line of Succession.

Article 3.

Qualification of Candidates

Section 1. Minimum Length of Citizenship to Hold Office

Every Elected Official, Principal, or Inferior Officer of the United States and the States must be a Citizen of the United States for no fewer than twenty years.

Section 2. Minimum Age and Residency Requirements to Hold Office

The following are additional requirements:

The President, Vice President, Governor General, and any Elected Official or Officer in the Line of Succession for the Presidency must have attained the age of thirty-five years and be a Birthright Citizen of the United States. No person may hold the Office of President for more than twelve years during their lifetime, and they may not appear on a ballot for President or Vice President if, upon completing a full term in Office, they would serve more than twelve years; if serving as Secretary or Minister after serving as President, they may not be in the Line of Succession.

Members of the House of Representatives must have attained the age of thirty and may not serve in the House of Representatives for more than twenty years during their lifetime. Every Member must be a Citizen of the State containing the district they represent or a resident of the Federal House District containing the Federal Districts and Territories.

> Members are not required to live inside their district boundaries, so they won't have to move their residence after redistricting. The minimum age is raised from 25 to 30, and the term limit is 20 years.

Members of the Senate must be forty years old and serve no more than twenty years in the Senate during their lifetime. Every Senator must be a Citizen of the State they represent.

> The minimum age is raised from 30 to 40, imposing the 20-year term limit.

No person may appear on a ballot, receive any write-in votes, serve in an elected office, or be an employee of any Government if they have been convicted in a Federal Court for treason or for participating in or planning an attack using weapons or other means of sabotage against persons or operational systems employed by the military, domestic police forces, elected officials, or Government facilities.

> This paragraph provides an alternative to the ambiguous language of Section 3 of the 14th Amendment, which prohibits oath-breaking insurrectionists from federal office. Requiring a conviction in Federal Court avoids problems created in *Trump v Anderson* [2] where the Supreme Court reversed Colorado's disqualification of Trump. The Federal Government has the sole power to disqualify a candidate.

Section 3. Prohibition Against Running for More Than One Office

A Candidate may only appear once on a ballot for one office during any biennial election for a Federal Office. The Elections Board shall not count write-in votes for candidates for another office on that ballot.

Section 4. Legal Status of Political Parties

Political Parties sponsor candidates on Federal Ballots for the House of Representatives, the President, and the Vice President. The Government shall not prohibit Political Parties from sponsoring candidates for Offices in the States, Federal Districts, and Territories. The Government shall make no laws abridging the right of Political Parties to determine their own rules for membership or selection of candidates that meet the Eligibility Requirements of this Constitution.

Political Parties may organize separate National, State, and regional corporations, with by-laws that prescribe their governance, raising and spending contributions, the qualification of Party Members, and the selection of Candidates. However, the Elections Board shall recognize the National Party for sponsorship of all Candidates for Federal Offices governed by this Article.

> This Section formally recognizes Political Parties and their role in the political process. It protects them from government interference because the Parties are the medium by which Eligible Voters can cooperate and organize to change the government. Incumbent parties will want to enact laws to impede the formation of competitors, so it is necessary to provide Constitutional protections for political parties.

Section 5. Candidate Status as Affiliated or Unaffiliated

Candidates for the Elected Office may qualify to appear on a ballot through sponsorship by a Political Party as an Affiliated Candidate or by sponsorship from Eligible Voters as an Unaffiliated Candidate.

> A candidate can appear on a ballot through affiliation with a Party or as an independent, unaffiliated candidate.

Section 6. One-Sixth Threshold – Affiliated Candidates on Ballot

A Political Party qualifies to nominate one candidate for every district of the House of Representatives in every State and the Federal House District if no fewer than one-sixth of the office holders in the House of Representatives were sponsored by that Party at the prior election.

> If House Members switch parties after their election, the 1/6th calculation of their former party will remain the same, based upon sponsorship at the prior election. Mathematically, it is unlikely that more than three or four parties could meet this threshold. The 1/6th floor should screen out extremist, fringe parties from automatically qualifying their candidates.

A Political Party qualifies to nominate one candidate for every district of the House of Representatives within that State if no fewer than one-sixth of the office holders of the most numerous Legislature within that State were sponsored by that Party at the prior election. However, it may not nominate more than one candidate from the same Party for that ballot for a single district.

> This paragraph describes a second-tier method for gaining automatic qualification for the ballot. Nascent parties will likely be regional phenomena that gain footholds in State Legislatures before Congress. This method promotes these regional parties' ability to gain ballot access.

If no fewer than one-sixth of the Members of the House of Representatives were sponsored by that Party at the prior election, a Political Party qualifies to nominate a Presidential Slate containing the names of candidates for President, Vice President, and up to five additional Cabinet Secretaries in the Line of Succession.

> This method is simple and streamlined instead of fifty different rules and regulations currently prevailing in every state to qualify for a ballot. The popularity of the political party in getting representatives elected to the state and federal legislatures is the measurement used to qualify a candidate for nomination by a party. This rule strengthens the role of political parties.

A Political Party that sponsored a current Office Holder at a previous election may deny that current Office Holder its sponsorship at the following election. At its discretion the Political Party may sponsor a different qualified candidate for that Office on the ballot at the subsequent election.

Being elected as a Democrat or Republican doesn't guarantee that a candidate will qualify as the Party's standard bearer in the next election. The Party controls the nomination of its Standard bearer.

Section 7. Ballot Access for Unaffiliated Candidates, Dual Sponsorship

Unaffiliated Candidates who qualify as a candidate for President must nominate a Vice President, and they may nominate up to five additional names of Cabinet Secretaries in the Line of Succession to form a Presidential Slate.

The pairing of the President and Vice President is required for a Presidential Slate. Nominating Cabinet Secretaries to appear on the Slate alongside the President and Vice President is optional. Putting Cabinet Secretaries on the Slate bypasses delays by the Senate's approval process. A full Slate is also a good advertisement to the electorate of how the President plans to govern.

Unaffiliated candidates who qualify for a Presidential Slate or the House of Representatives may solicit the sponsorship of a Political Party for that office on the ballot, provided that the Political Party sponsors no other candidate on the same ballot.

A current officeholder elected as an Unaffiliated Candidate qualifies for the ballot.

This paragraph describes an alternative to Party Primaries. Parties are limited to one nominee under their banner. A Party might endorse an unaffiliated candidate instead of selecting their own candidate through their party primary. A new or small Political Party below the 1/6th threshold qualifies its candidates through the Unaffiliated procedures to get on the ballot after the Party sponsors the Unaffiliated Candidate to run under their Party banner.

If a State Party selects a candidate without broad support, a more popular renegade member of the Party could run as Unaffiliated. If he wins, he could caucus with his original party and be the standard bearer at the next election.

Any Office Holder sponsored by a Party who fails to be sponsored for the subsequent election must obtain Unaffiliated sponsorship from Eligible Voters to appear as a Candidate on the ballot.

> If a candidate is elected without sponsorship by a Party, they are guaranteed to appear on the ballot for the next election. However, if the candidate is elected as the Standard bearer of a Party and the Party does not renominate them for the next election, that candidate must get signatures to qualify on their own as an Unaffiliated Candidate or as the nominee of another party.

More than one Political Party may not sponsor the same person for Elected Office on a single ballot. A candidate affiliated with a Political Party for Elected Office may not qualify as an Unaffiliated candidate on the same ballot. Two candidates from the same Party may not appear on the same ballot for the same office. Presidential Slates must be uniform in every voting precinct.

The Elections Board may not charge any filing fees for Unaffiliated Candidates.

Section 8. Signature Requirements for Unaffiliated Candidates

A Citizen qualified for membership in the House of Representatives at the time of taking the oath of office may qualify as an Unaffiliated Candidate by gathering signatures on a petition from Eligible Voters within that District exceeding one-twentieth of the number of votes for all Candidates for the House of Representatives cast during the prior election within the district. Eligible Voters may only sponsor one Unaffiliated Candidate for each office for each election. The same rules apply to the candidates for the Federal House District or the Federal Districts and Territories. Candidates may not offer, nor may Eligible Voters receive, pecuniary or non-pecuniary forms of compensation as an inducement to sponsor an Unaffiliated Candidate.

A person qualified to hold the office of President may qualify as an Unaffiliated candidate by gathering sponsorship from Eligible Voters exceeding one-fiftieth of the votes cast at the prior Federal Election for President in every State and the Federal House District, provided at least one thousand valid signatures are submitted from one-half of the districts in a State. The period for obtaining sponsorship shall not exceed nor be restricted to less than three-hundred sixty-five days, terminating no later than one hundred twenty days before the Final Voting Date. The Elections Board will only place names of Unaffiliated candidates for a Presidential Slate if they qualify in every State and the Federal House District.

> Requiring at least one thousand signatures from one-half of districts prevents someone from collecting all their signatures in a single urban area. Presidential candidates must demonstrate broad support by building a campaign infrastructure sufficient to meet this threshold.

Section 9. Verification of Sponsors for Unaffiliated Candidates

The Elections Board shall mail forms to the residence of Eligible Voters proposed as Sponsors for an Unaffiliated Candidate for Elected Office. The person seeking to qualify as an Unaffiliated Candidate may submit signatures as they are received and identifying information for Eligible Voters to the Elections Board to confirm the Eligible Voter's sponsorship. The Eligible Voter may directly solicit the Elections Board to mail forms that they will use to verify the Eligible Voter's sponsorship.

Section 10. Six Candidate Limit and Order of Ballot Appearance

In addition to a write-in option, up to six Candidates may appear on a federal ballot for a single office. The ballot order for candidates is:

- eligible incumbents
- number of House Members affiliated with a Party

- number of State Legislators in the chamber with the most members affiliated with a Party having fewer members than one-sixth of the House of Representatives
- candidates submitting the largest number of Eligible Sponsors

The ballot will offer a seventh option for the voter to write in the name of a Candidate who had tried and failed to qualify for a displayed position. The Elections Board shall publish the names of candidates who are not eligible to be displayed on the ballot and display their names in the order of the number of valid signatures submitted. The Elections Board shall provide at least one copy of this list at every precinct and in an electronic medium accessible to everyone.

> At most, six candidates will appear on the ballot for any Federal Election. This six-candidate limit avoids ballot clutter and makes it easier for voters to decide. The six-candidate limit is a tradeoff between allowing challenges to the two major parties and only allowing serious candidates to appear on the ballot. However, this paragraph guarantees a write-in option as a protest outlet.

If a voter selects more than one candidate for any office, the vote for that office is void.

Article 4.

Political Parties and Campaign Donations

Section 1. Exclusive Citizen Support of Political Parties & Candidates

Political Parties are legally chartered by the Federal or State Governments as non-profit corporations. The minimum annual contribution for a party member to select candidates for elective office and to select the corporation's officers cannot exceed one one-thousandth of the Compensation Index for two consecutive years before an election date. All party member votes shall be weighted equally. Political Parties shall establish by-laws to govern their procedures for membership, dues, and rules for sponsoring Candidates to appear on a ballot for elected office.

> Limiting political parties to nonprofit corporations eliminates the existence of shareholders who can obtain control by explicit purchases of shares. This Section limits the membership criteria by capping the annual contribution limits to $174/year based on 2021 salaries and mandating that all members have equal votes in governance. It is likely that most parties will reduce the annual membership fee to broaden outreach. Having committed members who donate money as persons in charge of selecting who gets to represent their values is better than allowing anyone with money to put themselves on a ballot and go around the Party Leadership to buy an election.

Candidates for Government Office and Political Parties can only receive monetary donations and in-kind contributions from Eligible Voters of the United States. They may not receive monetary donations and in-kind contributions from legal persons, foreign and domestic Governments, non-citizens, and non-eligible Voters. The Elections Board shall suspend a Political Party's candidate sponsorship privileges of the Office for which the offense was committed for twenty-four months. Congress may enact additional financial and criminal penalties. The limitations on political donations shall apply during the four years before the Final Date of Election for the office.

Section 2. Restrictions on Party Support of Candidates

Political Parties may not donate to Candidates not affiliated with their Party. Political Parties may not be limited to donating less than three times the Compensation Index to a Candidate Committee for the House or less than four hundred times the Compensation Index for a Campaign for a Presidential Slate.

> Only natural persons who are US Citizens may donate money to Political Parties and Candidates. This provision keeps foreign influence and corporate money out of political parties. No public financing of campaigns by the State or Federal Governments is allowed.
>
> While Political Parties may continue to utilize the state election apparatus for Primaries, they can also use caucuses to select their standard bearers.

Section 3. Restrictions on Taxation and Use of Political Donations

Political Parties may not pay in-kind or monetary compensation to the Candidate, their spouse, parents, or direct descendants. Congress shall enact laws defining eligible expenditures for Political Parties. Donations received by Candidate Campaigns and Political Parties are not subject to taxation provided that the expenditures are for a lawful purpose to support or oppose candidates and Political Parties and that they only employ Citizens on a paid or volunteer basis. If at least fifty candidates affiliated with a Political Party qualified on ballots for the State Legislature or the House of Representatives collectively, then Party donations are not taxable.

> This paragraph prevents candidates from using tax-advantaged donor contributions for personal use. These donations are a tax-advantaged source for Political Parties and Candidate Campaigns, but they cannot employ non-citizens if they wish to receive this tax benefit. Also, these tax-advantaged contributions are reserved for serious, viable parties that sponsor candidates appearing on ballots and not fringe movements.

Excepting Political Parties and Candidate Campaigns defined under this Article, no expenditure of money, labor, or other resources to solicit or broadcast support or opposition to candidates for Government Office, for Political Parties, or legislation may be applied to reduce the amount of income subject to taxation by the Government.

> This paragraph addresses the Independent Expenditure Committees, the sources of Dark Money in campaigns. Under this paragraph, the Independent Expenditure Committee could not deduct any expenses to reduce its taxable income. 100% of its gross income would be taxed at the corporate income tax rate.
>
> This tax rule contrasts with non-political corporations taxed on their net income after deducting expenses. The Independent Expenditure Committee expenses are treated the same as after-tax personal consumption. This paragraph uses the tax code to preserve the freedom of expression to spend your money as you please while providing prejudicial treatment in favor of political expenditures routed through regulated campaign committees. Currently, the 501 {c]{4} and {c}{6} portions of the tax code permit these political non-profits to deduct expenditures and avoid taxation of their gross revenue.
>
> From a personal perspective, it's essential to understand that individuals can spend their after-tax dollars on political action without donating to a candidate's campaign or a political party. However, if they choose to form a legal person or partnership to collaborate and coordinate with other individuals, then any donations that they

make to that entity will be subject to taxation. For instance, if you give $1,000 to a political campaign and the entire $1,000 is spent by the candidate, there are no tax implications. But if you give $1,000 to some other entity, then that $1,000 is subject to a tax of $250, and the remaining $750 is available for expenditures, assuming a 25% corporate tax rate.

Suppose a Church or for-profit company spent only 5% of its budget on political activities. In that case, the Church has the burden of keeping records to prove it did not commingle political expenses with regular operating expenses. Otherwise, the government will tax all their revenue. This will lead companies to be very careful to have segregated Political Action corporations so that this co-mingling of expenses won't occur.

Vendors paid by Political Actors shall not be subject to an additional prohibition against using their expenditures to reduce their taxable income if they publicly disclose proof of payment from political actors and that their service charges are uniform and equally available without discrimination. Political actors cannot deduct these expenditures to reduce their taxable income. Vendors and their beneficial owners may not create subsidiaries to evade the requirement for uniform charges and non-discriminatory services.

If a Political Actor hires a printer or law firm or pays for advertising, those vendors are not subject to this restriction. However, the vendor could not offer preferential rates or deny service based on the political affiliation of their clients.

Any corporation that donates money for this purpose, or if it directly supports or opposes a candidate, would be treated as personal consumption (spending on meals and entertainment) that could not be used to reduce net taxable income.

If a corporation is established to receive donations and spend them outside the political parties and candidates, then all its donations would be taxable, not the net income. Using the tax code is the best way to discriminate against these independent actors. *This provides a strong financial incentive for routing money directly to the campaigns and the Political Parties instead of through Independent Expenditure Committees.*

Consider the potential implications for media outlets like FOX, ABC, NBC, NY Times, and MSNBC. Could they be subject to this interpretation? Could the fraction of expenses devoted to endorsing or tearing down a candidate or Party be disallowed for reduction of taxable income? This raises important questions about the role of the media in political campaigns and the potential impact on their financial operations. This paragraph may incentivize Political Parties to own media companies, promoting their partisan ideas more honestly than is currently done by media outlets pretending to be objective, non-partisan purveyors of information. These pretenders will be subject to punitive taxation because there is no other way to write a general rule to stop dark money in politics.

If a Candidate fails to qualify for the ballot, its Candidate Campaign privileges to receive donations free of taxation shall terminate on the Final Voting Date of that campaign period.

Without this paragraph, you would see unserious candidates running and seeking donations merely for their tax advantages. They could run a political news company under the guise of a campaign. This termination date gives real candidates who have failed to qualify for the ballot enough time to pay off vendors and creditors. However, it also forces failed candidates to go through the motions of re-qualifying for the ballot for the next election.

Section 4. Self-Financed Federal Campaign Contribution Limits

A Candidate may contribute up to three times the Compensation Index for their campaign for the House of Representatives. A Presidential Candidate's maximum donation to their campaign is four hundred times the Compensation Index. A Vice-Presidential Candidate's maximum donation to their campaign is two hundred times the Compensation Index. Candidates cannot use their personal or spouse's funds for expenditures on their campaign that do not originate from their Campaign Committee.

The current 2024 salary for a Member of the House is $174,000. Therefore, the President's compensation would be $3,480,000. $522,000 would be the maximum self-funded contribution for a House campaign. The President could self-fund $69,600,000, and the Vice President half that amount. Tying these limits to the compensation of a House Member adjusts for inflation. The amount of the limitation is something up for discussion.

Section 5. Political Contributions Restricted to After-Tax Funds

A donor may only contribute funds to a political campaign for Government Office if the donor has paid all income, estate, and inheritance taxes due on those funds. Any person found guilty of acting as a conduit for accepting funds and making Campaign Contributions on behalf of other persons shall serve no less than five hundred days in prison and be barred from all future employment by the Government.

This Section prevents the use of dark money, or undeclared income, and schemes to hide the identity of the actual backer.

Section 6. Political Contributions Routed Through Elections Board

Donors shall send all monetary donations for Political Parties and Candidates through the Elections Board escrow accounts to confirm that they derive from Eligible Citizens, complying with any donation limits. Donation limits apply during the forty-eight months before the Final Voting Date.

A serious and thorough campaign donation system must adopt these procedures. The Elections Board and the Census Board will have a database of people legally capable of making donations, and they can continuously track the contribution limits and make timely reports. This also offloads a lot of overhead from the campaign. The limits apply per candidate over four years.

The Elections Board shall develop procedures to ensure that donations are promptly deposited from their escrow accounts into the accounts of Political Parties and Candidates complying with these procedures no later than seventy-two hours after receipt. The Elections Board will pay a one-twentieth penalty and daily compounded interest payments of one-one thousandth on the unremitted deposits payable to every Campaign Committee sponsoring a candidate for that office. The Elections Board shall publish a daily report of the outstanding donations in escrow awaiting confirmation.

> Centralizing donation collections with the Elections Board poses the risk that campaigns won't promptly receive their donations. The late penalties imposed on the government are stiff in discouraging this behavior. There is a risk that the Elections Board could intentionally reject donations to harm a candidate's chances, so there is an appeals process. Penalties exist to discourage a campaign by someone to intentionally overload and sabotage the Elections Board's capacity to review donor qualifications. Every campaign receives an equal amount of the fine to deter the Elections Board from favoring a campaign by intentionally transferring late donations to boost their collections.

The Elections Board must notify the donor and the intended recipient of a donation, as well as the amount and reason for rejecting that donation. The Board shall not disclose the name to the intended recipient if the donor requested anonymity. Donors who disagree with the rejection may submit appeals for review of any rejections to the Elections Board and the Courts. Persons making disqualified donations are subject to criminal prosecution and fines enacted by Congress.

Section 7. Campaign Finance Reports

Beginning six-hundred twenty-nine days before the Final Voting Date, every one-hundred and eighty days, the Elections Board shall issue reports of total donations for the entire duration of the campaign for every person who has opened a campaign account with the Elections Board and every Political Party.

Beginning eighty-nine days before the Final Voting Date, every seven days, the Elections Board shall issue reports of total donations for every candidate. The Elections Board will not accept donations during the Ordinary Voting Period. After that, the Boards shall resume issuing reports seven days after the Final Voting Date, and the Board will issue additional reports every thirty days.

> This Section establishes a specific timetable for the Elections Board to report campaign donations. Legislation can specify the contents of the Expenditure Reports.

Section 8. Contribution Limits for Non-Anonymous Donors

Donors who openly disclose their identity and contribution amounts may not be limited to an amount less than one-fourth of the Compensation Index for no more than one active Candidate for the House of Representatives in each district and one active Presidential Slate for any election cycle. Except for candidates subject to Section 4 of this Article, the cumulative amount of all donations to every candidate from a single donor over a forty-eight-month period may not exceed the Compensation Index.

> There are two classes of donors. The first are non-anonymous donors who disclose their identity and get to contribute larger amounts of money than those who remain anonymous. $43,500 is the maximum 4-yr. donation is limited to a single candidate when the donor isn't anonymous. Then, there is a separate limitation for total contributions of $174,000 to all candidates.

Section 9. Restrictions and Reporting for Political Loans

Political Parties and Candidates may only accept loans from an Eligible Voter who immediately discloses the entirety of the written loan agreement to the Elections Board that publishes the agreement. The outstanding balance of all loans owed to an eligible lender by any Political Party or Candidate may not exceed the Compensation Index. If the Candidate or Party does not repay the loan within twelve months following the Final Voting Date, the Eligible Voter may not make any contributions or loans to any Candidates or Political Parties for thirty-six months following the twelve-month anniversary of the Final Voting Date. A lender cannot offer loans to more than one Candidate and one Political Party over a forty-eight-month period.

> Banks and other financial entities cannot loan campaigns and political parties' money. This prohibition protects banks from political pressure, and it shields candidates from being unduly influenced. An individual cannot loan more than the maximum amount, but if the candidate defaults, this loan converts to a campaign contribution. The penalty is severe to deter loans that are not made as a serious business proposition. Disclosing the entirety of the loan agreement allows for scrutiny of the conditions under which it was made.

Section 10. Contributions and Loans for One Candidate Per Office

Individual Citizens may not donate or loan money to more than one Candidate per office or one Political Party during a forty-eight-month period unless the candidate who received a donation or loan withdraws from the ballot.

> This Section stops the practice of buying access employed by many donors who are not committed to a candidate's policies and virtues.

Section 11. Prohibition of Government Employee Contributions

Excepting Citizens drafted into military service or other involuntary servitude for the Federal Government, Citizens voluntarily employed by the Federal Government are prohibited from donating or loaning money or in-kind goods or services to Candidates for Government

Offices. Citizens employed in the military reserves who are not Federal Government employees are exempt from this prohibition.

> This prohibition provides stronger protections than The Hatch Act to prevent an incumbent power from using the government's resources to protect its loss of power. It also establishes a hierarchy of master and servant. Government workers are servants of the citizens, and they have a conflict of interest in protecting their jobs and thwarting any decisions to reallocate resources away from these jobs.

Section 12. Disposition of Contributions After Election

Any candidate for office who withdraws their name from the ballot must pay all outstanding debts and remit any remaining balance of all donations to the Elections Board. The Elections Board will return this remaining balance pro-rata to the donors. Returned donations are not taxable income.

> This section protects donors and assures them that candidates who withdraw from an election cannot carry those donations over to another race, which the donor didn't consider for its decision, as is commonly done today.

Within sixty days after the Final Voting Date, a Candidate or Political Party must extinguish any outstanding liabilities using Campaign or Party funds. Political Parties are not required to refund contributions to donors after the Final Voting Date. Candidates are required to extinguish the balance in their Campaign Accounts subject to the following conditions:

Within fifty days of the Final Voting Date, and after repayment of liabilities, a Candidate Campaign may transfer all or part of the remaining balances in its Campaign Account to the Political Party that sponsored the Candidate. Any remaining balances in the Campaign Account must be returned to the Elections Board within sixty days. Then, the Board distributes these balances pro-rata to donors making contributions during the prior forty-eight months of the Final Voting Date. The Government may not levy taxes on funds transfers from a Campaign Account.

This Section prevents candidates from fundraising by amassing huge campaign warchests to donate to other candidates and extract commitments. This Section favors Political Parties over personalities. Once a campaign ends, the candidate closes their Campaign Account, and they must start fundraising again. Presumably, their political party will reimburse candidates for the portion they transferred to the party as seed money for their next election to reward their fundraising prowess. Unlike political parties, this Section is biased against unaffiliated candidates, who may not carry balances in their accounts after the election.

Section 13. Opening Campaign Account With The Elections Board

Only candidates who have applied to qualify as candidates or who have already qualified as candidates for office may open a campaign account with the Elections Board to accept donations.

Section 14. Restrictions for Anonymous Campaign Contributions

Donors who elect to make their identity and the amount of their donations a secret shall be subject to any donor limitations enacted into law. The maximum donation shall be no less than one-twentieth of the Compensation Index. It shall not exceed one-fourth of the non-anonymous donation limitation. Except for candidates subject to Section 4 of this Article, the cumulative amount of all donations to every candidate from a single donor over a forty-eight-month period may not exceed one-fourth of the Compensation Index. Any person who discloses or publishes confidential information about a donor's contributions shall be imprisoned for no fewer than five hundred days, be permanently barred from employment or elective office in the Government, and pay damages to any donor in the amount of the Compensation Index.

Anonymity comes with a tradeoff. A 5% maximum donation is $8,200 today, and the limit will adjust with inflation as compensation of House Members increases over time. Anonymity will also encourage greater donor participation because the Elections Board won't name them, exposing them to retribution. Even the candidate won't know their donors' names, making it difficult to reward someone for their donation. Donors will have to volunteer their support directly to the campaign. Harsh penalties for non-consensual disclosure will cover media outlets that won't be able to claim they were reporting the news revealed by an anonymous lawbreaker.

Section 15. Financial Disclosure Requirements for Candidates

No later than ninety days before the Final Voting Date, any Candidate for Federal Office and their spouse must disclose the following amounts for the previous ten years of income taxes, but only the current year for assets and liabilities:

The amount of taxes owed and paid to the states and their political subdivisions, territories, federal districts, and federal government, as well as any disputes and the amount of taxes in arrears.

The gross and taxable income reported on personal federal tax returns and any companies in which the candidate owns more than a one-tenth interest or receives more than one-tenth of the income.

All monetary and in-kind gifts and inheritance over one-tenth of the Compensation Index during any calendar year.

The names of any source of income that accounted for more than one-fifth of their Gross Income during any calendar year.

A Personal Financial Statement that lists all assets and liabilities as cumulative totals and an itemized enumeration whenever a single asset or liability exceeds the Compensation Index.

This Section makes the custom of Presidential candidates who disclose their tax returns a legal requirement. This Section has more stringent disclosure requirements than current House and

> Senate rules. This Section doesn't require the disclosure of entire tax returns, just the summary figures. However, it does require the disclosure of a detailed statement of assets and liabilities.

After vacating the offices of President and Vice President, the former officeholders must continue to submit these financial reports annually until ten years have passed.

> Bush, Clinton, and Obama have made a fortune after leaving office. If they were promised future compensation in exchange for favors given during their term, this Section could unveil those bribery schemes.

Section 16. Dispute Resolution Regarding Audits of Statements

Any candidate elected to office shall provide all necessary financial records to facilitate an audit to authenticate these Section 15 disclosures by the Elections Board. The Office Holder may contest any discrepancies uncovered by the audit. The Elections Board shall publicly disclose any findings of differences along with any rebuttal provided by the Office Holder no later than two years after the Final Voting Date. If the Elections Board fails to deliver its findings, the Board shall transfer all records to a Special Prosecutor if the Senate votes to appoint one. Tax collection authorities of the States, Federal Districts, Territories, and the United States shall promptly provide all records requested by candidates to fulfill the requirements of this Section.

> This strengthens the previous section and only applies to elected officials. The Elections Board will verify their financial disclosures. If fraud is uncovered, the Senate can appoint a Special Prosecutor to pursue it as a criminal matter.

Section 17. Primary Elections

Political Parties may contract with the States, their political subdivisions, Federal Districts, and Territories to operate primary elections and use the vote tabulations to assist in selecting their nominee for a federal ballot. The by-laws of the Political Party determine which Eligible Voters are eligible to vote for their candidates in the primary election. The by-laws prescribe which candidates may be sponsored by the Political Party on the primary ballot and which candidate appears on the Federal ballot. States are not obligated to host primary elections. However, States that host primary elections may not discriminate in their treatment of Parties that have qualified for the Federal Ballot, and they may not prescribe any rules for the number or qualifications of Candidates appearing on a Party's Primary Ballot.

Section 18. Disclosure of Campaign Advertisements

Fifteen days before the Final Voting Date, a Political Party or a Candidate Campaign Committee(s) complying with Article 4, Section 3 to receive preferential non-taxation of donations must submit to the Elections Board and the opposing Campaign Committees any new information for public broadcast at least forty-eight hours before its disclosure to the public. The Campaign Committee, the Opposing Campaign Committee(s), the Elections Board, or any other person violating this disclosure limitation shall pay fines no less than the Compensation Index. Any Campaign Committee, Political Party, or person violating this disclosure limitation, including news media, shall be subject to taxation of all donations, revenue, or income received thirty days before the disclosure and sixty days after the Date of Election.

> This Section deters the release of false information late in campaigns intended to blindside the competition and not give them adequate time to prepare a response. A 48-hour embargo gives the other side time to rebut charges. Campaigns cannot leak to the press and get around this prohibition because the media will be subject to fines.

Article 5.

The Executive Authority of the President

Dividing Executive Authority between the President, the Governor General, and the Executive Directors of the Boards is a significant innovation of this Constitution. The President is responsible for nonpartisan military and foreign affairs and domestic security that demand national consensus. The Governor General handles more divisive partisan issues of domestic policies. The Executive Directors handle nonpartisan tasks, insulated from political pressure.

The President will spend more than half his time focused on national security and diplomacy rather than subsidies for farmers, subway construction, high-speed rail, and solar panels. The remainder of his attention will be on managing the nation's public debt and fiscal health.

Section 1. Oath of Office For The President

Before entering on the Execution of the Office, the President shall take the following Oath or Affirmation: *I do solemnly swear (or affirm) that I will faithfully execute the Office of President of the United States, and will to the best of my Ability, preserve, protect and defend the Constitution of the United States.*

Section 2. Authority and Restrictions Upon the Use of Military Force

As the Commander in Chief, the President holds the authority and responsibility for all Armed Forces in instances of war beyond the United States' boundaries, including its territories, embassies, offices, or military bases. Without the House of Representatives' consent, the President may only initiate the use of force outside the United States boundaries for a maximum of thirty days during any consecutive three hundred sixty-five-day periods.

> This Section recognizes the necessity for the President to act quickly and secretly in certain circumstances, but it doesn't give the President an open-ended mandate to wage war. Theoretically, the House could always use the Power of the Purse to terminate these adventures, but the Presidential veto was always a tool to thwart that. This provision limits Presidential discretion to 30 days of war per year, and then he's forced to terminate a war after 30 days if he cannot gain consent.

Except in defense from an attack initiated by the enemy forces, at the end of thirty days, the President must discontinue hostile engagements, absent the majority consent of the House through a War Powers Resolution. Any War Powers Resolution by the House expires after twelve months unless terminated by a majority vote of the House before expiration. A War Powers Resolution may prescribe the extent of lethal and non-lethal attacks, sabotaging an enemy's property, information systems, and the territory over which such activities may occur. The use of force under a treaty obligation shall not abrogate the requirements of this Section.

> The War Powers resolution just requires the consent of the House, not the Senate. Its 12-month expiration date prevents a repeat of the War on Terror authority, which is still used after over twenty years as a justification for the President to launch attacks. Congress's power to Declare War in the 1787 Constitution was toothless. The Anti-Elitist Constitution restores this important check upon reckless military adventurism by a President.

The President, with majority consent of the House and the Senate, may command armed forces to combat domestic violence and rebellion within the States. This is subject to a Domestic Force Resolution that expires after ninety days. However, the President can command armed forces of the States and the Federal Government to defend

Military Bases, the Federal District, Federal Territories, Federal Property, shipping ports, interstate highways, airports, space launch facilities, and territory within three miles of the land Borders, without a Domestic Force Resolution.

> The Senate and the House must approve a Domestic Force Resolution. In this case, the president cannot unilaterally act without these consents, and the resolution expires after 90 days instead of 12 months.

The House may pass a resolution to request a ruling by a two-thirds vote of the Supreme Court that the President violated the restrictions of this Section or the terms of a War Powers Resolution or a Domestic Force Resolution. If that occurs, a six-elevenths vote of the House of Representatives removes the President.

> This method is an alternative to an impeachment trial. This lower threshold requires a two-thirds tenure percentage vote of the Supreme Court to agree that the President abused his war powers or domestic use of force. This sanction improved Congress's toothless declaration of war power in the 1787 Constitution.

Section 3. Use of Force, Appointment, And Executive Authority

The remaining Powers of the President are enumerated in this Section:

Faithfully executing all laws of the Federal Government that subject any person to fines, detainment, imprisonment, or expulsion from the United States, and command all personnel who enforce these laws.

Guard the borders, regulate the entry of persons and vehicles, and protect the media for distributing power and communications through the electromagnetic spectrum from disruption by natural events and deliberate attacks.

Maintain the safety of air and sea traffic.

> Because air and sea traffic control are intimately connected to military concerns and invariably are interstate in nature, the President has authority in these areas.

Collect taxes and disburse funds through an Appropriations or Taxation Bill enacted by Congress and manage the borrowing of money on the credit of the United States.

Commission all the United States Armed Forces Officers, whom the Senate can remove by a majority vote within ninety days after their appointment. Persons removed by a majority vote of the Senate may not be re-appointed during the lesser of the remaining term of the President or two years.

Make Treaties if three-fifths of the Senate concur.

Appoint Ambassadors whom the Senate can remove with a seven-thirteenth vote within one hundred twenty days of appointment and who may not be re-appointed during the remaining term of the President, provided that the Senate did not approve their nomination by majority vote.

> This paragraph permits the President to staff up his administration quickly and avoid the delay tactics of the Senate. While he retains the discretion to submit nominations to the Senate for approval before posting ambassadors, he doesn't have to. However, the Senate still has the discretion to remove someone after the fact with a supermajority, presumably because they are unqualified or have performed some egregious act after their appointment. In the current Constitution, the Senate doesn't have the ability to remove ambassadors today, so the Senate gains additional power.

Appoint Justices of the Supreme Court, judges of inferior courts, Adjudicators, and Board Members whom the Senate can remove by a majority vote within ninety days after their appointment. Persons removed by a majority vote of the Senate may not be re-appointed during the lesser of the remaining term of the President or two years.

> The President does not need to wait for the Senate to fill vacancies in the judiciary, but unlike ambassadors, the threshold for removal

> is a simple majority vote. Therefore, what would likely occur is that the President will fill a vacancy but still submit the nomination for approval by the Senate. There would be a gentleman's agreement that the Justice would resign his post if he failed to secure a majority vote of the Senate, sparing the Senate and the Judge from suffering humiliation from initiating a resolution to remove the judge or Justice.

The President may not appoint themself to an office.

Receive or expel Ambassadors and other public Ministers of foreign entities.

Grant Reprieves and Pardons for enumerated Offenses against the United States committed before the date of the reprieve or pardon. The President may not grant reprieves or pardons for persons convicted of failure to pay taxes, illegal entry into the country, or Electoral Fraud. The President may not grant reprieves or pardons for themself, their spouse, siblings, or those in their line of descent, or the Line of Succession, or in cases of Impeachment. Unless annulled by a three-fifths vote of the Senate before taking effect, any Reprieve or Pardon takes effect ten days after the President submits the pardon order to the Speaker.

> This paragraph corrects a weakness in the 1787 Constitution's overly broad pardon power. Ambiguity, whether a President could pardon himself, is resolved. This paragraph adds persons convicted of Electoral Fraud. Adding family members is another non-controversial addition. For other cases like the pardons made by Trump, Obama, and Clinton to ex-terrorists, siblings, or persons who did not cooperate with prosecutors, the Senate can annul a pardon within ten days. The President could pardon illegal aliens, but other provisions of this Constitution prevent these aliens from becoming Citizens. Restricting pardons to enumerated Offenses committed before the date of the pardon prevents blanket pardons for any crime that could be committed in the future.

Within ten days of passage, The President may veto any Bill not solely related to Appropriations and Revenue. This veto can be overridden by a three-fifths vote of Congress no later than thirty days after the veto.

The President can borrow less than the maximum amount of Public Debt authorized by the Resolution for Borrowing by the House of Representatives under Article 6, Section 5. The President has the discretion to reduce any expenditures to the extent that expenditures exceed revenues plus any borrowed funds.

> The Anti-Elitist Constitution does not allow the President to veto a Congress-approved budget. Removing this veto power prevents government shutdowns. In exchange, the President gets a line-item veto over the amount of spending that relies upon borrowing whenever Congress engages in deficit spending. Therefore, the President has the power and responsibility to control additional Public Debt accumulated under his watch. Congress surrenders control to the President over that portion of the Appropriation not covered by taxes. This arrangement is a workable substitute for a balanced budget amendment that would be riddled with exceptions and subjective calculations.

No Appropriation may supersede the obligation to repay the Public Debt held outside the Federal Government and the Federal Reserve Bank, per the covenants of the Public Debt instrument. Expenditures guaranteed under this Constitution shall be fulfilled after debt obligations. After that, the President shall have the discretion to prioritize the funding of Expenditures whenever revenue collections and the Authorization to Borrow do not support the amounts of expenditures authorized by the Appropriations Bill.

> This paragraph addresses complaints about defaulting on debt obligations routinely heard during the Government Shutdown crises. The government prioritizes payments to bondholders over all other expenditures. Second, in the event of a shortfall of cash flow compared to the amount Congress wanted to spend, the President gets to decide which programs get cut to avoid borrowing more money than was initially authorized.

Section 4. Division of Powers Between Governor General, Executive Director, President

The Powers of the President, Governor General, and Executive Directors of Boards are exclusive to each office. These powers may not be shared or delegated. The President, Governor General, or Executive Director, and a minimum of thirty Members of the House of Representatives or three Members of the Senate shall have standing in any disputes arising from the exercise of these powers. The Supreme Court shall have original jurisdiction. Persons serving under the President may not hold office while Members of the House or Senate.

> Under the Anti-Elitist Constitution, Executive Authority is split among three Branches of Government. This Section is one of its most important innovations. Giving Members of the House and Senate standing in complaints before the courts is crucial for enforcing this division of Executive Authority. Even if the President, Governor General, and Executive Directors wanted to collude to blur the lines of separation of Executive Authority, Legislators could challenge this subversion.

Section 5. Vice President

If the President dies, is impeached and convicted, or resigns from office, the Vice President shall assume the Office of the President. In cases of temporary incapacity, the President may delegate authority of the Presidency to the Vice President for at most ten days in any ninety consecutive days. The Vice President is a member of the President's Cabinet who, in addition to duties as Vice President, may be appointed to serve as the Secretary of any Department or as the subordinate of any Secretary without the consent of the Senate.

> Suppose a President has a chronic condition that renders him unable to function over long periods. In that case, this provision limits the President's ability to an extent where he must resign or be removed by authority granted in a later Section.

The Vice President can do far more than attend the funerals of foreign dignitaries and cast tie-breaking votes in the Senate. The President can make a Vice President act as a Cabinet Officer, chief of staff, or hold other positions.

The Vice President may not grant any pardons during the suspension of the President per Section 18. When the Vice President becomes President through Section 18 or the resignation of the President, then the preceding President is ineligible for a pardon.

This paragraph prevents a President from resigning office or feigning incapacity to allow his Vice President to pardon him.

Section 6. Term Limits for President

No person may serve more than twelve years as President during their lifetime. No person thrice elected to the office of President, or upon completion of a full term would exceed twelve years, may appear as a candidate on a Slate, nor hold office in the Executive Branches of the United States in the Line of Succession.

Three terms for a President are not a problem because he is limited to national security, foreign policy, law enforcement, and other matters that don't present the danger of doling out domestic welfare to buy influence for himself and his party. If the Vice President is groomed as a successor, then the President could resign after ten years so that the Vice President could run as the incumbent two years later in an election.

Section 7. Minimum Length of Service for Cabinet Appointments

Except for the Vice President, the President may terminate the employment of any Person in the Line of Succession after they have completed three hundred sixty-five days of service.

This Section balances the need for the President to choose the team he wants and stability. If a Secretary appeared on Slate and helped get the President elected, this prevents simply using a Slate member as a cut-out who was merely a political prop. The minimum of twelve months of service only applies if the Secretary doesn't resign.

Section 8. At-Will Staff

The President may hire At-Will staff who are not subject to any civil service or collective bargaining protections or requirements for approval by the Senate. The President shall determine or delegate the responsibility for assigning positions to At-Will staff and the chain of command in every Department regarding employees or those who are not At-Will staff.

Excepting the President or the Secretary of War, only active, commissioned officers in the military chain of command may issue orders to armed forces members. Only the President or the Secretary of War may issue orders for the armed forces of the United States to serve under a non-commissioned authority under treaty obligations or other arrangements authorized by law.

The President shall not spend more than one-twentieth of the total appropriation for staff compensation in Departments during a fiscal year on the At-Will staff of the Departments in the Executive Branch under the President. The compensation of any At-Will staff member and Cabinet Secretary shall not exceed the compensation of the Vice President.

At-Will staff is a very important innovation. It permits the President to install his own team throughout lower levels of management below the Secretary Level without being held hostage by the Senate. The President gets 5% of the staffing budget to hire qualified citizens on an At-Will basis, not hamstrung by Civil Service pay grades. Also, Cabinet Secretaries' compensation is not set by the House or Senate, placing a cap on the size of White House staff levels.

At-Will staff shall be citizens of the United States who are twenty-one years old and not covered by civil service protections. The children, siblings, or parents of the President or the President's spouse are ineligible. The employment and compensation of At-Will staff terminate immediately after the inauguration of a new President following an election unless they are re-appointed to their positions. The President is not required to spend the entire appropriation allocated for At-Will staff.

Persons who served as At-Will staff may not be employed in positions covered by Civil Service protections during the term of the President who hired them.

> This paragraph clarifies the disposable nature of the At-Will staff and the importance of a President's ability to populate these departments with people he can trust. However, we also acknowledge the importance of not succumbing to the shortcomings of cronyism and incompetence that the Civil Service legislation remedied. There is a balance between the continuity of human capital in these departments and having an ossified bureaucracy that can thwart a President's agenda for change. In exchange for Civil Service protections of Federal Administrators, these Administrators must become Political Celibates. Leave the partisan policy management to the At-Will staff, who can be held politically accountable. The President can hold administrators responsible when entire programs and departments are eliminated, which is a very blunt instrument. At-Will staffing is a compromise solution.

Section 9. Circle of Executive Privilege

The President shall designate twenty persons employed at any time as privileged staff. The President shall designate up to thirty persons during a four-year term in office, fifty during an eight-year term, or sixty during a twelve-year term. Communications between the President and privileged staff are confidential. Congress may not compel the President and privileged staff to divulge the content of their communications to any Government official or representative, absent a three-fifths vote of the Senate or the House of Representatives for each instance of a request to inquire about a specific matter. These communications shall receive the same protections for no less than thirty years after the President has vacated the office.

This Section clarifies the doctrine of Executive Privilege that has evolved through court cases. Executive Privilege is not absolute, and a three-fifths supermajority in the Senate *or* the House may breach it in extraordinary circumstances. It is limited to the most trusted circle of persons, so it cannot be claimed by lower-level persons in the departments under the President.

Section 10. Expiration of Executive Orders

All the President's Executive Orders expire upon vacating the office. Executive Orders are administrative commands to personnel in Departments subject to the President's Authority, and they do not have the force of law upon persons not employed by these Departments. Any Executive Order in conflict with the law may be challenged by three Senators or thirty Members of the House for a hearing by the Supreme Court.

This Section eliminates the controversy created by DACA, in which the Courts treated President Obama's executive order like a law preventing his successor from reversing this policy. This Section relegates Executive Orders to something less than laws enacted by Congress.

Section 11. Authority Over Foreign Relations

Except for matters of international trade, tariffs, and sanctions against foreign governments and organizations supported by foreign governments, only treaties approved by a three-fifths vote of the Senate can bind the president's conduct in foreign affairs. Agreements made by a President with a foreign power or laws enacted by Congress about recognition of and relationships with foreign governments or organizations do not bind future Presidents unless under the provisions of a Treaty ratified by the Senate. The President may submit trade and tariff agreements to Congress for a vote without any opportunity for amendments by Congress.

This Section strengthens the President's authority to conduct foreign affairs at his discretion without interference by Congress. It carves out an exception to the 3/5th Senate approval on trade-related matters. This also formalizes the Fast-Track powers currently granted to the President to facilitate his credibility and authority to negotiate trade agreements with foreign powers.

Section 12. Executive Immunity

During their tenure in office, the President and Vice President are immune from prosecution by Government authorities. Cabinet Secretaries in the Line of Succession are immune unless the President revokes their immunity. Only a Special Prosecutor commissioned by the Senate may conduct a criminal or civil investigation of the President, Vice President, or Cabinet Members.

This Section protects the President from harassment by State and local governments while they are in office. It clarifies the disputes that arose during the Clinton and Trump administrations. The innovation of the Senate's Special Prosecutor will be discussed later.

Section 13. Proposing Appropriations For Departments

If Congress does not enact an Appropriations Bill for a fiscal year, the existing Appropriations for Departments for the current fiscal year is renewed for the following fiscal year.

The President shall submit new Appropriation Bills for Departments to the House of Representatives for their advice and consent. When the Speaker receives an Appropriations Bill from the President, the Calendar of the House may not consider any other business until the Committee of the Whole House votes on this Appropriations Bill—any other Bills enacted by the House before this vote shall be null and void. Congress may not offer amendments to this Appropriations Bill. This expedited consideration is limited to no more than six Appropriation Bills from the President during a fiscal year.

These paragraphs empower the President to write his own budget for Departments under his control and submit it to the House on a Fast-Track basis for consideration without amendments. Because Departments will always be funded based on the previous budget that was approved, there is no risk of shutting them down due to an impasse with the House.

In practical terms, the President collaborates with the House to formulate a budget that is more likely to be passed. This approach has advantages, as it reduces the risk of the President's plans for an efficient military (such as closing underutilized bases, canceling outdated weapons programs, etc.) being influenced by House Members' parochial interests. The Congress establishes maximum total spending on Departments. This constraint enables the President to make the necessary tradeoffs.

The President can submit a single Omnibus spending bill that encompasses all Departments or divide the budget into separate bills. However, this authority is limited. The President is restricted to a maximum of six Bills per year, preventing the potential misuse of this fast-track authority to manipulate the House Calendar by submitting numerous Bills to wear down the House until it relents to pass his Bills.

The Triune Executive Structure of the Anti-Elitist Constitution combines a Parliamentary System for domestic programs while preserving the separation of powers between Congress and the Presidency for Treasury, law enforcement, military, and foreign affairs.

If the House does not enact an Appropriations Bill for Departments, it may submit amendments to the Appropriation Bill for the President's review. If the President consents to the amendments, then the Bill is enacted.

The House gets to provide feedback to the President, but their feedback will be self-executing if the President accepts their terms. This Section solves the problems noted by many Political Scientists about the inefficiency of our form of government compared to a Parliamentary system. The current separation of powers between the President and Congress makes building coherent, well-functioning government laws and programs nearly impossible. Accommodating parochial interests weakens the effectiveness of legislation. The separation of powers in the 1787 Constitution diffuses political accountability between the branches. The Anti-Elitist Constitution corrects this weakness.

Section 14. Impound Accounts

The President may refuse to spend an Appropriation of funds by the House of Representatives if the purpose of said expenditure is outside the powers enumerated in this Constitution. The Governor General is a party to a controversy to petition the Supreme Court to adjudicate this dispute.

While most Presidents would like to enlarge their sphere of control, this provision allows a President conscientious about the separation of powers to refuse the temptation. Members of the House and Senate could also get involved based on their standing before the Court to file suits in constitutional controversies.

The history of the past eighty years is evidence that, instead of jealously guarding its powers, Congress willingly surrenders its powers to the bureaucracy and the Presidency. Unlike Congress, the Anti-Elitist Constitution expects the President, the Governor General, and the Executive Directors to fight tenaciously against the other executives when they encroach on their powers.

Section 15. Financial Trustee

At the commencement of the term of office for the President, Vice President, and those in the Line of Succession, their financial affairs shall be managed in a blind trust by a Trustee selected by the Office Holder. If the Senate rejects this Trustee by a four-sevenths vote within ten days after the commencement of the term of office, the Speaker of the House shall appoint a Trustee other than those initially rejected by the Senate.

This Section lessens the probability of a financial conflict of interest arising in the conduct of the State's affairs. It also ensures that the officeholder doesn't select a lackey who does the officeholder's bidding by giving the Senate the ability to reject the Trustee.

Section 16. Pension

Except in cases of conviction by the House, the President shall receive a life pension with an annual benefit equal to the Compensation Index multiplied by years of service as President.

The President is the only employee or officeholder of the Federal Government entitled to receive a pension. The pension will be scaled by years of service and less than the pay he received during his presidency. It is best to make this an exception to clarify to the Courts that this document understood that, in Article 16, Section 14, it intended to prohibit Governments from paying defined benefit pensions.

Section 17. Line of Succession Before and After Inauguration

The Line of Succession to the Presidency shall be the Vice President and Secretaries named on the Presidential Slate in the order specified by the Candidate for President before the inauguration. After the inauguration, the President may deliver an order to the Speaker to alter the Line of Succession. After Department Secretaries, the Line of Succession continues with the Governor General. The Governor General delivers an order to the Speaker for the Line of Succession of Ministers. All persons in the Line of Succession must satisfy the requirements of Article 3, Section 2.

The President can determine his own line of succession after the Vice President. The Governor General has the same authority. Should the President die before the inauguration, the replacements are already determined.

Section 18. Extraordinary Removal of the President

The Vice President and three Cabinet Secretaries in the Line of Succession may transmit a written declaration to the Speaker that the President cannot discharge the powers and duties of the Office. A two-thirds vote of the House supporting the declaration suspends the President's term in Office, and the Vice President shall immediately assume the powers and duties of the Office as Acting President. Within sixty days, a majority vote of the House may terminate the suspension of the President, and the President shall assume the powers and duties of the Office. Otherwise, the Vice President shall be sworn in as President and serve the remainder of the term.

> This Section streamlines the current mechanism for removing the President. There is a 60-day assessment period where the President could be reinstated before the initial removal becomes permanent.

Section 19. Custody and Classification of Records

The President may designate a sphere of private communication and recording of events outside the scope of this Section if they are not used for the official duties of the Presidency. All other communications, records, and documents produced by the President and the Departments are the property of the Federal Government. The Research and Records Board shall archive these unclassified communications, records, and documents throughout the term of the President. The President shall manage the procedures for classifying, storing, and handling secret documents in accordance with the law.

Section 20. Limiting Number of Departments

The maximum number of Departments and Cabinet Secretaries is five: War, Treasury, State, Justice, and Domestic Security. An amendment to this Constitution can add one Department and Cabinet Secretary.

This Section is intended to limit the scope of Presidential Power and make it very difficult to expand. The governor general will be biased toward expansions of Federal Power under his authority, while the President's powers are confined to war, foreign affairs, law enforcement, revenue collections, and expenditure disbursement. Congress could not add ten additional Departments using one amendment—just one per amendment.

Article 6.

House of Representatives, Governor General

Section 1. Powers of Legislation, Taxation, Spending and Speaker

All legislative powers herein granted shall be vested in the House of Representatives. Only this Constitution may restrict the activities of the House. No money shall be drawn from the Treasury, nor any Federal debts forgiven (excepting a bankruptcy Court judgment), but in consequence of Appropriations made by Law. The House of Representatives may not delegate the authority to any agency to draw money from the Treasury except by Appropriation made by Law. The actions of the Committee of the Whole House are the sole lawmaking authority of the Federal Government, and the House may not delegate any authority to make Law to any other body.

A regular Statement and Account of the Revenues, Expenditures, Assets, and Liabilities of all Federal Accounts shall be published for each fiscal year using the same generally accepted accounting principles that the Government requires from commercial persons who pay taxes.

The Government shall collect no revenues unless an Appropriations Bill or statute authorizes a tax, fine, sale of assets, license, or fee for goods and services voluntarily procured from the Government. Except as provided by this Constitution, The Government may not segregate Revenue Collections apart from the General Fund to support any Government expenditures not authorized by an Appropriation every fiscal year. Congress may not enact any law to delegate the discretion to execute the postponement, forgiveness, or alteration of the maturity or the amounts of principal and interest for loans receivable to the Federal Government.

> These paragraphs contain language like the 1787 Constitution but add assets and liabilities to the accounting. It added a sentence regarding the collection of taxes and fines. Unlike the 1787 Constitution, the Anti-Elitist Constitution does not have enumerated powers that limit the scope of the legislation to matters covering interstate commerce and what is necessary and proper. The courts have given such loose interpretations to these enumerated powers that they rarely strike down federal laws that intrude on State powers. This Anti-Elitist Constitution ends the continuation of this dishonesty at the core of our Constitutional Jurisprudence. Also, it curtails the Executive Branch so that it cannot forgive debts as Biden did with Student Loans.

The first and second vote taken at the start of a new session of the House of Representatives is the selection of its Speaker and Vice Speaker. The Speaker from the Previous House of Representatives shall preside over this selection until the House chooses the successor. The Speaker's term shall be the duration of the House of Representatives until the subsequent seating of Members for the next term unless three-fifths of Members vote to terminate the Speaker's term at an earlier date.

The Speaker and Vice Speaker shall be Birthright Citizens who have attained fifty years and have never held an elected office in any Government except as Speaker or Vice Speaker of the House of Representatives after the adoption of this Constitution.

When absent, the Speaker delegates authority to the Vice Speaker. If the Speaker vacates the office during their term, then the Vice Speaker shall become the Speaker for the remainder of the term. During the House of Representatives term, the President may fill the vacancy if the House does not replace a vacancy for the Speaker or Vice Speaker after fifteen days.

The Speaker shall appoint a Sergeant at Arms responsible for carrying out the Speaker's orders, maintaining the security and safety of Members, and conducting the House in an orderly manner. These powers include the power to arrest and imprison persons on the grounds of the House of Representatives. The grounds are the chambers of the House and the offices and meeting rooms for its Members and staff. Within these grounds, the President and persons with Executive Authority under the President may not enter without the permission of the Speaker.

> These paragraphs adopt the British Parliament's model for a Speaker as a non-partisan authority to ensure the fair and orderly proceedings of the House. This paragraph creates the Vice Speaker position as a backup. Presumably, a State Justice, university President, or similar non-partisan public figure would be a popular choice. The Speaker has a 4-year term, so a simple majority of the Members cannot eject them because they are displeased by his rulings. There is a division of power between the Speaker and the Governor General. The Members elect both, so both are ultimately accountable to the voters. One oversees running the House, while the other oversees running his portion of the Government.

The compensation of each Member is paid monthly, on a pro-rata basis, based upon their hours of attendance compared to the hours the Subcommittees and the Committee of the Whole are in session according to the House Calendar. The Speaker has plenary authority to determine Members' absences and calculate their adjusted compensation.

Section 2. Calendar and Conduct of Business of the House

The Majority of the House of Representatives shall provide the calendar of its proceedings of the Committee of the Whole and subcommittees to the Speaker, who shall provide no less than twenty-four hours advance notice to all members. If the Majority provides no calendar, then the Speaker shall write the calendar. The House cannot conduct official business outside the calendar without a three-fifths vote of all House Members.

A vote on a bill by the Committee of the Whole cannot occur within seven days' time after the majority submits the bill to the Speaker for placement on the House calendar. However, the House can waive this requirement with a three-fifths vote.

The Speaker and Vice Speaker shall forfeit compensation pro-rata if neither of them Preside over any Proceedings of the House listed on the calendar.

> The Calendar forms the basis for operating the House transparently. The 7-day minimum requirement before a vote can be taken ends the practice of submitting a 4,000-page Omnibus Spending Bill to Members the day before the vote.

The House may determine the Rules of its Proceedings, punish a Member for disorderly Behavior, and expel a member with the concurrence of two-thirds.

> Language from the 1787 Constitution.

The Speaker shall be the arbiter of the Rules of the Proceedings of the House and can be overruled by a three-fifths vote of the House.

> The Speaker shall judge the rules but can be overruled in extraordinary cases.

A majority of House members signing a Petition to the Speaker can demand a vote of the Committee of the Whole for any Resolution or Legislation within seven days of receipt by the Speaker.

> This prevents the party leadership from throttling consideration of bills that have bipartisan support.

Section 3. Quorum and Attendance

The Majority shall constitute a Quorum to do Business, but a smaller Number may adjourn from day to day and may be authorized to compel the Attendance of absent Members, in such Manner, and under such Penalties as the House may provide.

Language from the 1787 Constitution. Because the President's Departments have evergreen budgets that are funded even if Congress doesn't Appropriate Funds, there is no need to give the President the power to force the House to be in session.

As determined by the Speaker, Members of the House shall not receive compensation for absences from the proceedings on the House Calendar. Except for the Governor General and up to eight ministers, a separate three-fifths vote by the House is required to grant a single member an exception to this requirement for up to thirty days.

If Members embark on overseas fact-finding missions, the House must grant an exception. Otherwise, if a Member is absent, they are not paid. The Speaker and his staff are responsible for these bookkeeping duties.

Section 4. Selection and Powers of the Governor General

The third vote taken at the start of a new session of the House selects the Governor General. A majority vote elects the Governor General.

This paragraph adopts the British Parliamentary model for selecting an Executive authority accountable to the House's majority party.

The Executive Power over all Ministries not under the Authority of the President or the Boards established by this Constitution and subsequent legislation shall be vested in a Governor General of the United States. Laws enacted by Congress shall define the extent of the Executive Power of the Governor General and shall not encroach upon the President's or Board Director's Executive Powers. The Governor General, Ministers, and employees of the Ministries may only enforce laws by detainment and use of force on the Property of the Federal Government governed by a Ministry. Any violators must be transferred to the custody of the President within two days of detainment or be released unless extenuating circumstances prevent it.

This model of this Constitution is betting that the President and the Governor General will compete against each other to enlarge the domain of their authority and ensure that no one officeholder concentrates excessive power into the Executive Branch. This Section merges the legislative and executive branches under the Governor General for matters of domestic social policy. The President has authority for foreign policy and enforcement of laws. The wager for this Constitutional model is that domestic social policy is more fraught with political conflict and is better managed under a system with unambiguous political accountability. Matters of foreign policy and law enforcement should be outside the bounds of partisan bickering and decided more as a matter of the competence of the President to act as a unifying, national figure.

Ministry and *Minister* denote agencies and subordinates under the Governor General, and *Department* and *Secretary* denote agencies and subordinates under the President. The use of force limited to Federal Property allows Park Rangers employed by the Ministry of the Interior to carry guns and arrest lawbreakers. The same applies to crimes in Federal buildings under the control of a Ministry. However, this authority is limited until the President can take custody of persons charged with a criminal act.

The Governor General shall be a Member of the House. Each Member of the House may nominate one candidate for Governor General. The two candidates receiving the most nominations by Members of the House submitted to the Speaker shall stand for election by the Members of the House. The Speaker announces the nominee receiving the most votes as the Governor General. The term of the Governor General ends after Members are seated after the next election for the House of Representatives or if the seven-thirteenth of the Members pass a resolution of no confidence.

Typically, we should expect the leaders of the two major political parties to be the nominees. Forcing Members to nominate only a single candidate enforces more party discipline to avoid risking that the minority party that doesn't split its nominations could beat the majority party that did.

The Governor General shall govern the Ministries authorized by law. The Governor General shall appoint Members of the House to be Ministers with executive authority over each Ministry with the concurrence of a House majority. The House may remove a Minister with a seven-thirteenth majority.

> Apart from Secretaries on the Presidential Slate, the President requires the Senate's consent to appoint Principal and Inferior Officers. The Governor General must seek the Members' consent to install and remove a Minister. Unlike most Parliamentary systems, this no-confidence vote requires a 7/13th supermajority.

Any Ministry administered by the Governor General must petition the President regarding any enforcement of laws related to the Ministry's operations.

> To implement this paragraph, units in the Justice Department will specialize in enforcing laws related to each Ministry. The Justice Department personnel report up the chain to the President, not the Governor General. The President could fail to faithfully execute his responsibility to enforce laws required for the Ministries to operate effectively. Later Sections will respond to this concern.

The Governor General has the authority to summon an individual Secretary in the President's Cabinet or a particular employee of the President's Executive Branch for non-consensual testimony before the Committees of the House of Representatives for no more than two hours every thirty days without the President's consent.

> This paragraph endows congressional authority to oversee the departments under the President. Because Congress is accountable for the Ministries it creates, authorization is not required. Hopefully, most persons under the President will voluntarily attend hearings of the House. The Governor General does not possess a police force to compel someone to attend.

With the consent of seven-thirteenth of the Members of the House, the Governor General may summon other persons not employed by the Government before the Committees of the House of Representatives without their consent for up to eight hours over no more than two days every twelve months, and reimburse reasonable travel, lodging, and meal expenses. This testimony may be under oath. The penalty for non-cooperation may be either a fine not to exceed one-fifth of the Compensation Index or not to exceed ten days in prison.

> This paragraph gives Congress the authority to haul corporate executives to testify before their committees. But anything beyond eight hours should merit a formal charge by the Justice Department. Otherwise, it is harassment. Only the President can enforce these Congressional edicts so Congress cannot act tyrannically.

The Governor General must answer questions from Members of the House for no less than one hour every fourteen days. Each Minister has the same obligation. All Members' names will be drawn randomly by the Speaker to determine the order of appearance over a twelve-month period to submit questions. Members may assign their position to speak to another Member. The failure of the Governor General to appear and answer questions about the allotted time results in the loss of fourteen days of compensation for each occurrence unless three-fifths of the Members grant a waiver.

> Institutes the British practice of question time.

Section 5. Limitations and Authority for Debt Financing

Article 16, Section 15 prescribes the powers of the House of Representatives to borrow money on the Credit of the United States.

> This provision dispenses with the Debt Limit as a tool for the Treasury. Article 16, Section 15 defines *Public Debt* as distinct from *Special Obligation Debt* within the Social Security Trust Fund. The House must commit to establishing a maximum amount of money to borrow. The President will use that amount to determine his ability to make line-item vetoes of expenditures that could reduce the amount of borrowing. It also prevents the issuance of indexed bonds.

Section 6. No Binding Obligations for Future Appropriations

No enactment of law or a court decision can obligate a future appropriation by a Legislature.

> This Section clips the wings of the courts that assumed legislative powers when mandating expenditures by Legislatures to enforce its rulings. A classic example was a federal judge forcing the Kansas City School District to drastically increase spending to remedy its desegregation judgment.

Excepting provisions of this Constitution that require an Appropriation, no promises of expenditures outside an Appropriations Bill for a single fiscal year are binding and enforceable. An exception to this prohibition is that Congress, with a six-elevenths vote, may Appropriate funds for transfer to a separate custodial entity under the oversight of the Federal Reserve Board that disburses these funds for a maximum of four fiscal years according to a law or contractual obligation.

> Under this paragraph, loan guarantees are not enforceable. This paragraph terminates SBA, Fannie, Freddie, Ex-Im Bank, and other loan guarantee programs with large and powerful constituencies. Loan guarantees are obligations for Appropriations for a future Congress imposed by the current Congress, which violates democratic control of the purse. This Section also thwarts the artifice of transferring funds outside the Federal Government to an entity that is required to disburse funds in future fiscal years according to the demands of a prior Congress. An exception is permitted, provided there is a 6/11th vote of Congress. This exception applies in cases like long-term military contracts or other projects where funding stability is essential. This paragraph only applies to the federal government. States can establish loan guarantee programs for homeowners and small business owners.

Section 7. Continuing Appropriations for Departments

The Bill for Appropriations of Departments and Boards and the Bill for Raising Revenue last enacted shall not contain expiration provisions. These Bills remain in force until replaced by another Bill for Appropriations or a Bill for Raising Revenue. Bills for Appropriations of Ministries expire at the end of every twelve-month fiscal year. Congress may not enact new Bills for Appropriations of Ministries in a fiscal year before the enactment of The Bill for Appropriations of Departments and Boards. The Governor General manages Social Security, Medicare, and Medicaid programs.

This Section prevents shutdowns of the Departments essential for national defense and law enforcement. It guarantees a continuing resolution that a new Appropriations bill can replace. These Departments receive uninterrupted funding. Because the House Majority controls the Ministries, the House can ensure that there are no funding interruptions for them.

Because Ministries will receive funding after votes to fund the Departments and Boards, the House must approve the federal government's most essential functions before it gets to the business of domestic pork barreling.

Section 8. The Congressional Record and Compensation Restrictions

The House shall keep a Journal of its Proceedings and publish the same in writing, excepting such Parts as may in their Judgment require Secrecy. The Yeas and Nays of the Members on any question shall, at the Desire of one-fifth of those Present, be entered into the Journal.

Language from the 1787 Constitution.

Excepting such parts, in the judgment of the Speaker or three-fifths vote of the House, requiring secrecy, The Committee of the Whole and the Subcommittees must broadcast the audio and visual record and transcription of their proceedings. The Board of Records shall archive this record and make it available for Citizens to retrieve.

Representatives, the Speaker, Vice Speaker, and Sergeant at Arms shall receive a Compensation for their Services, to be ascertained by Law, and paid out of the Treasury of the United States. They shall in all Cases, except Treason, Felony and Breach of the Peace, be privileged from Arrest during their Attendance at the Session of the House of Representatives, and in going to and returning from the same; and for any Speech or Debate, they shall not be questioned in any other Place.

Language from the 1787 Constitution.

Representatives are employees of the Federal Government, and they shall not receive compensation for services derived from their labor outside the House of Representatives, nor shall they receive any gifts other than an inheritance from the estate of their spouse or parents.

This paragraph minimizes conflicts of interest. While Representatives may earn investment income outside of their salary, they may not receive compensation for consulting or other labor income apart from their House salary. No book publishing deals, speaking gigs, inflated prices paid for artwork, or other compensation for labor is permitted—no gifts from friends seeking influence and favors.

No Representatives shall, during the Time for which they were elected, be appointed to any civil Office under the Authority of the United States, which shall have been created, or the compensation shall have been increased during such time.

Language from the 1787 Constitution.

Section 9. Compensation Calculations of Elected Officials

The Compensation Index defined in Article 23 is the basis for computing office holder compensation by the following multiples: President is twenty times; Vice President and Governor General are ten; Chief Justice five; Speaker of the House and Justices of the Supreme Court four; Vice Speaker, Sergeant at Arms, and Judges of the Inferior Courts three; Adjudicators of Administrative Law Courts two.

> Fixing officeholders' compensation and fines using House Members' compensation as the index is a way to remove partisan gamesmanship and posturing. It is an excellent proxy for keeping up with inflation. Also, a 2.5% limit on annual salary increases is a fantastic deterrent against promoting inflation!

Forfeiture of the compensation of individual House Members for absences shall not affect the compensation of other office holders. Except during the first term of the House of Representatives elected under this Constitution, the Members' annual compensation may not increase by more than one-fortieth of the preceding fiscal year.

Excepting the Governor General and a maximum of eight Ministers, each Member of the House of Representatives shall receive the same compensation. Ministers may not receive more than five times the Compensation Index.

The total Appropriations for operations of the House, use of facilities, and compensation of Members and staff shall be calculated and enacted in the Bill for Appropriations. The House shall equally apportion amounts for equipment, utilities, Member and staff compensation. Subsequently, each Member may enter arrangements to utilize their apportionment to cooperate with other Members to share staff, equipment, and utilities.

Use of building facilities shall be allocated by lottery if one-third of Members petition the Speaker, who shall then draw lots.

> These paragraphs protect the ability of each House Member to perform without succumbing to threats from the Majority Party that controls the House.

Excepting Citizenship, criminal and civil convictions, the staff hired by Members shall not be subject to any labor laws governing hiring, hours, compensation, insurance, and collective bargaining. The staff hired by Members are at-will employees. The House may adopt procedures for receiving complaints by staff against a Representative and administer sanctions according to its rules but may only deny a Representative its vote in the Committee of the Whole by expulsion.

> This paragraph prevents setting wage and hour conditions, requiring union representation, and other restrictions that could threaten a Member's independence. However, the leadership could still deny a member's participation in subcommittees.

Conforming to this duty to equally allocate resources among the Members, the Governor General and Ministers must operate a transparent process to ensure nondiscrimination when responding to reasonable requests by Members of the House and Senate submitted to the Ministries. The Speaker's ruling in a dispute in these matters shall be final. Ministers and staff responsible for a violation shall forfeit thirty days compensation for each violation.

> This Constitution sets the Governor General's compensation and his Ministers' compensation at 50% of his. However, this preferential compensation is limited to eight Ministers. Additional Ministers earn the standard House Member compensation. Having a proportional allocation of resources is fair and prevents the majority from abusing power in the operations of the House of Representatives. The Governor General cannot use control of the Ministries to evade the equal allocation of resources devoted to each House Member or for Senators required in prior paragraphs.

Article 7.

THE SENATE

Section 1. Mission of the Senate

The Senate is an independent body representing the States, separate from the Federal Government but granted authority in the Federal Government. This Constitution grants the Senate powers to restrain the Executive and Legislative powers of the Federal Government and to provide advice and consent to the President for appointments and Treaties. States select and employ their Senators to represent the interests of their State's Citizens, legal residents, State Government, and its political subdivisions. Ex-officio members of the Senate represent the interests of Citizens and legal residents of the Federal Districts, Territories, and the nation as a whole.

> Defining the Senate as a body independent of the Federal Government is a novel innovation. It is a separate branch of government, which gives it the independence and position to exercise oversight in a way that the current Senate cannot.

Whenever the Executive Branch of the Federal Government does not adopt an adversarial relationship investigating and prosecuting wrongdoing and is likely to collude with a person who should be prosecuted, the Senate may employ a special prosecutor with the full legal authority afforded to prosecutors in the Executive Branch before the Federal and State Courts.

> The appointment of a Special Prosecutor outside of the Executive Branch solves the conflict-of-interest problems and lack of accountability that have afflicted all prior attempts to insulate prosecutors from control by the officers entrusted by the voters to control these prosecutors.

The Majority of State Senators shall constitute a Quorum to do Business, but a smaller Number may adjourn from day to day. Two-thirds of Senators may vote to expel a Member. If a State's Senator fails to answer a roll call for more than three consecutive days while in session, then the senator is excluded from the majority calculation until they affirmatively reply to a roll call. Ex-officio members do not count toward a Majority.

Excepting the expulsion of a Senator, any simple or super-majority vote of the Committee of the Whole Senate shall only take effect if the States represented by those Senators in the Majority constitute a majority of the Citizens of the United States, according to the most recent Census. Ex-officio members of the Senate do not represent any Citizens for purposes of this test.

> This paragraph mollifies critics who dismiss the Senate's democracy bona fides due to its anti-majoritarian traits. This modification means that the Senate still needs a majority of Senators to pass anything, but that majority cannot represent a minority of the Citizens. This requirement differs from the House because a State coalition with a majority of Citizens cannot pass anything in the Senate if that coalition is a minority of the States.

When the Senate is in session, each State Senator must display their State Constitution at their desk as a condition for voting and participating in debates in the Committee of the Whole Senate and its Subcommittees.

> The State Constitution symbolizes the source of sovereign power vested in the Electorate of each State that sent the Senator. Emphasizing the State Constitution elevates the stature of Constitutional authority and restraints about how representatives govern the people.

The Senate shall appoint a Sergeant at Arms who will be responsible for carrying out the orders of any majority vote by the Senators, maintaining the security and safety of Members, and ensuring the orderly conduct of the Senate. A vote of the Senate shall set the compensation of the Sergeant at Arms, and each State shall bear it according to its percentage of the total population of Citizens according to the most recent Census. The Sergeant at Arms shall have the power to arrest and imprison persons on the grounds of the Senate for a maximum of three days. The grounds include the chambers of the Senate and the offices and meeting rooms for the Senators and their staff. Within these grounds, the President and persons with Executive Authority under the President may not enter without a resolution passed by the Senate. The Senate shall display this Constitution when the Senate is in session, and it shall be removed when the Senate is in recess.

> Symmetrical with the House of Representatives, the federal Constitution on display is analogous to the Mace in Parliament. It is the symbol of power.

Section 2. Selection of Senators

One Senator shall be chosen no sooner than seven days before the President's Inauguration Date by a majority vote of the most numerous House of the State Legislature for a four-year term that begins on the date of the Inauguration of the President. If a Senator vacates their office before the end of their term, the State Legislature may appoint a member of their Legislature to complete the remaining term.

> State Legislatures select their one representative for the State. That makes that Senator more prestigious than the current two per State. Fifty senators comprise a more collegial body than 100 Senators. However, not being selected by voters at large lowers their prestige. Nevertheless, their role as a separate branch of government that represents their Legislature makes this appointment by the Legislature mandatory. The Legislatures select their Senators in the same election cycle as the President. The voters chose the Members of the House two years later, providing periodic feedback. If a State did not send a Senator, then that does not impede the Senate from conducting its business. In fact, if the Senate did not ever meet and conduct business, it would not impede the other branches from acting.

A former President and Vice President, no longer serving in another State or Federal office, are ex-officio members of the Senate with equal voting rights. Except for the pension of the President and any private pensions earned before election to office, an ex-officio Senator may not receive any compensation for labor services from the Federal or State Government or other persons, gifts outside their parents or spouse, nor may they have been convicted by the House for an impeachable offense.

An ex-president would not likely participate as a full-time member of the Senate, but he could occasionally participate in crucial debates and votes. It is more likely that a former Vice President with Presidential ambitions will participate. They would also most likely assume leadership roles in the Senate. It is a place to retire gracefully and pass along the wisdom learned over the years. It is the only place in the US Government that resembles a House of Lords where your vote in a Representative body is not dependent upon a current election. An ex-officio member must declare their participation in the Senate, and during that term in the Senate, they cannot receive outside income for the entire term. They cannot earn income, so they could decide to participate for a month without outside income and then return to the private sector.

Section 3. Eligibility Requirements

No Person shall be a Senator who shall not be a Citizen of that State employing them for the Office of Senator. A State Legislature may only elect a Senator for their first term whom the eligible voters of that State elected and who was serving as a member of that State's Legislature when they began their first term in the Senate. If a Senator vacates their Office, the Legislature can only elect them if they are a Member of the State Legislature.

The first time a Senator is selected, they must have been elected as a Member of their Legislature. While serving as Senator, they will vacate their seat in the State Legislature, but they could still be selected to serve additional terms in the Senate. Limiting initial

> eligibility to members of State Legislatures limits the ability to reward Senate appointments to cronies, as was common before the adoption of the 17th Amendment.

Section 4. State Loyalty and Fixed Compensation

Senators are employees of their State Government, and their sole compensation for employment is from that Government.

> This paragraph explicitly defines their role as a representative of their State because they can only receive compensation from their State, not the Federal Government. Therefore, Senators from different States could receive different compensation packages. Because the Federal Districts and Territories receive Federal Funding to support their operations, they could not select a Senator independent of the Federal Government. Including Senators from federal districts and territories violates the rationale for the Senate.

The compensation of a Senator by their State shall be fixed during their four-year term of office. No person may serve more than twenty years in the Senate during their lifetime. The State Legislature may fill any vacancies arising during the four-year term in accordance with Section 2.

> Once elected by their State Legislature, the Senator serves 4-years instead of 6-years served by existing Senators. The state cannot reduce the senators' compensation to punish them or increase their compensation to reward them for votes. Large States will likely pay their Senators higher salaries and have larger staffs than small States. These differences ensure that larger States will have more influence and attenuate some of the Senate's anti-majoritarian critiques.

Section 5. Federal And State Funding of Senate Operations

The Federal Government shall provide offices, utilities, police protection, and meeting space for the Senators, Special Prosecutors and Staff to conduct business in the Federal Districts like the Members of the House. The States are responsible for the compensation of Senate staff and Special Prosecutors. Senators, Senate Staff, and Special Prosecutors may not receive compensation from the Federal Government or any non-government persons during their service to the Senate.

> The Federal Government is responsible for providing a meeting place for the Senate, which is the extent of Federal support. But their staff are the responsibility of the States. Likely, the Senate will allocate expenses for general overhead on a per-capita basis. The Senator's State will fund their staff. Senators from the same party will likely share staff per capita, too.

Section 6. Privilege from Arrest and Free Speech

Senators shall in all Cases, except Treason, Felony and Breach of the Peace, be privileged from Arrest during their Attendance at the Session of the Senate, and in going to and returning from the same; and for any Speech or Debate, they shall not be questioned in any other Place.

> Language from the 1787 Constitution.

Section 7. Legislative Veto

No Bills may originate in the Senate.

> This paragraph placates the left-wing critics of the Senate's anti-majoritarian nature. The Senate only has a restraining and oversight role, not a creative role in the Legislative process. This paragraph renders the filibuster a moot point.

Excepting Bills solely for Appropriations and Raising Revenue, no Bills passed by the House of Representatives with less than a two-thirds majority and signed by the President will be enacted sooner than ninety days from the date of passage unless a majority of the Senate votes to reject before enactment. Bills passed by a two-thirds majority of the House shall be enacted without the consent of the Senate.

This paragraph ensures that legislation cannot be rushed. Unless a 2/3's vote passes the bill, the Senate has 90 days to consider whether it wishes to initiate a rejection of the bill. The Senate's consent isn't required, but the Senate can be pro-active and reject something.

Article 8.

Impeachment, Conviction, Removal from Office

Section 1. Immunity While In Office

No trial for a criminal or civil offense against the President, Vice President, Principal Officers of the Executive Branch under the President's authority, Justices of the Supreme Court, and Judges of the Inferior Courts may proceed before they depart from office without their consent.

> This paragraph gives officeholders immunity while serving. It prevents interference with the performance of their duties.

After departing their office, only a Special Prosecutor appointed by the Senate may bring criminal or civil charges against these officeholders for acts committed under their duties during their service in the office, and only after a conviction by the House for an Impeachment.

> This paragraph solves the problem of state or local prosecutors and private parties suing or bringing indictments against the President or other officeholders for killings in war, damage to property, or other offenses committed in the ordinary course of performing their duties. This paragraph applies to officers who have departed from the government and then been prosecuted or sued. Now, this decision is assigned as an exclusive matter for a Special Prosecutor, and only after the office holder has already been convicted of an impeachable offense by the House for performing official duties in a manner meriting impeachment. This Section makes it a

political decision through impeachment to determine whether the acts by the officer were so egregious as to merit punishment, first by removal from office and then later by a court.

If a President commits an ordinary crime while not performing the duties of his office, then he can be prosecuted like an ordinary person *after* he leaves office.

Section 2. Trial For Impeachment and Conviction in the House

The House of Representatives has the sole Power to try all Impeachments of The President, Vice President, Principal Officers of the Executive Branch under the President's authority, Justices of the Supreme Court, and Judges of the Inferior Courts. The Speaker of the House shall Preside over the Trial. Conviction requires a three-fifths majority of the Members voting yea or nay. The Trial shall not exceed two hundred hours over thirty consecutive days.

Any person convicted by the House is ineligible to hold any elected or appointed public office, receive compensation or, in the case of the President, their pension, or be employed by the Government. If convicted before their term of office is concluded, they shall be removed from office.

This Section reverses the current regime, in which the Senate tries Impeachments, the House votes to impeach, and the Chief Justice presides over the President's trial in the Senate. This Constitution has the Senate appointing a Special Prosecutor and the trial in the House with the Speaker presiding—no mention of the grounds for an impeachment relating to high crimes and misdemeanors. America's experience with Clinton and Trump is that impeachment is a political process, not a judicial one.

Subject to Section 1 of this Article, they may be subject to Civil or Criminal Prosecution in Federal or State Courts after conviction.

Prosecutors seeking a criminal indictment or Parties filing a civil suit for adjudication in a State or Federal Court against a former President or Vice President regarding acts, not under their official duties must petition the Senate for review and approval by a majority vote. By a majority vote, the Senate may elect to change the trial venue and pay reasonable attorney fees incurred for the defense against the charges.

> This Section protects the President or Vice President from prosecutorial misconduct and bias after leaving office. Unfortunately, the precedent of New York prosecutors running for office promising to indict and sue Donald Trump is an example of political lawfare that needs to be curtailed. This Section prevents the proliferation of politically motivated retaliatory prosecutions by ambitious, elected prosecutors. This protection is limited to unofficial, private acts and only requires a majority vote of the Senate for approval to allow a prosecution to proceed. The Senate has the additional discretion to change the venue and pay for the defense cost as additional protections against politically motivated lawfare.

Section 3. Senate Appointment of Special Prosecutor

By a vote of seven-thirteenths majority, the Senate may pass a Resolution to appoint a Special Prosecutor with the power to subpoena witnesses, conduct investigations, and try cases in the Federal and State Courts identical to rules applied by the Department of Justice for all other citizens under Federal Law and by the laws of the States, with jurisdiction over any violations committed by President, Vice President, Principal Officers of the Executive Branch under authority of the President, Justices of the Supreme Court, and Judges of the Inferior Courts. This Resolution is limited to a single defendant. This investigation shall not commence any later than twelve months after they depart from the Office.

> The appointment of a Special Prosecutor by this non-Federal Senate is an important innovation. It solves the problems vexing prior Special Prosecutors. The first Special Prosecutors were a law to

> themselves. They were fiscally and legally unaccountable. They pursued matters outside their original mandate. Later reforms placed Special Prosecutors under the Attorney General, compromising their independence whenever the target was the President or other Executive branch members. Their budgets and the time they took to conduct investigations were out of control. The Special Prosecutors under this Constitution will have the same authority as Attorneys working in the Justice Department, and Senators will probably recruit Special Prosecutors from the ranks of current and former employees of the Justice Department. A 7/13ths super-majority (27 Senators and majority population of Citizens) is not too high of a hurdle and increases the likelihood that there is some bi-partisan consensus that something is amiss.

The Special Prosecutor may request the Supreme Court to overturn any plea agreements by the Executive Branch that obstruct the pursuit of justice against elected officials and officers of the Executive Branch. The Special Prosecutor may request an extension of any statute of limitations that expired because the Justice Department refused to file charges promptly.

> This paragraph handles situations like the plea bargain arrangement with Hunter Biden that would remove any leverage to obtain evidence against his father, the President. When the Justice Department allowed the statute of limitations on Hunter Biden's tax violations to expire, later administrations could not reverse this malfeasance under the current rules. This paragraph fixes that problem.

The Senate will employ a Special Prosecutor and staff by a Senate Resolution defining the scope and cost of the investigation. The expenses of the Special Prosecutor are the responsibility of those States whose Senators supported the Resolution.

> Those Senators supporting a Special Prosecutor will have to raise funds from their States to pay for the assignment. This requirement gives larger, wealthier States with a greater capacity to support these Special Prosecutors more influence in the decision to

appoint these prosecutors. While in theory, each State gets one vote, the reality is that supporting a Special Prosecutor is a costly proposition that is easier for the larger States to back. This structure ensures that the Special Prosecutor will be independent of the Executive Branch, but he will be more accountable for time and expenses than is currently the case.

The Special Prosecutor's term commences immediately upon the vote of the Senate. The initial term of the Special Prosecutor shall not exceed five hundred days, and any extension no greater than two hundred days of this initial term requires a three-fifths majority vote of the Senate before the end of the initial term. Otherwise, three hundred days must pass before another Investigation and Prosecution of the same Office Holder may commence.

Setting a 500-day deadline is reasonable. Requiring a super-majority to extend the deadline allows a promising investigation to continue for 200 days. Requiring a 300-day interlude deters never-ending, open-ended investigations.

Section 4. Impeachment for Obstruction of Oversight by President

The Governor General may authorize Articles of Impeachment with the consent of seven-thirteenths vote of the House of Representatives and a majority vote of the Senate if the President refuses to cooperate with the House of Representatives in its exercise of oversight of the Departments under the control of the President. By majority vote, the Senate may appoint a Special Prosecutor and conduct the trial under the rules of Section 2 of this Article.

This tool imposes accountability upon the President to cooperate with the House's oversight responsibility.

Article 9.

The Judiciary

Section 1. Vesting of Judicial Power and Judicial Review

The text of this Constitution defines and constrains the Judiciary's authority. As a symbol of the Judiciary's submission to this higher authority, the text of this Constitution shall be displayed in front of the Chief Justice when the Supreme Court is in session and removed when it is in recess. The same applies to every Federal and State Court Judge, and the State Court Judges must also display their State Constitution.

> This submission is an admonishment against Justice Charles Evan Huges, who remarked, "The Constitution is what the Judges say it is."

The Judicial Power of the United States shall be vested in one Supreme Court and in such Inferior and Administrative Courts as the Congress may from time to time ordain and establish. The Judiciary must ensure that the laws enacted by Governments do not transgress this Constitution in part or whole.

> This paragraph places the Court in a subservient position to the Constitution and puts a stake in the creative interpretations of the document. "In part or in whole" means that the Court cannot ignore an explicit prohibition contained in a Section of the document by appealing to the entire document's purpose. Judicial review is adopted as the remit of the Court. The two-year lag for increasing the number of judges, circuit, and appellate courts deters court-packing while that party is in power.

Judges in Martial Courts are not members of the Judicial Branch. Enactments of Congress govern their conduct and supervision by the President.

Adjudicators in Public Benefit Ministries who dispense pecuniary and non-pecuniary benefits to persons are not members of the Judicial Branch. Enactments of Congress govern their conduct and supervision by the Governor General. The Government must afford public benefit recipients a pre-termination evidentiary hearing before discontinuing their aid. Judges and Adjudicators of all other courts shall be members of the Judicial Branch.

> This paragraph eliminates the current distinction between Article 1 and 4 Judges found in bankruptcy courts and administrative tribunals and Article 3 Judges, with lifetime tenure and protections against pay reductions. It also ends the confusion caused by a series of challenges [3] to adjudicators in public rights cases and ensures that Administrative Law Court Adjudicators are independent of partisan whims. Adjudicators in Military Courts and those handling disputes concerning Social Security, Medicare, Section 8 Housing, and other welfare programs are not part of the Judiciary.
>
> The *Goldberg v Kelly* [4] requirement for due process for the denial of aid to welfare recipients is recognized.

Whenever Congress enacts laws to increase the number of Judicial seats, the President may not nominate a Judge to fill these new seats before two years elapsed. This restriction does not apply to Adjudicators.

> This paragraph thwarts opportunistic expansion of the courts when one party is dominant and wishes to pack the courts with its preferred candidates. With a two-year delay, another Presidential election will occur, so Congress cannot be sure that the next President will be from their party.

Computation of compensation for the Supreme Court's Justices and the Inferior Court Judges depends on two thousand hours of work during a fiscal year. The Research and Records Board computes this compensation for each Justice, Judge, and Adjudicator on a pro-rata basis of the maximum compensation defined under Article 6, Section

9. Congress shall have oversight authority and issue reports regarding the volume of cases heard, the number and cost of clerks and other assistants, thoroughness of opinions, and the treatment of litigants for each Judge and Adjudicator who appears in Court. Congress shall appropriate a minimum amount for clerks and staff for every Justice and Judge under this Article equal to the Judge's or Justice's compensation.

> This paragraph establishes the principle that the Judges are not above scrutiny from outside their own peer group. Congress cannot do much other than embarrass the Judges, short of impeachment and conviction. Public reports about laziness, maltreatment of litigants, and poorly drafted opinions will affect the reputation of the Judges and thus be a great motivational tool. The two thousand hours equals 50 weeks times 40 hours/week, yielding two weeks for vacation. If they work 42 hours/week, then they can work 48 weeks and get four weeks' holiday. Of course, judges can claim that they are working at their desks outside of the courtroom, beyond the scrutiny of the Research and Records Board, but then the expenditures for clerk salaries should reflect this tradeoff.

Section 2. 9 Permanent and 2 Provisional Seats on Supreme Court

One Chief Justice and eight Associate Justices occupy the Permanent Seats of the Supreme Court that may try and rule on a case. There are two Provisional Seats. The senior Provisional Justice ascends to a Permanent Seat of the Supreme Court whenever a Justice vacates a Permanent Seat.

Excepting matters of recusal, all majority and super-majority votes by the Supreme Court and Inferior Courts shall be computed using the Tenure Percentage Vote method described in Article 23. Provisional Justices are assigned a four-year term to calculate the Tenure Percentage Vote when they serve as Temporary Members.

> Assigning a four-year term for Temporary Members thwarts a Justice with lesser tenure recusing himself so that a Provisional Court member with a longer tenure could ascend as a Temporary Member and have greater voting strength to decide a close case.

A Permanent Justice vacates their seat if they die or if the Justice is absent for more than thirty days within any twelve consecutive months when the Court was in Session. Congress may enact laws governing the minimum time for a Court to be in Session.

> This innovation permits the Court to function fully without interruption from Senate hearings for a nominee to replace an open seat. A president cannot immediately affect the voting balance in the Court with an appointment. It might take several years before an appointee moves onto the Permanent Court. Congress's ability to enact laws governing the Court's behavior establishes the precedent that the Court does not possess plenary authority over its work schedule.

The Senior Provisional Justice serves as a Temporary Member of the Supreme Court whenever a Justice cannot serve due to a recusal or illness. Temporary service does not count toward the maximum term of service as a Permanent Member.

> Provisional Justices are convenient replacements, ensuring that the Court nearly always operates at total capacity unless more than two recuse themselves.

Section 3. Term Limits, Minimum Age, Recusal

The President shall nominate a Provisional Justice of the Supreme Court and Judges of the inferior courts. No Justice or Judge may serve more than eighteen years during their lifetime as a Permanent Member, excepting those most senior nine Permanent Members who served before the ratification of this Constitution. Upon attaining eighty years, a Justice or Judge is retired from service. Except for the justices serving before ratification, a Justice must be a Citizen of the United States who has attained the age of fifty years upon assuming the position of Justice. A Judge of the inferior courts must have attained an age of thirty-five years.

> Judges get 18-year maximum terms instead of a lifetime appointment. Setting the minimum age at 50 means that justices will have more experience and a position on the Court will be near the end of their legal careers.

Six Permanent Justices may compel the recusal of only one other Justice from hearing a case before the Supreme Court. Two-thirds of the Judges on an Inferior Court may compel the recusal of another Judge from hearing a case before their Court. Recusal votes are not based on the Tenure Vote Percentage.

Section 4. Term Limits According to Senate Vote Majority

The President nominates Justices, Judges, and Adjudicators for a Provisional, Inferior, or Administrative Court seat. If the Senate does not reject the nomination by a majority vote within ninety days, then the nominee may serve a maximum term of six years.

If a majority vote of the Senate rejects the nominee, then the nominee may not be nominated for another Seat until four years after the vote. If the President refuses to nominate someone within ninety days after someone vacates a Permanent, Provisional, Inferior, or Administrative Court Seat, the Senate may nominate and appoint someone for a two-year term.

If the Senate approves a nominee by a five-ninths majority, the nominee serves a maximum term of thirteen years. Senate approval by a two-thirds vote serves a maximum eighteen-year term. No Justice may serve more than eighteen years in a Permanent Seat during their lifetime as a Justice.

> Like Ambassadors, the President can nominate Justices who will be seated on the court if the Senate doesn't reject the nominee by a majority vote. Any justice seated by this method can only serve a maximum of six years. Therefore, the President is encouraged to let the Senate approve most of his nominees before they are seated. The President is also incentivized to nominate a judge with a moderate record to secure an 18-year term instead of six years. The Tenure Percentage Voting method demonstrates the importance of securing an 18-year term for a nominee.

Suppose three justices each had eighteen, thirteen, and six-year terms. According to the Tenure Percentage Voting method described in Article 23, the total number of years in the denominator used for the calculation would be:

(3 x 18) + (3 x 13) + (3 x 6) = 121 years

121/2 = 60.5, so a coalition of Justices equal to 61 years of tenure is a simple majority. 121 x (2/3) = 80 2/3, so a coalition of Justices equal to 81 years is a two-thirds majority.

Three Justices with eighteen-year terms plus one Justice with a thirteen-year term equals 67 votes, a majority vote with only four Justices.

The President may not nominate, and the Senate may not approve a Justice to the Provisional Court after they vacate their Supreme Court seat before the end of their term. The President may not nominate a Justice serving on the Permanent Court to the Provisional Court.

A justice who gets a six-year term cannot resign and be re-appointed for another six years on the Supreme Court. They must serve their full term and hope to be renominated by whoever is President then, but then they would become a Provisional Member instead of a Permanent Member of the Court.

During their tenure, Judges, Justices, and Adjudicators may not earn compensation for labor services outside of the Judiciary, nor may they receive gifts other than an inheritance from their parents or spouse. Upon retirement from the Supreme Court, a Permanent Member of the Supreme Court shall be randomly assigned to a Seat on an open seat on an Inferior Court with decreased compensation. Justices, Judges, and Adjudicators must make annual disclosures of all gifts and income derived outside the Judiciary and a statement of assets, liabilities, and equity for themselves and their spouses.

This Section deals with the Ethics controversy of Justices who receive outside income from book deals, lectures before groups, or gifts from friends and political supporters.

Section 5. Setting Staggered Terms, Chief Justice Selection

On the thirtieth of June, immediately following the adoption of this Constitution, the names of the nine most senior members of the Supreme Court shall be assigned their remaining tenure on the Permanent Court based upon a lottery. The Speaker of the House shall draw these names randomly. The first name drawn has one year remaining on the Court. The second name has two years and repeats until the last name has nine years remaining on the Court. Any remaining Justices beyond these nine shall immediately vacate their seats on the Supreme Court.

After the Supreme Court, the names of all the Judges of the Inferior Courts shall be drawn by the Speaker of the House and placed in random order on lists with nine names. Starting with the first through the ninth name, the remaining tenure of each judge shall be one to nine years. The Speaker shall repeat this assignment of remaining tenure for each subsequent group of nine Judges until all Judges are assigned their remaining tenure on their courts.

> This staggered set of retirements and term limits lessens the anxiety and pressure surrounding nominees to the court because the major parties know they will get an opportunity for an appointment. The current politicized environment encourages strategic retirements to permit replacements with ideological clones. This process removes any Justices appointed in any court-packing scheme before the ratification of this constitution. This process will winnow the ranks of the Supreme Court and the lower courts.

When the Chief Justice vacates their position, the most senior Associate Justice shall become the interim Chief Justice. The President may nominate a Chief Justice from the nine Permanent Members of the Court, whom the Senate approves with a majority vote.

> Because of the staggered terms, the most senior member of the Court will likely have only a few years remaining to serve. If the President nominated a junior Associate Justice, they could serve as Chief Justice for the remainder of their term.

Section 6. Term Limits for Inferior and Administrative Court Judges

No federal judicial office of an inferior Court or Administrative Court may be held for more than eighteen years by any person during their lifetime.

Section 7. Scope of Judicial Authority

The judicial Power shall extend to all Cases, in Law and Equity, arising under this Constitution, the Laws of the United States, and Treaties made under their Authority; to all Cases affected. Ambassadors, other public Ministers, and Consuls; to all Cases of admiralty and maritime Jurisdiction; to Controversies to which the United States shall be a Party; to controversies between two or more States.

Language from the 1787 Constitution

The Judicial power of the United States shall not be construed to extend to any suit in law or equity commenced or prosecuted against one of the United States by Citizens of another State or by Citizens or Subjects of any Foreign State.

11th Amendment language

In all Cases affecting Ambassadors, other public Ministers and Consuls, and those in which a State shall be Party, the Supreme Court shall have original Jurisdiction. In all other Cases before mentioned, the Supreme Court shall have appellate Jurisdiction, both as to law and Fact, and it shall have the power to review and invalidate laws that conflict with this Constitution.

Language from the 1787 Constitution, except the clause *with such Exceptions, and under such Regulations as the Congress shall make*, was deleted and substituted with *and it shall have the power to review and repeal laws that conflict with this Constitution.*

Any case arising in a Federal District where the Supreme Court does not have original jurisdiction shall be assigned to a Trial Court or an Appellate Court outside the Federal District on a rotation.

> This paragraph prevents most significant cases from going to the District of Columbia District and Circuit Courts where the bias of that one Circuit could have a disproportionate impact, not reflecting the diversity of judicial philosophy throughout the Federal Courts.

Section 8. Right to Trial by Jury, Treason,

The Trial of all Federal Crimes, except in Cases of Impeachment, shall be by Jury, and such Trial shall be held in the State where the said Crimes shall have been committed, but when not committed within any State, the Trial shall be at such Place or Places as the Congress may by law have directed.

> Language from the 1787 Constitution.

Treason against the United States shall consist only in levying War against them, or in adhering to a Foreign Government, giving it Aid and Comfort. No Person shall be convicted of Treason unless on the Testimony of two Witnesses to the same overt Act, or on Confession in open Court.

> Language from the 1787 Constitution.

The Congress shall have Power to declare the Punishment of Treason, but no Attainder of Treason shall work Corruption of Blood, or Forfeiture, except during the Life of the Person attainted.

> Language from the 1787 Constitution.

No person who is not a State resident shall be subject to the jurisdiction of a State Court with Judges who win their seats by a popular election.

> This paragraph doesn't prohibit the election of judges, but it provides a strong deterrent against its practice.

Section 9. Abuse of Prosecutorial and Enforcement Discretion

If a two-thirds majority of the Supreme Court finds that the President has engaged in inconsistent, prejudicial, non-enforcement of statutes thirty days after a notice of complaint has been filed with the Court by five Senators or fifty Members, then the President shall forfeit one year of compensation for the first offense, and surrender the power to appoint judges of the inferior courts and Justices of the Supreme Court to the Governor General for the remainder of their term for a second offense.

> This Section addresses the abuse of prosecutorial discretion whereby the President refuses to execute laws faithfully. President Obama's episodes with Deferred Action for Childhood Arrival (DACA), lax immigration enforcement, and refusing to enforce the Defense of Marriage Act are examples of this abuse. A President can effectively repeal legislation he opposes by claiming prosecutorial discretion. The penalties have some teeth.

Section 10. Limitations on Court Injunctions

Only the Supreme Court may issue an injunction against the Government. If an Inferior Court recommends an injunction, the Chief Justice may assign the case to the Appellate Court or the Supreme Court for further review.

> This Section was inspired by the battle between liberal judges and the Trump Administration's immigration policies, which the Supreme Court later overruled. The Fifth Circuit placed an injunction against Biden's vaccine mandates for employers with more than 100 employees, which was another episode. This Section prevents the lower courts from issuing injunctions covering the entire government.

Whenever the Supreme Court grants a writ of certiorari, it must extend to the entire case and every question. Otherwise, the Supreme Court can answer specific questions the inferior courts certify.

> Ben Johnson wrote in The Atlantic [5] that ordinarily, the circuit courts get the final word, but there are two exceptions where the Supreme Court gets to speak:
>
> First, circuit courts can send specific questions to the Supreme Court. The justices may answer the question or bring the whole case for the justices to decide in full. Second, the Supreme Court could grant certiorari and decide the entire case. In 1939, the Court wrote its own rule, giving itself the power to limit its review to specific questions in all cases.
>
> Section 10 reverses that rule.

Section 11. Justices and Judges' Recommendations for Amendments

On November thirty of each year, the Chief Justice shall deliver a report to the Speaker of the House recommending any required statutes or Amendments to this Constitution. This report may contain text for statutes, Amendments, and arguments for Congress to propose Amendments for consideration by the State Legislatures to remedy ambiguities or omissions in this Constitution.

> This Section is an outlet for the Justices to let off steam instead of legislating from the bench. If cases raise matters where there isn't a consensus about how they should have been decided, then this is the forum for airing the problem.

Article 10.

Administrative Branch

The 1787 Constitution, while recognizing the Constitutional status of Regulatory Agencies in the Executive Branches, did not anticipate the later development of their unique combination of legislative, judicial, and executive authority [6]. This Section underscores the need for a comprehensive framework that acknowledges the role of the bureaucrat subject to the Executive Authority and the oversight of the House. While outside the control of the President and Governor General, Boards are not empowered to exercise legislative authority above Congress, emphasizing the importance of a clear regulatory structure.

This Section places a crucial responsibility on The House of Representatives to draft comprehensive and detailed legislation. This is a proactive measure to prevent the future House and administration from diluting the original statute or neglecting its implementation due to vagueness. While it is inevitable that a statute may need further clarification, this Article empowers the House to anticipate and address such gaps, with the input of bureaucrats, ensuring a robust and effective regulatory system.

Nevertheless, bureaucrats and Presidents sometimes use legal ambiguities to impose their ideological preferences and create rules that Congress did not originally intend when it passed the law.

This Section redefines regulations as amendments to existing statutes. Essentially, the executive authorities can submit clarifying amendments to existing laws to ensure that they correctly carry out the mandates of the statutes. The House gets to review the interpretation of the executive authorities, and it won't be approved

> absent a favorable majority vote of the House. A super-majority vote of the Senate could over-rule the adoption of the amendment as a further protection.

Section 1. Congressional Oversight of Administrative Branch

The employees of Boards, Departments, and Ministries of the Federal Government are Administrators. They serve under an Executive Director, President, or Governor General. Administrators may propose amendments to statutes or repeal prior amendments to statutes previously enacted by Congress. Any amendment proposed by Administrators shall be germane to their scope of authority. Departments, Ministries, and Boards shall submit an amendment to the President. If the President approves the amendment, the President may submit the amendment to the Speaker. If the House of Representatives approves the unaltered amendment submitted by the President within one hundred eighty days of its receipt by the Speaker, it submits the amendment to the Senate. The amendment is enacted in ten days if a seven-thirteenth vote of the Senate does not deny the amendment.

Section 2. Unenforceability of Administrative Rules

Only violations of statutes enacted by Congress may be the basis for a fine, tax, or imprisonment of a person, denial of a license, or expropriation of their property. Regulations or orders adopted by Administrators or their superior officers are not enforceable upon the public.

The Judiciary owes no deference to the interpretation of vague and ambiguous statutes by Administrators, their superior officers, or Prosecutors.

> This Section repudiates the Chevron Doctrine where the Courts gave deference to the bureaucracy's interpretation of regulations. Because this Article has dispensed with the bureaucracy's power to make regulations without Congressional approval, there is no need to have a Chevron Doctrine. When Congress writes vague and ambiguous laws, the Courts are empowered to make them

unenforceable in specific cases. Courts could recommend clarifying amendments in these circumstances.

Whenever a plaintiff sues the Federal Government and reaches a settlement, the terms of every settlement are subject to review and approval by the House of Representatives. Statutes may not be amended or enacted by a consent decree but solely by the House of Representatives enactment.

The Department of Justice (DOJ) currently enters sweetheart arrangements with litigants. First, the DOJ settles a lawsuit and enters a consent decree that effectively enacts a new regulation favored by the plaintiff and usually also by the Administration. Also, the DOJ often awards generous fees to the plaintiff's attorneys. The DOJ uses a slush fund called the "Department of Treasury's Judgment Fund." The DOJ dips into the fund as it sees fit to reward Environmental Activists and others. This provision preserves the role of the Legislative Branch to approve any changes in the law and appropriations of funds. This may be cumbersome, and it is likely that Congress will routinely approve dozens of cases, but a few questionable settlements will be flagged. Also, litigants will file fewer suits now that litigants know this gravy train is ending.

Section 3. Administrative Law Courts

Administrators shall submit requests for prosecution to the Justice Department of persons who violate statutes related to their administrative functions. The Attorney General is responsible for prosecuting cases tried in administrative law courts. These administrative courts shall try cases solely related to matters arising from violations of laws about a specific Board, Department, or Ministry. The appointment, confirmation, maximum term of service, and conduct of proceedings in these courts by these Adjudicators shall be governed by Article 9. Adjudicators are members of the Judicial Branch. Only Administrative Law Courts may issue orders, and only Adjudicators may issue warrants pertaining solely to the subject matters of their respective Board, Department, or Ministry.

In any proceeding before an administrative law court, the defendant has the right to counsel and a jury of a Panel of Experts of no fewer than four persons whose majority vote may decide a case unless the defendant waives this right. These Experts are paid the Compensation Index on a pro-rata basis, but they may not receive more than thirty days of compensation during any twelve-month period. Except for military service, no more than two persons may serve on a panel of experts who were prior Government employees, and none may serve if the Government currently employs them. Administrative law court trials may use remote transmission of audio and visual information.

> The *Securities and Exchange Commission v Jarkesy* [7] case discussed in this NY Times article [8] covers a 2023 Supreme Court case grappling with these very issues. This Section overturns a 1977 Supreme Court decision *Atlas Roofing v Occupational Safety Commission* [9], that held it was proper to combine prosecutorial and judicial powers with OSHA and that the failure to have a jury trial did not violate the 7th Amendment because this case was not a Suit at common law.

If the penalties for a defendant, occurring within a twelve-month period, exceed one-half of the Compensation Index or one-hundred eighty days in prison, then the defendant is entitled to a trial held in a common law court. This trial will include a jury and the same rights of discovery for any criminal or civil trial, ensuring the defendant is afforded the same protections as in an administrative law court.

> In Philip Hamburger's book, *Is the Administrative State Unlawful?* [10], he demonstrates that the administrative State's wielding of executive, legislative, and judicial power violates the 1787 Constitution's separation of powers and, in Madison's words, is the very definition of tyranny. Section 3 moves the judicial authority outside the agency and into the Judicial Branch. The Judicial Branch can create special administrative law courts staffed by judges with the appropriate expertise in the regula-

tions that Judges in the regular courts would not have the ability to master. The President and his Justice Department oversee prosecutions. This preserves the separation of powers in contrast to the current situation where the regulators have the combined power to prosecute and adjudicate violations. Admittedly, this Section is redundant to Article 5, Section 3 description of the President's exclusive authority, but it is a belt and suspenders affirmation of this separation of powers. This Section replaces the Petit Jury of twelve commoners with a 4-person jury of unbiased experts with the technical knowledge required for adjudicating matters.

Section 4. Rules for Warrantless Searches and Seizures

Congress may enact laws that allow executive authorities under the President to inspect properties, buildings, and financial records, seize contraband, and order the cessation of illegal conduct without a warrant, only under restricted conditions related solely to commercial activities or taxation. The Government must obtain a warrant for any property used solely as a residence.

The IRS cannot operate if required to get a warrant for every tax return audit. The same is true for inspections of workplace safety, nuclear plant operations, aircraft manufacturing, food safety, etc. The warrantless requirement is limited to commercial activities and tax revenue collections, so warrantless searches of a home are not allowed.

Persons selected for warrantless searches to detect law violations must be identified according to a random, unprejudiced procedure unless all persons in the category of interest under that executive authority are subject to searches at least every two years. The Government may only order non-random selections of persons for warrantless searches based on facts and behavior highly correlated with prior violations.

> The Government must have a neutral rule for conducting warrantless searches. For example, *Every meat packing plant must be inspected, without notification, at least twice a year*. Or *based upon a random number generator, we will inspect shipping containers according to the number pattern*. Or *all containers arriving from Nigeria will be inspected.* Or *the Government shall audit individuals with sole proprietorships deducting more than $100,000 at a rate of 1 per 75, while W2 salaried persons at a rate of 1 per 1,000.*

As time permits, all persons and the basis for their warrantless searches shall be submitted to the Judiciary for review and approval at least ten days before the search. The Government shall submit all other warrantless search orders to the Judiciary to ascertain compliance with warrantless search requirements. Any violations by the executive authority shall be punishable by the Court.

> The Judiciary gets oversight to curb abuses by the prosecutors in the Department of Justice. At least some responsibility is assigned to ensure due process in warrantless searches. There is always the danger that the Judiciary will behave as they did in the Foreign Intelligence Surveillance Acts (FISA) Courts.

Article 11.

THE CENSUS BOARD

Section 1. Responsibilities and Non-Partisan Mandate

The Census Board shall establish offices and hire staff to maintain an accurate and current registry of births, deaths, and records of every person residing and traveling within the United States and its Federal Districts and Territories. It shall record the Citizenship, age, sex, and residence address of persons and transmit information to the Elections Board to assist with compiling a list of Eligible Voters. The Census Board shall terminate employees or vendors if they engage in partisan activities supporting or opposing Political Parties or Candidates for any Government Office. At least five Citizens must petition the Federal Courts for the termination of any Employee engaged in partisan activities whom the Board did not terminate.

> Whereas counties are currently responsible for birth and death records, the national government will assume this responsibility. The goal is to have a real-time Census accounting for every resident of the United States. The Census Board's database will support the registry of Eligible Voters to clean up our elections.

Section 2. Minimum Appropriation Guarantee

The minimum appropriation for the Census Board is one-five hundredth of the federal government's expenditures in the previous fiscal year.

> This Section places the Census Board funding beyond partisan manipulation because the Census Board's work is fundamental to the operation of the Electoral system.

Section 3. Sharing Data with States, Audit Trails, False Records

Every State may establish its records of births and deaths, but the Census Board shall transfer records it maintains of residents within a State to the State, and the State shall report any discrepancies in its records to the Census Board.

> The Census Board will share its findings with States, but States are free to run their own systems of births and deaths.

The Census Board shall establish procedures to ensure that citizens' records are corroborated through contact by Census Board Staff and that it corrects errors. Procedures shall establish a chain of custody to support allegations of misconduct and corruption against individual Census Board Staff who falsify records.

Section 4. Duties of Citizens to Report to Census Board

All Persons residing within the United States and its Districts and Territories must notify the Census Board of any changes in residence, contact information, and births and deaths in their households.

> Persons evading the law or collections agencies might neglect to notify the Census Board. However, that will have repercussions for other privileges based on Census data.

When a Citizen has attained eighteen years and fails to submit a return for an accounting of individual income taxes, whether any taxes are owed, the Census Board shall classify the Citizen in an unknown residency status and report this to the Elections Board.

> Even if you don't owe any taxes, you are still obligated to file a tax return with your address on it. The IRS and Census Board will be comparing addresses for individuals. The Census Board may presume that if someone fails to file a tax return, they could be deceased or put to prison, which is sufficient grounds to question their eligibility to vote.

Section 5. Annual Census Report, Content And Disclosure of Records

On the first Monday of March each year, the Census Board shall prepare and distribute a report to the President and the Governor General of the total number of the following categories as of the previous thirty-first day of December: Citizens, Legal Permanent Residents, foreign visitors, Refugees, and persons of unknown status. It will also report the total number of births and deaths of all persons for the previous calendar year and entries and exits by foreign visitors. These records shall form the basis of all Per-Capita State Expenditures. The report shall also provide this information by House District, State, Federal Districts, and Territories.

A later Section covers Per-capita state Tax Payments in greater detail. The point of this Section is that there is an annual accounting of Citizens and persons in the United States that will form the basis of calculations related to taxation, revenue, and spending.

A person's minimum standard record contains the date of birth, place of birth, citizenship, sex recognized at birth, aliases, current name, parents' names and their citizenship, residency status, current address, and date of death. The record shall also contain birth certificates, name-change documents, death certificates, passports, identification records like fingerprints and other unique physical markers, and photographs. The Census Board shall restrict access to records solely to government officials on a need-to-know basis and disperse the storage and accessibility of records to minimize the loss of confidential information resulting from security breaches.

This is fundamental information for a secure election system.

Section 6. Confidentiality Protections

The Board may only release a Citizen's record to law enforcement and voter registration officials. Unless a court grants an exception, the Government will notify the Citizen within three days whenever it releases their record and to whom.

A Citizen has the right to confirm the contents of their record and appeal for a correction of any errors to an administrative law court to adjudicate their dispute.

Section 7. Enumeration of Population, Fact Checking

The Census Board shall undertake an actual enumeration of all persons within the United States within a twelve-month period, at least once every eight years, concluding December thirty-one of the year of a Presidential election. It shall collect and utilize information to conduct ongoing audits and make corrections to ensure the accuracy of its records.

> Ideally, this enumeration should be ongoing to maintain the highest accuracy of the database. Concluding the census during the year of a Presidential election permits redistricting to conclude one year before the following House elections.

Article 12

THE ELECTIONS BOARD

Section 1. Certification of Election Returns, Integrity of Voter Lists

The Elections Board certifies the winner of all Federal Elections. The Board shall only use Census Records to create a National Voter Registry of Eligible Voters for every precinct, administer elections, count ballots, certify election results, and once every eight years, draw boundaries of districts for the Members of the House of Representatives in each State. States are not required to use the National Voter Registry for their elections and shall continue to administer their elections with State employees. States may appeal for corrections of discrepancies between their Voter Registries and the National Voter Registry in Federal Court.

The Board shall mail notifications to the residence of every Eligible voter every twelve months to the physical address on record. The Board shall suspend the assignment of an Eligible Voter to a precinct if they do not respond to three solicitations within one hundred eighty days to confirm their place of residence and qualification to appear on the registration list of their precinct. The Government shall transfer that Eligible Voter to the Federal House District until the Government resolves their voting status.

> Citizens 18 and older are automatically registered as voters in the precinct associated with the address in the Census database, eliminating the hassle of keeping track of voter registrars in counties with inaccurate databases. The Federal House District is the catch-basin for the homeless, nomads, persons who have moved during the Voting Period, etc. Everyone can vote, but they cannot vote for a representative of a district in a State unless they register as a resident eligible to vote in that district.

Section 2. Duty to Notify Census Board to Update Voter List

Eligible Voters must notify the Census Board of any change of residence, their name, additions to their household, and other contact information. Eligible Voters are responsible for ensuring their Voter Registration is accurate or missing and notify the Census Board of any errors transmitted to the Elections Board. The Government shall transfer an Eligible Voter to the Federal House District if that voter fails to file a tax return or uses an address different than their census record.

> While not everyone will owe income tax, everyone is obligated to file a tax return. In addition to the postcard mailings, this is another way to track people who aren't residing at the address in the database. Someone could falsely complete a postcard while failing to file a tax return. Or they could file a return from a different address, providing evidence that they did not register at a proper address.

Section 3. Size of House Districts, Number of Districts Per State

The Elections Board shall create District Boundaries for Seats of the House of Representatives. The Board shall calculate the number of Representatives for each State by dividing the total population of Citizens in a State by four hundred thousand. The Board assigns one Representative to States with fewer than four hundred thousand Citizens.

When the calculation yields a whole number plus a remainder less than one-half, the State receives the whole number of Representatives. When the calculation yields a whole number with a remainder equal to or greater than one-half, the State gets the whole number plus one of the Representatives.

If the total number of Representatives for all States by this calculation is not evenly divisible by two, then the Board adds one Representative to the most populous State.

The Federal House District shall comprise Citizens from the Federal Districts, Territories, those with an unverified address, and those Citizens in transitory, non-permanent situations. This District shall be assigned only one Representative for Membership in the House even if its population of Citizens exceeds four hundred thousand.

> The States have an even number of Representatives, and the Federal Districts and Territories have one member at large to create an odd number of seats in the House to minimize tie votes. The number of Representatives grows with the population of Citizens. With approximately 310,000,000 US Citizens in 2020, there would be about 775 seats in the House of Representatives. Alaska and Vermont would get two instead of one representative under the current Constitution. Current policies count the number of residents. This Constitution bases representation upon the number of Citizens.

Section 4. Redistricting of House

The Executive Director is responsible for drawing district boundaries for House seats before June thirty, following the completion of the eight-year Census on December thirty-one. The Board adopts these maps for the Elections for Members of the House of Representatives the following year.

The district boundaries must adhere to specific requirements:

The difference in the population of Citizens between the House district with the most and least number of Citizens within that State shall not exceed one-twentieth of the total population of Citizens residing within the smallest District.

The District's boundary must be inside one State.

The boundary must be continuous and unbroken by another District boundary.

The Board may not use information about voting history or membership in the political parties. If the Executive Director fails to submit a map for a State before June fifteen, then the Executive Director shall be discharged from their office.

> The Elections Board could assign a computer program to generate various maps using these conditions and allow a committee to pick one of the randomly generated options. These conditions effectively remove much of the discretion required to gerrymander a state into partisan pieces. While some specialists use a Reock Score [11], this Section adopts a different version. Recognizing that a beehive with equilateral hexagonal minimizes the length of perimeter boundary lines (wax walls separating honeycombs), this Section adopts the minimization of the perimeter boundaries as a ranking criterion. The Rock uses a circle as the standard, but you cannot create a Map with multiple adjacent districts using only circles. Hexagonal would be the most efficient shape to use whenever there are more than five districts in a State. But with odd-shaped State Boundaries and other criteria to consider (like municipal and county boundaries, rivers, lakes, mountains, and other physical boundaries), you cannot impose a single mathematical standard. However, you can establish a way to rank Maps with each other to eliminate the most egregious forms of gerrymandering.

The Board shall submit the House District Map for every State to the most populous Legislature of the State before June thirty. If three-fifths of members of the Legislature reject the Map before July fifteen, then the Legislature may submit its Map to the Senate. A three-fifths majority of the Senate adopts the Legislature's Map. Otherwise, the Elections Board's Map is adopted.

> This paragraph provides a modicum of political accountability for the Elections Board, but obtaining those majorities in state houses and the Senate would be highly unusual.

Section 5. Minimum Guaranteed Appropriation

The minimum annual appropriation for the Elections Board equals the following product: Divide the total population of Citizens of the United States by two thousand. Multiply that amount by the annual salary of a Member of the House of Representatives. Each House District shall have no fewer than one hundred separate voting precincts, each staffed by two or more Elections Board Employees.

(310,000,000 Citizens/2,000) x $175,000 annual compensation = $27,125,000,000 annual appropriation. This is substantial for an annual appropriation when elections are held every two years. One hundred precincts per House District ensures that there cannot be longer lines in underfunded Districts with fewer voting places.

Section 6. Safeguards Against Partisanship

The Executive Director, Employees, and contractors performing duties of the Elections Board must be Citizens, and they must swear an oath of partisan celibacy each year and sign a statement outlining the prohibited activities. The Board shall dismiss employees and contractors who violate non-partisan restrictions.

The Board Members, Executive Director, employees, and contractors may not contribute labor, money, or in-kind donations to campaigns for candidates or legislation. They may not express partisan opinions in public, orally or in writing, nor may they participate in public demonstrations or otherwise tarnish the non-partisan reputation of the Elections Board. Furthermore, they and their parents, siblings, and children may not have held elected office before or during their employment. Employees may not serve more than twenty years in the employment of the Elections Board during their lifetime. At least five Citizens have the right to petition the Federal Courts to terminate any Employee engaged in partisan activities whom the Board did not terminate.

These extraordinary restrictions upon Elections Board employees are necessary to create a trustworthy, nonpartisan, impartial body operating the government accountability system. The Framers didn't have a good solution other than letting each State do its own thing. Dispersing political power and minimizing the damage that one party could inflict if everything were centralized have benefits. Recognizing that centralizing this power is dangerous, the guardians of democracy must be spotless.

Article 13.

The Federal Reserve Board

Section 1. Exclusive Control of Money Supply and Banks

The Federal Reserve Board controls the supply of Money used as legal tenders for all debts, public and private, in the United States. The Board shall regulate Member Banks and is prohibited from regulating other financial institutions.

The States may not issue any Money or regulate banks subject to the oversight of the Federal Reserve Board. Money created by the Federal Reserve is a liability for an eligible asset that the Federal Reserve purchased or a loan to a Member Bank. Eligible assets are the following: a debt instrument containing a promise of repayment to extinguish this debt at maturity and thereby reduce the supply of Money; gold, platinum, or silver bullion held in the custody of the Federal Government. The Federal Reserve Bank may not offer loans to Member Banks holding Federal Government Debt Instruments or pay interest on Reserve Accounts opened by its Depositors. Five years is the maximum maturity of loans to Member Banks.

> This Section eliminates Federal Reserve regulation of insurance companies, mutual funds, private equity, hard money lenders, and others who don't create deposit accounts that clear through the Federal Reserve system at par. The US Treasury can assume responsibility for that oversight. The Fed's mission is limited in scope because it is politically insulated.

> Prohibiting Federal Reserve loans to banks when they hold US Treasury Debt prevents the recurrence of the Bank Term Funding Program, in which the Fed gave loans to banks using the par value, rather than the market value, of Treasuries as collateral for the loan. Banks should be forced to sell Treasuries at market value to raise reserves and reveal the true status of their balance sheets rather than hiding the truth.
>
> The proposal also includes the prohibition of interest payments on Reserve Accounts. This measure is crucial as it prevents the Fed from creating money unrelated to the issuance of Debt authorized by Congress. This policy upholds the principles of congressional control over appropriations by ensuring that the creation of money is in line with the authorized Debt.

If the dollar, the current unit of account for Money, is redefined or redeemed in exchange for new units, all statutes and contracts denominated in dollars will automatically adjust to maintain the prior value based upon the previous unit of account.

Section 2. Limitations on Asset Purchases

The Federal Reserve shall not engage in activities that undermine the principle that any expenditures of money by the Government must derive from an Appropriations Bill enacted by Congress.

Applying this principle of Congressional authority, the Federal Reserve and the Federal Government cannot purchase the debt instruments of States or their political subdivisions or make payments on these debt instruments. The Federal Reserve cannot buy any person's debt instruments or ownership shares or make payments on these securities. Its asset purchases are confined to the assets, liabilities, and equities of its Member Bank and Public Debt instruments issued by the Treasury of the United States with a maturity date not exceeding ten years from the date of issuance. The Federal Reserve may not purchase Special Obligation Debt. The Board may only acquire assets from non-governmental persons or Member Banks. Congress must appropriate funds for the Secretary of the Treasury to purchase any assets prohibited for purchase and holding by the Federal Reserve.

> This Section confines the Fed to purchase the debt of the Federal Government, or bad loans of Member Banks. Congress can use appropriated funds to directly aid a state or private business because that goes through proper channels. The Fed cannot interfere in political and private affairs and avoid democratic accountability.

Member Banks may not be owned in whole or in part by the Federal or State Governments.

The Member Banks of the Federal Reserve System issue liability accounts to their depositors denominated in the currency of the United States. These deposits are transferrable to depositors of other Member Banks at par on the condition that Member Banks adhere to regulations governing their solvency. The Federal Reserve is responsible for regulating the lending policies of its Member Banks solely to reduce the likelihood of the non-payment of loans by borrowers, leading to the insolvency of Member Banks. Any other lending regulations are reserved for enforcement by other Agencies created by Congress.

> The Federal Reserve will stay out of regulating banks for the promotion of Climate Change and other partisan matters that should be the domain of Congress.

Section 3. Limitations on Deposit Accounts

Except for Member Banks in the Federal Reserve System, foreign governments, and supranational organizations, the Government may not open deposit accounts for citizens, residents, or legal persons domiciled within the United States at the Federal Reserve or any other Government-controlled bank. Member Banks of the Federal Reserve System may only refuse to offer or restrict the regular use of depository accounts and funds transfer services to persons violating the law, those engaging in legal commerce categories restricted by law, or those who overdraft their account balance, or who fail to pay the bank's fees.

> This article [12] outlines all the various ways the Government can abuse Central Bank Digital Currency to impose its will upon users

and curtail their independence. This Section allows imposing such restrictions upon non-citizens and corporations not domiciled in the United States. Without these protections, the Government could impose a social credit system like China's. This Section also protects persons and businesses from being frozen out of the banking system by a bank unless there is a lawful reason. Notice that discrimination in the offer of loans is not protected as a Constitutional right in this Section. That will have to be the domain of legislation.

Section 4. Financing and Independence of the Federal Reserve

The Federal Reserve funds its operations with income from interest earned on its assets and assessments from Member Banks to protect its independence and ability to conduct non-partisan monetary policy. The Federal Reserve may not financially support activities outside the responsibilities assigned by this Article. Any excess revenue not required to sustain the operations of the Federal Reserve shall be refunded to the Treasury and counted as Tax Revenue for budgetary calculations.

This Section prohibits funding agencies like the Consumer Financial Protection Bureau through the Federal Reserve to escape Congressional oversight and budgetary control.

Article 14.

The Research And Records Board

Section 1. Responsibilities to Collect and Report Information

The Board collects and disseminates impartial, non-partisan, accurate information about the Government, persons, geography, and commerce of the United States. The Board maintains standards for weights and measures. The Board shall publish this information for Citizens so that they may make informed decisions to hold their elected officeholders accountable.

The Board archives all records of the United States Government, including the President, House of Representatives, and Senate. It shall fulfill public information requests by Citizens for documents, complying with laws protecting national security.

The Board, operating independently, provides assessments of the work of Departments and Ministries upon requests submitted by the President or the Governor General, supported by an appropriation.

All States shall report information about criminal convictions to the Board, which will be used to enforce restrictions on weapons purchases, employment, and other activities.

The Board shall terminate its employees and vendors if they engage in partisan activities supporting or opposing Political Parties or candidates or standing for election or appointment to any Government Office.

These tasks should not be subject to partisan influence. This Section centralizes all the data collection and reporting responsibilities into one Board. With political donor reports compiled by the Elections Board, Citizens will have easy access to the information required to fight corruption.

Section 2. Public Disclosure of Expenditures, Political Donations

The Board shall publish the disbursement register of every government entity of the United States. All government entities must submit their disbursement records monthly to the Board. When a State or its political subdivisions have not filed a report by the deadline, their membership in the Senate is suspended until the report is received. The State and its political subdivisions shall provide the name of the payee, the amount and date of payment, the government entity, the department within the entity, and the identification of the account from which the payments were made.

Each State and its political subdivisions must submit a regular Statement and Account of the revenues, expenditures, assets, and liabilities of all its accounts that shall be published for each fiscal year using the same generally accepted accounting principles that the Federal Government requires from commercial persons that pay taxes. The Board shall develop a standard format for government entities to submit these reports. The Board shall develop tools to facilitate the ability of persons to access this data. The Government may not exclude more than one-tenth of Federal disbursements from these reports and only for items related to national security. Congress may enact exceptions to this limitation for no longer than one fiscal year by a three-fifths vote.

This Section enables Citizens to hold every elected official accountable at every government level. Transparency is maximized.

Section 3. Audits of Tax Returns

The Research and Records Board employees shall conduct all audits of Federal tax returns. Using attributes correlated with tax payment evasion, the Executive Director shall adopt policies to select persons for random audits. The Attorney General submits audit requests to the Board pursuant to an investigation approved by an Adjudicator from the Department of the Treasury.

> This paragraph thwarts a President using the IRS as a weapon to attack political enemies. It entrusts audit powers within a non-partisan entity.

The Board shall complete a lifetime audit of Supreme Court Justices, the President, the Vice President, and any person in the Line of Succession six months after ascending to the office. The audits shall include all Federal personal income tax and business income tax returns where the officeholder had a beneficial interest greater than one-fifth or exceeding the Compensation Index. The Board discloses any violations and accrued tax liabilities to the public.

Any taxpayer may request a lifetime audit of their federal tax returns by the Board. The Board's charge to prepare this report cannot exceed the Compensation Index. The Board shall refer any violations and accrued tax liabilities to the Department of the Treasury for enforcement. The Government may publish the report with the taxpayer's consent or during a judicial proceeding. Persons illegally disclosing and disseminating the contents of this report or the Federal or State tax returns of any taxpayers shall be fined no less than the Compensation Index and banned from any Government employment.

> Executive Branch officeholders, the Governor General, and anyone else in the line of succession are now subject to an audit. No one will likely want to assume office without prior knowledge of the results of this audit. Political donors will likely require public disclosure of this report as a condition for launching a campaign. Anyone with political aspirations can pay for their audit to prove they are clean or take care of any violations before running for office.

Article 15.

Appointment, Removal, and Regulation of Board Members

Section 1. Appointment, Removal, and Terms of Board Members

This Constitution empowers Boards to perform tasks insulated from partisan influence and ensure that their work is based on empirical, objective standards. All majority and super-majority votes by Boards shall be computed using the Tenure Percentage Vote method described in Article 23. A majority vote of Board members can propose statutes for consideration by the President and issue orders to their Executive Director.

A majority vote of the House of Representatives may enact statutes proposed by the Board. Statutes to regulate a Board not proposed by that Board require a five-ninths-majority vote of the House.

This Section regulates the structure and operations of the Federal Reserve, Census, Elections, Research and Records, and any Boards created in the future. The Board is a legislative body that commands its Executive Director to carry out its orders.

The Board can propose statutes and request that a majority vote of Congress enact them. However, going in the other direction, Congress has a 5/9th supermajority requirement to enact statutes to regulate Boards. This protects Boards from partisan influence, but if a Board goes rogue, Congress can still hold them accountable. However, the normal route for correcting a Board's errors will be proposed statutes of a future Board.

There shall be five seats on every Board created by this Constitution or subsequent laws enacted by Congress. The President shall nominate three Board Members, and the Governor General shall nominate two. All nominees will be appointed unless rejected by a majority vote of the Senate within ninety days. After ratification of this Constitution or the creation of a new Board, the terms for each Board member are contingent upon the number of approval votes by the Senate: a one-year term for less than a six-elevenths vote, a five-year term for a six-elevenths vote, and a nine-year term for a three-fifths vote. If a Board Member receives less than a six-elevenths vote, they are not eligible for nomination to any Board for ten years.

> This Section ensures that Board Membership continuously changes. Giving the Governor General appointment powers alongside the President and requiring Senate consideration prevents one person from packing a Board. Linking their term in office with the size of the majority vote of approval ensures that they will be selected for their knowledge of the subject matter under consideration by that Board. The Tenure Percentage Vote method motivates the President and Governor General to appoint competent technocrats.

Once a President's nominee creates a vacancy, the President shall nominate a replacement. Once a Governor General's nominee creates a vacancy, the Governor General shall nominate a replacement.

A five-ninth vote of the Senate may remove a Board Member. They would become ineligible to serve on any Board until four years had elapsed.

Board Members and Executive Directors shall have attained at least forty years and be Citizens of the United States. They shall not have been elected or appointed officials or employees of any Government for ten years before the start of their terms.

> This ten-year gap in government employment maximizes the odds of appointing non-partisan board members and executive directors.

Section 2. Executive Director of Boards

The Board shall select an Executive Director who serves at the Board's pleasure and for no longer than twelve years during their lifetime.

> The Executive Director should have executive experience related to the subject matter. For example, the Executive Director of the Federal Reserve should have experience running a banking or finance company or a large bureaucracy. Their term limit is 12 years, and hopefully, most of them will serve close to the maximum term if they act as technocrats rather than ideologues.

The Executive Director is responsible for budgeting and managing the Board's employees, contractors, and assets and for carrying out the Board's orders.

The maximum compensation for the Executive Director shall be eight times the Compensation Index and the compensation for Board Members shall equal three times the Compensation Index.

> This pay level should attract high-level talent from the private sector in their later careers. This profile is preferable to the political ideologue without much managerial talent, who is usually motivated by partisan ideologies.

Section 3. Establishment and Termination of Boards

After ratifying this Constitution, Congress, by a five-ninth vote, may enact laws to establish Boards where the provisions of this Article govern the selection of their Members and Executive Directors. Congress may terminate Boards established by Congress by two majority votes occurring no less than five years and no more than seven years apart. Congress shall enact no laws in conflict with this Constitution over the scope of and restrictions on powers of the Boards created by this Constitution.

Article 16.

Taxation, Appropriations, Debt

The Anti-Elitist Constitution's taxation authority is not a vague concept but a clear and precise enumeration between the States and the Federal Government. Unlike an enumeration of limited powers, taxation involves numbers. Judges could not easily apply creative interpretations to evade the language. It's important to note that most of these limitations on tax rates apply solely to Citizens, further emphasizing the clarity of the Constitution's stance on taxation.

The Anti-Elitist Constitution, while having few mentions of the enumeration of Federal Authority, places significant reliance on the division of Executive Authority and tax revenue sources to limit Federal Power's scope. The Feds can do whatever they want, but only within the limits prescribed by the Bill of Rights and the extent of revenue raised by taxation. This reassures us that protecting our rights is a fundamental aspect of this Constitution and that putting a check on their sources of tax revenue is the best restraint upon Federal authority.

Section 1. Phase-In of Income Tax Limitation

The provisions of this Article shall take effect six years after ratification. Per Section 5 of this Article, during this transition period, the maximum income tax rates shall be the following: four-tenths in the first, three-tenths in the second, one-fourth in the third, one-fifth in the fourth, one-seventh in the fifth, and one-eighth in the sixth fiscal year after ratification.

The Federal Government will receive 12.5% personal income taxes to fund Medicare and Social Security programs. The remaining sales, value-added taxes (VAT), corporate income, tariffs, and estate taxes will fund the rest of the federal government. The Balance of Power to tax personal incomes will shift to the States, and we rely upon the competition between States to limit the extent of individual income tax rates. It leaves the Feds to tax things of a national scope to simplify compliance and not have to deal with 50 separate jurisdictions. Taxing commerce through corporate, value-added, sales, pollution, tolls, tariffs, and other consumption taxes allows the Federal Government to match its current percentage of GDP tax collection power. More functions of national domestic policy will shift to the exclusive domain of the States because they will have more tax revenue at their disposal. Unlike the period before the 16th Amendment, where alcohol taxes comprised 1/3 of the Fed's revenue streams, in a modern economy with electronic banking, a negligible percentage of cash transactions, the mechanisms to easily levy taxes will be far more diverse. States will probably take over many domestic Federal Departments like Education, Agriculture, Commerce, Labor, HUD, and HHS.

Having a gradual reduction in the maximum income tax rate forces Congress to take immediate action and avoid a fait accompli cataclysm adjusting from 39% to 12.5% tax rates in a single fiscal year. Congress must adopt VAT, corporate income tax, utility taxes, pollution taxes, tolls, and other revenue sources to replace this lost income tax revenue.

Within six months after the ratification of this Constitution, each State must convene a Special Session of the most numerous House of its Legislature to remove any conflicts with this Constitution in its own Constitution or its Statutes. The Legislature shall amend any prohibitions in the State Constitution or Statutes about collecting tax revenue from sources permitted by this Constitution. A majority vote is authorized to enact these changes to the State Constitution and statutes, solely about State taxation and expenditure mandates, within two years after ratification of this Constitution. If the President determines that a State failed to enact sufficient changes to its Constitution and Statutes, the President shall draft alternative amendments and submit them to the Supreme Court. A majority vote of the Supreme Court is required to enact the President's amendments.

States like Texas, Florida, Tennessee, Nevada, and Washington prohibit income taxes. This prohibition will not be sustainable once the Federal Government has exclusive rights to collect corporate income and sales taxes they previously relied upon. Because the methods for amending each State's Constitution may take too much time, and voters may disapprove of making sensible changes, thereby fiscally ruining the State, this Section allows a one-time override of the State's amendment process. According to Article 17, Section 1, a State could, in theory, collect no income taxes. However, its Constitution could not contain a prohibition on the collection of income taxes or any limitations on property tax rates.

Section 2. Uniformity of Rates, Allocations of Revenue

All revenues collected by the federal Government are assigned to a general fund available for Congress to fund any appropriation. The Government may not receive or deposit Revenues into a separate account reserved for financing any Appropriation that Congress did not approve for the current fiscal year. Revenues include money received from tax collections, and any money received from the sale of assets and property, earnings from investments in securities, commercial enterprises, and other activities.

Taxes and other stuff comprise Government Revenue. If the government operates an electrical power system, Congress cannot segregate utility fees of the entity operating the plant like a corporation. Each year, Congress would have to authorize the corporate entity to operate like an independent business. Congress could not authorize the issuance of Revenue Bonds where the revenue from road tolls is reserved to pay off the bondholders. All that toll revenue must go into the General Fund.

All schedules of rates of Federal Taxation shall be uniform throughout the United States. There are four allowable methods for a government to calculate a tax: ad valorem, unit, tolls, and fees.

> This Section preserves the Legislature's power over the purse and prevents a prior Congress from overriding the authority of a future Congress.
>
> This Section prevents the Government from imposing arbitrary taxes. Local governments frequently abuse taxation authority by allowing bureaucrats to impose arbitrary taxes upon developers to pay for deferred maintenance on roads and infrastructure instead of raising general property taxes upon everyone in the tax district.

The Government has the burden to refute any allegation that the fee charged to a person is arbitrary, discriminatory, or exceeds the actual costs incurred. The Government must annually publish aggregate and job-specific information about work hours and resource costs incurred for all fees charged as evidence to support its claims that it only covers actual costs incurred.

> This paragraph forces the Government to publish these records. Taxpayers can use this information to verify government claims that its fees are solely for reimbursement of actual costs. A taxpayer could independently collate data about the number of employees, payroll costs, etc., to see if they can support the Government's claims.

Section 3. Limitations on Federal Payments to State Governments

The Secretary of the Treasury shall calculate the total Appropriations for payments to the State Governments for the current fiscal year minus Reimbursements for State services provided to foreign residents and Refugees from the prior fiscal year. The Treasury Secretary divides that number by the total population of Citizens from the most recent Census to determine the maximum Per Capita Appropriation for the current fiscal year. During any twelve consecutive months, payments by the Federal Government to a State government and its political subdivisions cannot exceed the number of Citizens of that State multiplied by the Per Capita Appropriation unless suspended for a single fiscal year by a two-thirds vote of the House and the Senate. Payments to State Governments shall include payments to legal persons partially or wholly owned or controlled by a State or its political subdivisions.

The Section impedes the Government's ability to share Revenue with the States. States currently offer lower tax rates and rely on Federal assistance for welfare, health, and education programs. Requiring the Federal Government to disburse equal per capita aid to States appeals to a sense of fairness that the Feds shouldn't show favoritism between the States. Also, it suggests that states should raise their taxes to pay for programs that benefit their residents. This regulation doesn't affect direct aid from the Federal Government to an individual recipient. However, it eliminates Revenue Sharing in programs like Medicaid, where the State receives federal funds and administers the program on a revenue-sharing basis. The last sentence prohibits violations of this provision's spirit in case States form entities in partnership with other States or private corporations to evade these restrictions.

What about cases of Emergency disaster relief? This Section provides a super-majority exception to accommodate those situations.

Section 4. Requirement to Submit Tax Return

Even if no taxes are owed, a Citizen or permanent resident eighteen years or older must submit a tax return for an accounting of individual income taxes due to the Federal Government. Citizens under eighteen must file a return and pay taxes if they earn taxable income.

This Section ensures that the Census Board can update its database. However, it also establishes the obligation to pay taxes.

Section 5. Limitation of Income Tax Rate

The income tax is an ad valorem tax. The accrual of individual federal tax obligations calculated as a percentage of income over any twelve consecutive months from a Citizen who is a Citizen of a State may not exceed one-eighth of income earned over that same twelve consecutive months. Violation of this provision requires the Federal Government to refund the excess taxes collected, plus a one-tenth penalty compounded annually, and the Government shall not count this penalty as taxable income. The Government may subject Citizens with residency in Federal Districts and Territories and Transitory Citizenship to additional taxes above this one-eighth limitation.

> Instead of setting the income tax to zero, the Federal Government must be a central repository of income collection for data collection purposes. Because residents of the Territories and the Federal Districts aren't paying State Income taxes, they're subject to higher federal income tax rates. The Federal Government can tax non-citizens at higher rates.

These limitations apply to a Trust established for the benefit of a living, natural person who is a Citizen. Taxable personal income includes business expenses, like insurance, transportation, and meals, that provide value enjoyed outside the ordinary course of business operations away from the business premises.

> Health insurance or a company car used for personal travel will be considered personal compensation subject to the federal income tax. A company kitchen on a factory or office grounds would not be classified as personal income because the company provides meals during the ordinary course of business on the premises. The Government would tax company reimbursements for employee meals at a restaurant. The Government would not tax employee income to receive services provided by a clinic staffed with doctors and nurses on the business premises. A group health insurance plan that pays for medical expenses at a hospital or doctor's office would be taxable personal income. This paragraph eliminates the tax-advantaged status of employer-provided group health insurance.

The Government may compel an employer to withhold personal income taxes from an employee's compensation. However, the Government may not levy any ad valorem tax upon an employer based on the compensation paid to its employees or its gross revenue or expenses. Only States may levy unit taxes on employers based on the number of employees.

> Federal or state governments cannot levy payroll taxes owed by the employer separately from the income tax owed by the employee. Otherwise, the Federal Government could evade the 1/8th income tax limitation by relabeling it as an employer tax proportional to wages paid. States are also prevented from levying these taxes as they would encroach upon the Federal Government's domain of taxing corporate income. States may charge head taxes to finance worker's compensation or similar programs whose costs are not proportional to employee earnings.

Section 6. Prohibition Against Tax Benefits

Differences in the income of natural persons before taxation shall be the only legal basis for discrimination in taxation rates on their income. Except for payments covered in Section 8 of this Article, value-added taxes in commercial transactions, and accrued taxes covered in Article 17, Section 24, no deductions are permitted. Prohibited deductions include payments of non-Federal taxes, excluding income categories, charitable donations, deferrals of payments of incurred tax liabilities, deposits into savings, insurance, or retirement accounts, receipt of non-pecuniary benefits in the form of goods, services, insurance, or other methods of reducing the amount of income subject to Federal taxation. This list of prohibited deductions is not exclusive.

> This Section makes Federal Income taxes neutral and fair. It removes the perception that if you can afford tax experts, you can game the system and hide your tax breaks, reducing transparency. In tax policy parlance, these are called *tax expenditures*. Under this Section, if the Government wishes to favor certain kinds of

investments or compensate persons for payments of taxes, it must be done with an explicit spending measure in the budget, renewed each year.

The 12.5% cap on income taxation will ameliorate opposition to the elimination of tax credits and deductions (Enterprise Zones, State Income Tax, Home Mortgage deduction, etc.) and deferrals (1031 Exchange). The States can incorporate those tax expenditures in their tax code. This Section eliminates a massive source of lobbying pressure by special interest groups to obtain these loopholes in the tax code. This Section also makes the tax system at the national level uncomplicated and fair without the sense that well-monied interests get special favors.

Federal politicians win more votes by extending tax breaks to individuals rather than businesses. Now that businesses cannot make campaign donations, they have far less leverage in lobbying for tax breaks. Also, with federal individual income tax rates capped at 12.5%, federal politicians have no room to offer individual tax breaks.

The Government may apply prior tax payments to the computation of the value-added portion subject to taxation on commercial transactions.

All earned subsidies are contingent Expenditures that do not represent a statutory obligation for an expenditure by Congress. Congress may include all earned subsidies for natural and legal persons in an Appropriation Bill for a later fiscal year. Calculated subsidies may not be applied to reduce the taxes payable to the Government.

Suppose the Federal Government wishes to reward nonprofit donations or compensate homeowners with mortgage interest. In that case, the benefits must be an overt cash subsidy paid to the taxpayer, not a tax benefit hidden from public scrutiny. The Government must pay the subsidy in the following fiscal year to allow Congress to make an Appropriation instead of crediting the subsidy against taxes earned.

To comply with Section 5 of this Article, subsidies and credits paid to a person may not be counted as a reduction in their tax liability for any fiscal year. Any discharge of indebtedness to the Federal Government or debt guaranteed by the Federal Government becomes a Federal Income Tax liability for the borrower unless discharged through a bankruptcy judgment of a Federal Court.

> The Government cannot tax someone at a rate higher than 12.5% and later argue that the subsidy paid netted out the excess taxes paid to yield a 12.5% net tax rate.
>
> The taxpayer cannot deduct donations to non-profits, mortgage interest, and State Taxes. However, with a 12.5% maximum federal tax rate, the marginal gain from these tax benefits is tiny, minimizing opposition to their exclusion. States can include these benefits in their tax code if they wish. Because the federal Government will tax pension and healthcare benefits as current income, the 12.5% rate will fall on a more significant sum of income. Again, if the Federal Government wishes to encourage pension and medical insurance, it can send subsidy checks. Forgiveness of loan balances counts as taxable income.

Section 7. No Deductions for Expenditures that Violate Laws

The Government shall not allow expenditures for activities violating Government laws or paying a Government fine as a reduction of the amount of income subject to Federal or State taxation.

Taxpayers may not deduct compensation payments to persons illegally residing in the United States and those without permission to work to reduce the amount of income subject to Federal or State taxation. The Government is responsible for promptly authenticating the legal work status of any person before a taxpayer may deduct that person's compensation to reduce the taxpayer's taxable income. Any employer requesting a deduction of compensation paid to any person must request that the person authorize the Census Board to transmit a message to the employer and the Treasurer of the United States authenticating their residency and work status and permission for the employer to claim their compensation to reduce taxable income.

> This Section requires companies to authenticate the legal work status of their employees to qualify to deduct their wages. The Census Board is responsible for communicating that information to the IRS before the employer can deduct payments to vendors and employees using something resembling the E-Verify system.
>
> Employers will want to deduct the wages of all employees so that they will subject all employees to this scrutiny and authentication. During this transition, the authentication process of the Treasury Department and the Census Board will expose the scale of identity theft when workers and employers discover millions of duplicate and fake social security numbers used by illegal immigrants.

Section 8. Mandated Expenses Are Taxes

If the Federal Government requires an involuntary purchase of a service, including retirement or insurance plans, or any other good or service provided by the Government, a person, or payment of membership dues in an organization, then that expenditure shall be classified as taxation of income of a natural person, subject to the limitations of Section 5 of this Article. Payments for occupational licensing fees under Article 19 of Section 19 shall be classified as expenses to reduce business income subject to taxation and not as taxation of individual income.

> This Section codifies Justice Roberts' definition of the Obamacare mandate to purchase health insurance as a tax. When the Government uses collective bargaining laws to compel payment of union dues, it also counts as a tax. Any attempt to pass legislation compelling union membership or purchase of insurance will bump up against the 12.5% maximum on federal income taxation. The Government counts licensing fees as business expenses, while Social Security and Medicare insurance payments are income taxes.

If a State Government or its Political Subdivisions requires an involuntary purchase of a service, including retirement or insurance plans, or any other good or service provided by the Government, a person, or payment of membership dues in an organization, then that expenditure shall be classified as taxation of income of a natural person for purposes of satisfying amounts owed to the Government based upon that person's taxable income.

Section 9. Exclusive Domains for Federal Taxation

The Federal Government has the exclusive right to levy taxes on the following: ad valorem taxes on the income of legal persons, partnerships, sole proprietorships, and the sales of goods and services; unit taxes on the volume and mass of poisonous and polluting emissions into the air, ground, and water; fees to register vehicles traveling on land, air, water, and outer space; tolls on interstate roads, railways, navigable interstate waterways, air travel, airports, shipping, and ports, travel into outer space; unit taxes on the weight or volume of the water drawn from underground or above-ground interstate bodies of water; unit or ad valorem taxes on the communications, information, and power transmitted through the electromagnetic spectrum for commercial exchange; fees for inspections or provision of services, and interstate commerce licenses.

The Federal Government shall be responsible for collecting these taxes. However, it may share portions of these collections with the States using the source of the tax revenue from within a State as a basis for its allocation. The Government must uniformly apply these allocation rules. Tax revenues from these sources shall not apply to Section 3 of this Article.

> This section simplifies things and gives the Feds exclusive powers of commercial taxation because it's tough to distinguish interstate and intrastate commerce for regulatory and taxation demarcation between the States and the Feds. From the States' perspective, this takes corporate income tax and sales tax breaks off the table in the bidding wars between States. The States will compete on property tax and personal income tax rates.
>
> The Federal Government has the option to split its revenue collections with the States. For example, the Federal Government could divert 20% of tolls on interstate highways to States based on the mileage driven within a State by all vehicles. The same could be done for sales taxes collected at hotels and restaurants.

Section 10. Taxes at Death on Estate and Inheritance

Estate Taxes are ad valorem taxes. Taxes at death on the value of an estate and amounts received by its heirs are exclusive to the Federal Government. The Federal Government establishes the basis for calculating future taxes on the appreciation or depreciation in the value of assets received by the heirs at the amount used to determine the estate tax revenue collected by the Government at the time of death of the Estate owner.

> This paragraph establishes the step-up of the basis for determining future capital gains.
>
> In 2024 this threshold for charging inheritance taxes would be approximately $5,200,000. The Feds cannot charge a 40% estate tax and a 10% inheritance tax at the time of death because that would violate the limit. Making this tax exclusive to the Federal Government eliminates competing claims by States on properties held by the deceased in their State and what is subject to taxation. The Feds could discriminate in their taxation for non-citizens.

The combined rate of taxation at death for the value of a Citizen's estate and amounts received by their heirs who are Citizens shall be calculated based on the Compensation Index:

The portion of an estate valued at less than thirty times shall not be taxed. The portion greater than thirty times and less than fifty times may not exceed four-tenths of the estate's value at the time of death. The portion greater than fifty or less than six hundred times may not exceed seven-tenths. The portion over six hundred times may not be lower than seven-tenths.

> This paragraph mandates the Feds to tax vast fortunes exceeding $174 Million at a minimum 70% rate. Estate taxes are a good tax because heirs of large fortunes seldom turn out to be a positive influence upon society. These tax rates break up dynasties.

Citizens have a maximum of ten years from the date of death, based upon the valuation on the date of death, to extinguish their Estate and inheritance tax obligations. The interest payments on outstanding Estate tax obligations shall accrue starting one year after the date of death. The interest rate shall not exceed the weighted-average interest rate on twelve-month maturity debt sold to the public by the Treasury during a fiscal year plus one fiftieth, calculated annually and compounded annually, upon the unpaid balance.

> This paragraph relieves persons who inherit businesses because the heirs cannot quickly sell these businesses to pay these Estate Taxes. This paragraph gives these heirs a ten-year time limit, but it is fair because they owe interest on the unpaid amount.

The value of any gifts received from all natural persons during a fiscal year by a Citizen exceeding one-eighth of the Compensation Index is taxable income. Citizens are subject to State taxation on gifts received during the donor's lifetime. Any distributions of money or things of value by legal persons are taxable income for the recipient.

> This paragraph simplifies the tax code by treating gifts and inheritance as income. Because gifts are not income received at the time of death, the State can levy income taxes upon them. There is an exemption on the first $21,750 received by an individual from all sources (as of 2024) so that people aren't paying taxes on birthday gifts and everyday gifting. Presently, persons can receive individual gifts below a threshold amount and not pay any income taxes if they receive gifts from multiple donors. In contrast, this provision values all gifts collectively from all donors to calculate this tax-free threshold. The government will not levy gift taxes upon the donor, although they might be required to file a report on the recipients of any gift they make. The government will only levy taxes upon the recipient of the gifts whenever they exceed 1/8th of the House Member compensation.

Section 11. Wealth, Property, and Other Taxes Reserved for States

Except by a three-fifths vote of Congress, the federal government may not levy taxes not listed in this Article.

The States have the exclusive right to levy ad valorem and unit taxes on property and other types of wealth during the life of a Citizen. The Federal Government may only levy taxes on property and other types of wealth owned by natural persons who are not Citizens, United States Nationals, United States Residents, or legal persons controlled by Citizens or Nationals.

> This Section prohibits a Federal Wealth Tax on Citizens, but States can adopt one. The Federal Government can only levy wealth taxes on foreigners.

States may levy unit taxes on the weight or volume of metals, minerals, soil, sand, stone, timber, or hydrocarbons extracted from underground or above ground within the State's land and lake boundaries and no further than three miles into the ocean. States may levy taxes on extractions from land owned by the Federal Government that are sold or leased for commercial purposes. Land owned by the Indigenous Sovereign Nations is exempt from this State taxation. States may levy unit taxes for nuisances and other conduct not covered in Section 9 of this Article.

Fees charged for licenses and inspections must be directly related to Government administration expenses, and they may not be applied based on a person's income or wealth.

> This Section prevents the States from effectively levying corporate income tax.

A State will have the exclusive right to levy ad valorem and unit taxes on land and buildings in that State that legal persons own.

The Federal Government and a State may levy an ad valorem tax on legal persons for the rental income derived from land and buildings in the State. If the taxpayer owns the land, buildings, and other assets in a commercial enterprise without rental expense, then the State may levy taxes on the fair market value of the implied rent. Disputes over the implied rent shall be under the jurisdiction of the Federal Courts.

This paragraph clears up any ambiguity about holding title to property in an LLC. States have the exclusive right to levy and collect property taxes. Like the income tax, there is a special carve out for a State and the Federal Government to tax rental income on properties located in their State. Because the attractiveness of properties is due to the efforts of local governments, then they should be compensated for rental incomes. Also, it eliminates the unfairness of taxing rental income on persons who own property in their name while not charging State taxes on rental income on properties held in an LLC owned by non-residents. With owner-user commercial real estate, if the property is held in the same corporation as the operating company, we want to close the loophole where that corporation doesn't pay any rent and deprives the State of tax revenue on the rental income paid to the property owner.

States have the exclusive right to levy ad valorem and unit taxes on property except for property owned by the Federal Government and the Indigenous Sovereign Nations.

States can levy ad valorem taxes on property value and income taxes on non-resident Citizens who derive income from property in that State. Tax rates for different categories of property (residential, retail, hospitality, agricultural) must be uniform within the State to prevent discrimination against non-residents.

Any annual charges by States related to the incorporation of a legal person are limited to actual costs incurred that are uniform for all legal persons and, in no case, may exceed one two-hundredth of the Compensation Index per annum.

States can charge annual fees for corporations and LLCs registered with their Secretary of State, but those charges cannot be a backdoor route to a corporate income tax. In 2024, the maximum annual fee would be $870.

The Federal government must share the Federal Tax Returns of Citizens of a State with that State. The Federal Government must notify any State Government where the taxpayer earned income or is a resident.

The States shall only register legal persons engaged in commercial activities after receipt of evidence from the United States Treasury of the legal person's intent to file Federal Tax Returns and the identities of all beneficial owners with more than one-tenth ownership or income distribution.

> This paragraph ensures taxpayers make consistent claims about their income for each State. The Federal Tax return provides a means of checking for that.
>
> Because the Federal Government will solely tax all corporations and LLCs, this Section ensures that States notify the Federal Government whenever these corporations register with a State. These requirements are also anti-fraud protections to defeat the lax registration regimes of States like Wyoming that are havens for entities engaged in money laundering. One-tenth ownership share is not a heavy burden to meet for disclosures.

State Citizenship shall determine which State has jurisdiction to levy income taxes upon Citizens, except when a Citizen is required to be physically present within another State as a requirement for earning a specific portion of their income that will be subject to taxation by that State. Income earned by natural persons through the interstate transportation of goods and persons shall be subject to taxation solely by their State, District, or Territory of residency. Federal law shall govern the apportionment of non-citizen income taxes among the States, and it shall resolve disputes between the States regarding the taxation of Citizens of one State compensated for work by persons located in another State. This Section also applies to citizens who are residents of the Federal District and Territories.

> Truck drivers and airline pilots won't have to pay State income taxes for each State they travel through. However, sports professionals and others earning income by performing work within a non-resident State will have to pay that State's income tax for the portion of income earned during their work stay.

Section 12. Super-Majority Requirements for Increasing Income Tax

Section 5 of this Article may be suspended for all or part of one fiscal year under the following conditions: a five-ninths majority vote of the House permits a rate no more than one-sixth; a three-fifths majority vote permits a rate no greater than one-fifth; a two-thirds majority permits a rate no greater than one-third. The Government shall reinstate Section 5 limitations at the end of the fiscal year.

Section 13. Taxation of Pension Contributions

Any promise of future compensation by an employer to an employee or by the Government to a taxpayer, based upon the present earnings of the person, shall be subject to income taxation during the current period when that promise of future compensation, both pecuniary and non-pecuniary, is received. This Section applies to Government and Non-Government employers, employees, and taxpayers. All promises of future compensation require taxable employer contributions of money or securities that shall be the property of that employee or taxpayer. A custodian may hold the assets for an individual beneficiary. Except for the President or the governor of a State, no government may offer guaranteed compensation to any person for more than one fiscal year.

> This Section eliminates the tax advantages of current defined benefit pensions. This Section requires separate accounting for the ownership amount per individual. All pension plans are taxed like defined contribution plans. Section 15 converts Social Security and Medicare programs to defined contribution plans with separate accounting for ownership shares in Personal Treasury Accounts. This requirement avoids the fiscal catastrophe experienced by Illinois' underfunded employee pension plans because it forces the employer to make current cash plan contributions out of current government expenditures. This Section requires federal personal income taxation on all compensation, with no tax-free harbor for

pension plans. The Federal Government can issue refund checks to persons or pension systems who contribute to a pension plan if it wishes to encourage savings, and it makes the expenditure, or size of the tax benefit, more transparent. This Section converts Social Security and Medicare into separate mutual accounting funds accumulating taxed contributions over time. The last sentence prohibits defined benefit pension plans for Government employees.

Section 14. Loan Guarantees and Government Retirement Plans

The current Congress may not obligate a future Congress to Appropriate Funds. Except for the debts of the Federal and State Governments and the pension of the President or the Governor of a State, no Government shall enact laws that guarantee the repayment of any financial obligation or contingent liability. Any loan guarantee or contingent liability in force at the time of ratification shall expire no later than thirty years after ratification of this Constitution.

Fannie Mae, Freddie Mac, SBA, Ex-Im Bank, and other agencies that offer loan guarantees will have to fold at the Federal Level and move to the States that want to adopt them. A 30-year transition period is permitted to let outstanding loans remain in force.

Section 15. Government Debt

The House of Representatives has the exclusive power to authorize the amount of borrowing on the credit of the United States by Resolution. The House authorizes two types of borrowing: Public Debt and Special Obligation Debt.

The President, in turn, is granted the exclusive power to borrow money authorized by The House of Representatives. This process is reset at the end of each fiscal year, aligning the maximum amount of borrowing on the credit of the United States with the outstanding amount of borrowing on that date plus one-fiftieth of that amount. The House may pass a separate resolution for every fiscal year to increase or decrease the maximum amount of borrowing.

> The House sets the Public Debt limit without consent from the President, but only the President, through the Secretary of the Treasury, may borrow authorized money. The debt limit resets every year. This requirement thwarts attempts to establish a high debt limit to avoid periodic review.

The primary issue of Public Debt must meet the following requirements:

The purchaser must pay with United States currency to have an enforceable claim for repayment. This exchange must occur in an open, competitive market with funding from taxable, non-government persons that are not controlled by the Government and are domiciled in the United States. The Government or the Federal Reserve may not purchase Public Debt before four days elapsed after issuance. States and Indigenous Sovereign Nations may not buy the primary issuance of Federal Government Debt.

> States and Foreign Governments can purchase Federal Debt on the secondary market from individuals and funds established in the US. This Section thwarts the use of straw buyers, including State governments, by requiring a minimum 4-day holding period for primary issues of US debt in a US-domiciled fund purchased with US currency to purchase debt in a rigged auction. This Section prevents the Federal Reserve from purchasing primary issues and subverting the market's debt pricing.

Whenever the sum of all payments for a Public Debt instrument exceeds five times the amount of money received at the time of its issuance, then that debt is extinguished. This requirement shall supersede any other terms and conditions in the Public Debt offering. The Secretary of the Treasury prescribes the coupon rate, maturity, repayment of principal, and other terms contained in a Public Debt offering.

> This paragraph thwarts the Treasury from evading debt limitations set by Congress by issuing bonds with extremely high coupon rates at a low face amount that causes investors to pay an astronomically

hefty premium above the face amount of the bond. It also restricts the ability of the Treasury to offer long-term maturities. If there are high interest rates, then the maturity of the bonds might have to be shortened to accommodate this five-multiple restriction. While Congress sets the debt limit, the Treasury retains discretion on the terms contained in the debt offerings.

Federal or State Governments can only issue Special Obligation Debt for a specific sum of money in their respective Personal Treasury Accounts. Only a natural person can own a Personal Treasury Account.

Special Obligation Bonds (SOBs) currently fund Social Security and Medicare. Payroll taxes don't purchase Federal Debt on the secondary market because that would send tax revenue outside the Federal Government and blow a hole into the Federal Budget. Instead, SOBs are a primary issue of debt. However, the Social Security Trust Fund – a federal government agency- holds this debt while the tax revenue goes to the Treasury for current expenditures. Essentially, SOBs are an accounting gimmick that creates a compulsory appropriation upon a future Congress to pay Social Security and Medicare recipients because these expenditures are repayment of debt obligations, not discretionary spending.

This Section retains the primary issuance structure so that Social Security and Medicare payroll tax revenue continues to flow directly to the Government. However, the taxpayers receive individual ownership of an account that is a fractional share of the Special Obligation Debt (SOD). This share is calculated based on the cumulative contributions of payroll tax. The Treasurer, instead of Congress, currently determines the amount of interest paid. This Section corrects the usurpation of the power of the purse by assigning Congress the responsibility for deciding how much interest to spend on these accounts. This Section enables federal and state governments to establish retirement plans. The assets in these plans are exempt from wealth taxes.

The Government can issue Special Obligation Debt when: the outstanding balance is less than the maximum borrowing limit of credit authorized by the House of Representatives or a State Legislature; a natural person exchanges personal income taxes paid to the Government in money; the House passes a resolution to authorize interest earnings for the account holders.

The aggregate amount of interest earnings credited to all Personal Treasury Accounts on the fifteenth day of the new fiscal year divided by the aggregate sum of Special Obligation Debt as of the last day of the prior fiscal year cannot exceed the weighted average rate of interest paid on Public Debt of twelve-month maturity or less during that prior fiscal year.

Only an account owner can receive distributions from a Personal Treasury Account, which are taxable and subject to accrued tax withholding. A Personal Treasury Account is not eligible as collateral to secure a loan.

> This formula has three parts:
>
> 1. Special Obligation Debt (SOD) cannot exceed the Debt Limit set by the House.
> 2. SOD must be exchanged for personal income taxes.
> 3. Congress can pay interest on the SOD, but it cannot exceed the rate of interest paid on one-year Public Debt.
>
> Interest earnings are credited to PTAs on January 15 to allow time for computations of interest allocations to each account. Prohibiting using a PTA to secure a loan and restricting distributions solely to account owners protects account owners from exhausting their retirement support.

The Secretary of the Treasury shall apportion aggregate interest earnings to each Personal Treasury Account according to that account's fractional share of the aggregate amount of Special Obligation Debt on a weighted-average basis throughout the year.

> This paragraph is a long-winded way to say that the Treasury Secretary considers interest compounding when paying interest in any year. Also, it prescribes that the allocation of interest must be proportional to the size of the account. The calculations can be complex. Someone who earns more at the beginning of the year

should get more interest paid than someone who ends the year with the same income taxes paid mainly at the end of the year. This paragraph inserts a weighted-average basis for the apportionment. Also, Congress cannot selectively subsidize one person's account with payments not proportional to their prior income tax contributions. This paragraph prevents Social Security from being used as a stealthy wealth distribution program. While Congress authorizes the total sum of interest earnings, the Treasury has the job of apportioning that interest to each account.

Interest earnings are not like payroll taxes. A discretionary appropriation by Congress credits interest payments through a discretionary Legislative Appropriation, but no money is actually paid to anyone. The interest earned increases the debt owed.

Currently, the first $168,600 (2024 limit) of income is subject to Social Security and Medicare tax. Under this Section, the amount of those taxes equals a credit to the taxpayer's PTA. Because the PTA doesn't allow stealthy wealth transfer of retirement benefits to taxpayers with less income, Congress will likely lower the ceiling to less than $100,000. Congress is limited to collecting 12.5% of income tax, so they don't gain any political points by raising the ceiling for the PTA. All they do is increase the future debt obligations upon a later Congress to deal with, without any present-day political benefits. The lower the ceiling, the greater the portion of personal income taxes available to fund other programs.

A Personal Treasury Account is the personal property of the account owner and part of that account owner's estate and living trust if established and referenced in the trust by the account owner. Congress or a State Legislature may enact laws regulating when and how much account holders may redeem from their respective Personal Treasury Accounts for money. If the deceased account owner has designated heirs to receive distributions from the Personal Treasury Account, then the Government may not delay or obstruct these distributions. No Government may tax the amount of the obligation in a Personal Treasury Account. Only the distributions from the account may be taxed. If an account owner did not provide instructions to the

Government for the amounts of distributions and named recipients of these distributions after death, the Government shall distribute funds to next of kin. If none can be found within twelve months, then the Government shall credit the remaining balance as interest earnings pro rata to all account holders.

Neither the Federal nor the State Governments may impose a wealth tax on balances in Personal Treasury Accounts (PTAs) while the account holder is alive. However, it could be subject to Estate and Inheritance Taxation.

Instead of a lifetime annuity payout formula, the PTAs would likely use a maximum distribution formula, similar to the IRS's Required Minimum Distribution formula for Individual Retirement Accounts. This requirement ensures that you cannot outlive your savings, but it also ensures that whatever you earned during your lifetime will pass on to your heirs if you die earlier than expected. This way, we can adapt the account's personal ownership concept to the paternalistic demand of ensuring that you cannot deplete your savings too early. It would be interesting to see if any States create their own Social Security programs with Personal Treasury Accounts.

This Section imposes a massive change upon the Social Security and Medicare programs by converting them into defined contribution plans. It will expose the heretofore hidden wealth transfers occurring under the current system. Now, Congress will have to explicitly increase taxes on wealthy PTA taxpayers and provide explicit welfare assistance to lower-income persons whose PTA distributions will be lower than current benefits provided under the current Social Security system. However, with a 12.5% maximum rate, Congress has little room to maneuver to conduct significant wealth transfers. Vote buying with wealth transfers is a game for State-level politicians not saddled with a maximum income tax rate.

After Ratification, the Social Security Administration would have to look back at each taxpayer under age 55 and their history of contributions and interest earnings credited by the Trust Fund.

The SSA uses this information to establish balances in each living contributor's newly established PTA. The Treasury Secretary must calculate this PTA account balance in six years. Those over 55 at Ratification will be grandfathered into the existing SS program and not have a PTA.

Section 16. Definitions of Income, Wealth, Commercial, Consumer

Income is the difference in flows of money or economic benefits paid as expenses and received as revenues over a unit of time that two methods can measure. These revenues and expenses may be recognized when money is received or spent; they can be recognized on an accrual basis, applying generally accepted accounting principles when the economic benefits or costs accrue. The Government shall follow the law to determine which method will be applied to calculate an income tax for a person.

The *Moore v. United States* case [13] demonstrates the importance of precise definitions of wealth [14] and income in the Anti-Elitist Constitution to remove the ambiguities inherent in the current Constitution.

Akhil Reed Amar argues that the 1787 Constitution permitted an income tax because *direct taxes* referred solely to head taxes and real estate taxes. (He was unclear whether only acreage taxation or property value taxes were prohibited. To be logically consistent, property value taxes should be permissible without apportionment among the States.) The delegates from slave-holding States insisted on this provision to prevent imposing head taxes that would render slavery unprofitable. Hence, the 1787 Constitution required direct tax apportionment according to the population of the States – and the 3/5th rule dampened the effect of taxing slaves. The Slave States then had to count Slaves as 3/5ths toward the apportionment of Representatives in the House and the Electoral College. *Pollock v. Farmers' Loan & Trust Co.*, 158 U.S. 601 (1895) was a mistaken interpretation of direct taxation that said a personal income tax was a direct tax. In Amar's view, the 16th Amendment corrected the Court's error in *Pollock* but would have otherwise been unnecessary. In his view, Congress has no limit on what it can tax other than head taxes and real estate taxes. Indeed, there is no obstacle to levying a wealth tax.

Therefore, under the Anti-Elitist Constitution, it is essential to precisely define which types of taxation the Federal and State governments permit — eliminating ambiguity.

If one party borrows an amount of money that the Government taxes as income, then the Government shall classify the amount of loaned funds as an equivalent expense for reducing the amount of income taxed for the counterparty. If the Government classifies loan proceeds as income, then the future repayments of principal and interest received by one party shall be taxed as income, and the payment of principal and interest by the counterparty shall be an equivalent expense for reducing the amount of income taxed.

This paragraph applies accounting symmetry as a deterrent to the Government's application of this tax to evade the prohibition on wealth taxes by redefining the common understanding of income versus debt. Suppose that the Government wants to apply an income tax against a borrower who receives money from a loan, which, under current tax law, is not classified as income subject to taxation. The Anti-Elitist Constitution must have clear demarcations between wealth and income taxation because Constitutional Scholars like Amar see no reason that Congress could levy wealth taxes. This paragraph explicitly defines this symmetry of revenue that increases income versus expenses that reduce income. This paragraph will make this kind of taxation less profitable for the Government. If the Government proposes this kind of tax, then it is saying that these kinds of loans are for consumer purposes and should be taxed as income for a natural person instead of a business.

It is too challenging to prohibit taxation on unrealized capital gains. While imposing taxes on unrealized gains seems unfair and impractical, it is not legally inconsistent. Because the government taxes businesses using an accrual basis, and if the Government

> classifies depreciation as an accrual expense, then unrealized gains are a kind of accrued revenue. It would be unfair to only apply the taxation of accrual items on the expense side, not the revenue side. Once you accept the principle of accrual accounting, then taxation of unrealized gains is fair game.

Wealth measures the value of a person's assets at a single point in time when the tax is assessed or of that person's equity — the difference in value between assets and liabilities at a single point in time.

> Defining *wealth* separately from *income* makes it easier to enforce the boundaries between Federal and State domains of taxation and protect the State's tax revenue stream from Federal encroachment. The concepts of *a point in time* versus *differences over a unit of time* provide the logical distinctions that should be impossible for a Judge to subvert without ridicule.

Commercial activity is exchanging money, credit, or other things of value for goods or services. The valuation of the expenditures is classified as expenses subtracted from the revenue received to calculate the income subject to taxation.

A *Sole Proprietorship* engages in commercial activity, and its assets are owned by a natural person who deducts expenses generated by commercial activity from its revenue to calculate the personal income subject to taxation.

Consumer activity occurs when a person spends money, credit, or other things of value on goods or services that cannot be subtracted from their revenue to calculate the income subject to taxation.

> A person could simultaneously be a consumer and a business owner, but the Government taxes his consumer activities differently than his business activities.

Ad valorem – a tax rate multiplied by the money value of the activity or good being taxed. Multiplying the assessed value of a building times the property tax rate is the property value tax.

> Ad valorem taxes are the most common. Income and sales taxes are ad valorem. Property taxes are most commonly ad valorem, too.

Unit – a measurement of the physical thing being taxed multiplied by the amount of money assessed for taxation per physical unit of measurement. Multiplying the number of square feet in a building times the dollars per square foot equals the property unit tax.

> Governments can levy Unit taxes for carbon or pollution taxes. Also, charging tariffs based on the number of goods instead of the purported valuation of goods applies this method. When the cost of providing a service to property owners is related to the amount of property rather than its value, then unit taxes are a good choice.

Toll — charges a uniform amount across categories of users based upon a published schedule of rates for the use of Government property or use of the Commons, not owned by any person or Government.

> Toll charges for highway use are the most common example. However, entry costs into National Parks are another form of toll. Tolls allocate scarce resources (traffic congestion) or preserve a resource against wear and tear (entry into National Parks), in addition to any recovery of actual maintenance costs of the roads or parks. Tolls can differ for trucks or cars, but they must be according to a published schedule. They cannot be arbitrary.

Fee — an amount not to exceed the actual cost incurred by the Government to provide a service, inspection, monitoring, remediate a nuisance, or issue a license to practice a trade. Fees must be uniform and charged according to a published schedule or to the actual costs incurred to perform a specific activity.

> Fees are the types of taxes most subject to abuse by the use of arbitrary assessments of liability.

For this Article, *Property Taxes*, are assessed against real estate — land and buildings fixed to the land. Chattel is not real estate and is reserved for taxation solely by the Federal Government.

Article 17.

General Government Mandates

Section 1. State Legislatures Cannot Delegate Authority

The States' Legislatures are composed of representatives who draft and enact laws of that State and are elected by Eligible Voters of that State. Any provision of a State Constitution or State law in conflict with this definition of the Legislature shall have no effect. These Legislatures may not delegate any power to appoint Senators, approve Proposed Amendments, or any other responsibilities this Constitution or Federal Law assigns.

> This paragraph regulates situations where state courts often arrogate powers to thwart the powers of the state legislatures guaranteed under the current Constitution. This paragraph prohibits the direct elections for Senators and other delegations of a legislature's authority.

The Constitution, statutes, ordinances, and regulations of a State or its political subdivisions cannot regulate levels of taxation or require Appropriations for an Expenditure by that Government in the future.

> This paragraph prevents amendments to State Constitutions like Propositions 13 and 98 in California. Proposition 13 limits the property tax rate, and Proposition 98 requires a minimum expenditure for K-12 Education. Both hamper the Legislature's ability to be responsive to the electorate by constraining their degrees of freedom to develop sound fiscal policies according to a coherent

plan. Initiatives that only focus on taxation or spending separately are not coherent with a specific action plan, and the sponsors bear no political responsibility for future problems caused by their constraints and mandates.

Section 2. Supremacy Clause

This Constitution, and the Laws of the United States which shall be made in Pursuance thereof; and all Treaties made, or which shall be made, under the Authority of the United States, shall be the supreme Law of the Land; and the Judges in every State shall be bound thereby, any Thing in the Constitution or Laws of any State to the Contrary notwithstanding.

Language from the 1787 Constitution.

However, any provisions of a Treaty in conflict with this Constitution shall not be enforced.

This paragraph thwarts using Treaties to trump the Constitution. Instead, the Congress and the President must amend the Constitution directly, not indirectly, through a Treaty.

Section 3. Admission And Creation of New States and Secession

A new State may be created from a Federal Territory, an existing State, or several States. A portion of a State may secede from one State to join an adjoining State. The most numerous Houses in the Legislature of the States forming the new State must consent, and the House of Representatives and the Senate must approve it with a three-fifths vote.

This paragraph corrects the 1787 Constitution Framers' failure to anticipate the problems created by adding new States to the Union. This failure first appeared during the addition of Free and Slave States during the Ante-Bellum period. This failure reappeared when Democrats threatened to admit Puerto Rico and

> convert Washington, D.C., into a state, thereby adding four additional Democrat Senators. These failures demonstrate that partisans can weaponize the creation of new States for political ends. The Anti-Elitist Constitution reduces the small State's powers in the Senate, so the stakes in admitting new states are less than with the current Constitution.

When the Census has counted a State's population of Citizens greater than one-sixth of the population of Citizens of the entire United States, then that State shall be divided into two States, neither having a population of Citizens greater than one-tenth the population of Citizens of the United States. The Senate shall pass a resolution to name the new State in cases of disputes.

> This paragraph undermines one aspect of State sovereignty. States are instruments of the Citizenry, so when a State becomes too large, it undermines the balance of power between the States and the balance between a State and the Federal Government. This doctrine is inconsistent with John Calhoun's views of State Sovereignty pre-existing in the Union.

Within one year of the Census finding, the State Legislature shall submit a map with the new State boundaries to the House of Representatives. The new map is adopted if four-sevenths of the House does not approve an alternative map. The Elections Board shall draw new district boundaries for the House of Representatives within the States.

If the State Legislature fails to submit a map within one year, the Elections Board shall use existing boundaries for the House of Representative districts to divide the State into two separate States that retain the exact district boundaries.

Two-thirds of the Congress must consent to the formation of additional Federal Territories after Ratification.

A State or Territory may secede from the United States under the following conditions: The State or Territory Legislature, by a five-ninth vote, supports a Resolution of Secession on two occasions separated by five years but not greater than eight years. Within one hundred eighty days of the approval of the second Resolution of Secession, the Resolution shall be submitted to the Eligible Voters of the State or Territory for a referendum. If four-sevenths of the voters approve the Resolution, then it shall be submitted for a Plebiscite by Article 18, Section 5. If approved, the Secession takes effect. The Citizens of the former State or Territory shall forfeit their United States Citizenship, and Legal Residents shall forfeit their residency privileges.

> This paragraph considers the possibility of a peaceful secession, negating the principle of the perpetual Union of States. The Anti-Elitist Constitution has Citizens as the sovereign authority where the federal and state governments are instruments of the Citizens. There is nothing inherently sacred about States that merit an irrevocable union with other States if this union doesn't serve the Citizens' interests. Because Citizens have the right to voluntarily surrender their Citizenship, this Section recognizes that a collective of Citizens might decide to secede and collectively surrender their Citizenship. Admittedly, this Section sets a very high hurdle for secession, but it is possible.

Section 4. Formation of a New Federal District

The federal government may only incorporate two federal districts: the District of Columbia and one other district, which cannot exceed fifty square miles nor lie less than eight hundred miles from the District of Columbia. Any new Federal District must receive the State or States' consent to offer territory. A five-ninth vote of Congress enacts the law to create a new Federal District. Congress may not convert all or part of a Federal District into a new State, but its territory and residents may be returned to its adjoining States with the States' consent and a three-fifths vote of Congress.

> A new Federal District should be created in the Midwest to lessen the average travel distance to the Capital and be in the middle time zone to ease meeting scheduling. Nearly doubling the number of Members of the House of Representatives in an age of security and terrorism concerns, a new district should be built to host new, modern facilities. It would also symbolize the adoption of a new Constitution.

Section 5. Residency Privileges in a Federal District

The Citizens of the United States may obtain Residency Status in a Federal District. Citizens with Federal District Residency forfeit the right to vote for office holders in a State or political subdivision of a State. They shall be subject to taxation by the Federal District authority in addition to any Federal Income Tax limitation provided by Article 16. By a three-fifths vote of Congress, the Federal Government may cede part of a Federal District and its Residents to an adjoining State.

This Section settles the controversy about converting Washington, D.C., to a state. If it is so important, the residents could be transferred to Maryland so that they could vote in that State's elections. Because the Anti-Elitist Constitution doesn't permit a direct vote for Senators, and the District of Columbia will have representation in the House, most of the steam behind this push will dissipate.

Section 6. Archive and Universal Library

The Federal Government shall have the duty to maintain an archive of written, musical, artistic, and technical works that protects the property rights of authors and publishers in any dissemination of their works. It is responsible for establishing a universal public library in cooperation with all nations to disseminate and preserve knowledge for future generations.

This Section addresses the controversy created by Google's project to capture images of books, art, and other works and who has rights over them. The US government should take over the project and cooperate with other nations to finish and maintain it.

Section 7. Storage of Commercial Records

The Research and Records Board must maintain a secure, duplicate system of all banking and financial records, property titles, liens, and other records. The Government shall prepare to restore these systems in the event of natural catastrophe or human sabotage of the private records that rely upon the Government's legal systems for enforcing claims.

> This kind of sabotage could end civilization in the US. This Section places responsibility for its prevention in the Federal Government's lap to ensure everyone understands who is in charge.

Section 8. Electrical Power Safeguards

The Federal Government has the duty to regulate the production and delivery of electrical power, minimize the risk of disruption of the delivery of power, disperse the generation of electricity, and minimize the vulnerability of electricity transmission to natural disasters and enemy attacks. It shall reduce blight and environmental damage and provide a reliable, continuous power source. It shall procure, store, and prepare for the provision of equipment held in reserve to restore electrical power.

> Electrical power grids are vulnerable to solar flares, Electromagnetic Pulse weapons, weather, and terrorism. The Federal Government must assume responsibility because the power distribution grid is interstate. Due to the externalities and vulnerability to regulatory and tort risks, the private sector would need assistance to provide the kinds of molten-salt, thorium/fluoride fission reactors that could meet these requirements. Wind and solar power methods are subject to natural weather conditions, and they rely upon transmitting power over long distances from wind and solar farms to urban centers. Wind and solar farms also cause visual blight and disruption to the land and sea. The Transmission lines from wind and solar farms are a huge vulnerability. A backup supply of voltage transformers is necessary for an EMP or Solar Flare event.

Section 9. Bankruptcies, Contracts, Republican Government, Inspections, Religious Test

Full Faith and Credit shall be given in each State to the public Acts, Records, and judicial Proceedings of every other State. And the Congress may by general Laws prescribe the Manner in which such Acts, Records and Proceedings shall be proved, and the Effect thereof.

Congress shall enact uniform laws on the subject of Bankruptcies throughout the United States.

Language from 1787 Constitution.

Subject to the exceptions of Section 10, States may not discriminate in applying laws, regulations, and procedures for due process against Citizens from other States.

States cannot discriminate against a Citizen based on their residence. This paragraph is a substitution for the privileges and immunities clause of Article 4 Section 2 of the 1787 Constitution.

A Person charged in any State with Treason, Felony, or other Crime who shall flee from Justice and be found in another State shall, on Demand of the executive Authority of the State from which they fled, be delivered up, to be removed to the State having Jurisdiction of the Crime. Congress may enact laws to enforce this requirement.

Language from the 1787 Constitution.

The United States shall guarantee to every State in this Union a Republican Form of Government with a Judiciary, Legislature, and Governor. The Eligible Voters elect members of the Legislature. The Legislature may elect the Governor, or the voters may directly elect the Governor by a majority vote. If the legislative bodies of the State's political subdivisions adopt geographical districts, the number of Citizens in these districts shall not exceed one-twentieth difference between the largest and smallest districts in that jurisdiction. A non-partisan commission with membership criteria like Article 12, Section 6 must draw legislative district boundaries. The commission must draw boundaries by applying the constraints and procedures of Article 12, Section 4. States and their political subdivisions are not required to adopt geographic districts for members of their legislative bodies.

Dividing the number of Citizens by the number of members in the State Legislature shall not exceed one hundred thousand. It shall not exceed fifty thousand in a political subdivision's legislative body. Five seats are the minimum number in a political subdivision's legislative body.

The *Baker vs. Carr* case of 1962 required equal-sized legislative districts in the States. This Section explicitly enshrines that requirement rather than inferring it from the 14th Amendment's equal protection clause. This Section compels States to have small districts so that the voters can be closer to their representatives.

The City of Los Angeles has 3,8220,000 people and 15 city council members for an average of 254,000/person. They would have to expand the number of council members to 77. At some point, the size of the council becomes unwieldy, and it would make sense to divide the city into one or more municipalities.

This Constitution, the State Constitution, and Statutes enacted into law shall govern a State's Judiciary. The United States shall protect each State against Invasion and on Application of the Legislature or the Governor (when the Legislature cannot be convened) against domestic Violence.

Any inspection and entry restrictions conducted by the States at their Borders to deter the spread of contaminants injurious to crops, plants, animals, and people shall be subject to approval by Congress.

The Anti-Elitist Constitution can omit many of the Sections of the current Constitution because it does not contain enumerated powers for Congress. Because of the Taxation powers in Article 16, many of the prohibitions upon State actions listed in the current Constitution are moot.

The Senators and Representatives before mentioned, and the Members of the several State Legislatures, and all executive and judicial Officers, both of the United States and of the several States, shall be bound by Oath or Affirmation, to support this Constitution; but no religious Test shall ever be required as a Qualification to any Office or public Trust under the United States.

Language from the 1787 Constitution.

Section 10. Power of State to Discriminate Against Non-Residents

Excepting emergency, non-recurring medical care, use of the courts, and police protection, a State may require no more than twenty-four consecutive months of residency as a condition for any person who has attained nineteen years to be eligible to receive direct financial or non-pecuniary assistance from the State. If a Citizen resides continuously in a State for sixty days, they can declare residency, vote, and pay income taxes in that State if they abandon their previous residency status.

> Children shall be eligible for full State support, including Public Schooling. Anticipating that States will be very competitive in their tax and spending policies, this ability to withhold welfare benefits for 24 months discourages persons from moving to States with generous benefits without first contributing tax payments.

Section 11. Federal Responsibility for Foreign Residents

The Federal Government must pay the States' expenses for foreign visitors, legally and illegally residing in the States. The State must promptly notify the Federal Government of the recipients' services, costs, identities, and addresses.

> The current Constitution makes the States bear the brunt of illegal immigration. Their public schools, welfare system, prisons, etc., burden the States' taxpayers. The Federal Government should bear these costs and incentivize the States to assist the Feds in enforcing immigration policies.

Section 12. No Government-Sponsored Personal Advertising

For any public or private notice of the responsibility for the provision of cash, goods, services, and property sponsored by the Government, the only permitted wording shall be: *Brought to you by the Taxpayers of the United States of America*, the State, Territory, or other political subdivision thereof. Other than a signature on a bank draft, no other attribution of responsibility for the provision of such benefits shall be allowed that displays the name of the office or the name, physical or electronic address, voice, or image of an office holder.

> This Section stops politicians from taking credit for pork-barrel projects in their districts or State or cash disbursements similar to President Biden's October 21, 2021 letter regarding the $1,400 American Rescue Plan.

No person may hold elected or appointed Government office if their name or likeness is affixed to or used in official communications identifying Laws, Property, Parks, Places, equipment, vehicles, and vessels of the Federal Government. A living person must consent to using their name and likeness in such a manner.

Section 13. Prohibition of Gifts to Officials by Foreign Governments

The United States and the States may not grant a title of nobility providing compensation to that person or their heirs. No Elected Official, Officer, or government employee shall, without the consent of the House of Representatives, accept any gift, payment for services, office, or title, of any kind whatever, from any foreign entity during their term in office and no fewer than five years from the date of vacating the office.

Section 14. Indigenous Sovereign Tribes

The Treaties with the Indigenous Tribes shall remain in effect, and all Members of these Tribes are Citizens of the United States, a State, and their Nation. Congress shall enact legislation regarding the States' authority to tax the Citizens of these nations. Otherwise, these Nations have the same powers and limitations of taxation as the States per Article 16. These Nations may not maintain relationships with foreign governments or organizations independent of the United States foreign policy. These Nations may only grant Citizenship in their Nations based upon biological descent from a male and a female who were both Citizens of their Nations and the United States at birth.

> Members of the Tribes can be Citizens of States for voting purposes. However, Congress could offer Citizens of the Nations an exemption from State taxation. Limiting membership to biological descendants eliminates schemes where tribal memberships could be exchanged for money.

Section 15. Bill of Attainder, Ex Post Facto Prohibition

Neither the States nor the United States shall make or enforce any Bill of Attainder; or Ex Post Facto Law about criminal, civil, equity, or taxation law where the defendant or respondent is held liable for acts committed before enactment of a statute.

Section 16. States Not an Administrative Arm of Federal Government

The Federal Government may not enact any laws to compel a State to enforce Federal Laws, administer Federal Programs, or force a State Judiciary to try cases covering Federal Laws. No State may enforce any penalties or sanctions against employees of the State Government who cooperate with the Federal Government without compensation by the Federal Government.

> Article 16, Section 3 requires that per capita federal assistance to States be equal. This section indirectly impacts federal programs that base assistance on states' compliance with federal rules as a condition to qualify for federal dollars. This section should eliminate most Block Grant programs as currently designed. The federal government cannot force States to act as their agents, thereby preserving federalism. On the flip side, a State may not block its employees from aiding Border Control agents in tracking down illegal aliens, furthering a national purpose.

States may enter compacts with other States to incorporate entities for the joint administration of services, which may be exclusively for the Citizens of their States unless a majority of Congress passes a Resolution opposing a compact.

> For example, if the Federal Government disbands the Small Business Administration (SBA), a consortium of States might want to pool resources to establish a joint entity that replaces the SBA. These States wouldn't need to seek permission from Congress, but Congress could block it.

If the Federal Government leases all or part of its property to a person within a State to conduct commercial activities, then that person must comply with the laws and regulations of that State.

> This paragraph safeguards against the Federal Government using its buildings, military bases, or national parks as a sanctuary for businesses thwarting State laws. It doesn't prevent the Federal Government from using Federal employees to perform activities in conflict with State laws.

Section 17. Intellectual Property

The Federal Government shall have exclusive jurisdiction for promoting Science and Useful Arts by securing the Rights of Persons to their respective Writings, Inventions, and Discoveries. If an author or inventor is a Citizen and the owner of the protected work, they have exclusive and modified Rights during their lifetime. Congress may enact laws requiring compulsory licensing of protected works with maximum ad valorem or unit rates accruing to the author or inventor for a period not to exceed the lifetime of, or twenty years after, the author's or inventor's death.

If a Citizen leases, transfers, or hypothecates their intellectual property rights during their lifetime, then the protection of Property Rights shall not exceed twenty years from the lease date, transfer, or hypothecation.

> This Section introduces the concepts of Exclusive Rights and Compulsory Licensing. This Section balances the need to develop an invention but doesn't protect a monopoly privilege. At its discretion, Congress could give heirs twenty years of additional income.
>
> This Section prevents the favoritism shown to Hollywood when Congress extended copyright protections for motion pictures to preserve the revenue stream of the studios that owned the rights. These extensions have nothing to do with furthering invention and are political payoffs. This Section closes that loophole. The limitation on the sale of the patent or offering it as collateral in a loan eliminates a loophole where a corporation could get a patent for a period exceeding 20 years.

If an author or inventor is a legal person or non-citizen, then the exclusive Rights shall be at most twenty years or be more than fifteen years from the date of approval by the Government. A legal person may transfer or hypothecate its intellectual property rights for the remainder of the protected period of exclusive Rights.

Upon expiration of the protected period of exclusive Rights or compulsory licensing, the property shall revert to the public domain or, by an act of Congress, become the property of the Federal Government.

Section 18. Qualified Immunity for Government Officials

Government officials performing discretionary functions are shielded from personal liability for civil damages, but their employer, the Government, must compensate the victims of any tort. The President decides whether a suit filed against a federal official can proceed outside a Federal Court.

When a Court finds that a Government Official threatened to use their power or to abstain from using their power under color of law to influence a person's political contributions, speech, commercial activity, affiliation with or support of persons, they shall be removed from office, imprisoned for at least one thousand days, and fined at least the Compensation Index.

> This paragraph responds to the case of *National Rifle Association v Vullo* [16]. A state official threatened insurance companies with adverse treatment unless they canceled insurance policies with the National Rifle Association. The Supreme Court ruled unanimously against Maria Vullo, the head of New York's Department of Financial Services.

Section 19. Prohibition of Government Resources for Campaigns

Government employees and officials cannot use Government property, or appropriations and expenditures of funds, to support or oppose candidate campaigns, legislation, political actors, or political action committees. Elected Officials may only use government employees, government-controlled communication channels, and property to support or oppose legislation during the public exercise of their duties on government property reserved for this purpose.

No elected official or government employee may use government funds for housing, security, and transportation expenses to travel to events and solicit political contributions from any candidate, political party, or political actor. A limited exception for the President is the ability to use government funds for security and transportation expenses to solicit contributions and campaign solely for the President's re-election to office no earlier than three hundred days before the Final Voting Date. Guilty parties must pay a fine of twelve months of compensation and reimbursement of prohibited expenditures.

House Members may be reimbursed for reasonable transportation expenses to their District for up to twenty separate dates in a fiscal year. The Secretary of the Treasury shall manage reimbursement of transportation expenses. These eligible transportation expenses shall not be added as non-pecuniary income of the Member used to compute the Compensation Index.

All elected and appointed officials and Government employees must only use Government-controlled property and communication channels to conduct or provide information about any Government business. Only persons who violate the law may be excluded from these channels.

> This Section prohibits Hillary Clinton's private email server. It also prohibits government personnel from using private social media to disseminate information not otherwise publicly available and excluding critics from viewing their accounts.

Section 20. Prohibition Against Privatizing Law Enforcement

No Government shall bar its officials from enforcing a law and substitute enforcement by non-government persons to sue persons who violate that law in civil court.

This paragraph prevents States from adopting the legal strategy employed by Texas in its 2021 SB 8 law that evaded federal enforcement of *Roe v Wade* directly against the State of Texas because the law deputized private citizens to sue abortion clinics. The private citizens could win at least $10,000 in damages if a court rules that the clinic provided an abortion.

No government shall enact a law granting powers to private persons to file lawsuits on behalf of persons who did not consent to representation as a member of a class of injured persons in the controversy.

This paragraph prohibits using Private Attorney General laws authorizing private persons to sue for the public interest and their plaintiff. Instead, attorneys must follow the established rules governing a class action lawsuit.

Any fines or settlement payments arising from a judgment in a case filed by the Government must be paid into the Government's General Fund, and this money may not be redirected to a non-government person without an Appropriation by the Legislature.

This paragraph thwarts the Obama-era practice of awarding judgments to Progressive non-profit organizations. The principle at stake is that revenues earned by the Government may only be appropriated by legislation and not by the Executive branch's discretion.

Section 21. Standing In Lawsuits For Violations Of This Constitution

Three Senators or Thirty Members of the House of Representatives may petition the Supreme Court to review any allegations of violations of this Constitution. In their petition, they must designate one lead counsel and one co-counsel to present their case to the Court. A Senator or Member is limited to filing no more than one petition per twelve-month period. These officials may not pay their legal expenses with Federal funds.

This Section establishes a balance between a Court's abuse of the standing doctrine [17] to deny the resolution of essential controversies and the proliferation of cases that would arise if persons without a material interest in the controversy could get a hearing and inundate the courts. For example, the Supreme Court nearly denied hearing the Student Debt case (*Biden v Nebraska* [18]) on the grounds of standing even though weighty Constitutional principles were at stake in this controversy.

Section 22. Limitations on Rule By Decree

Congress may enact a law granting the President the limited power to rule by decree under enumerated circumstances when it supersedes the authority of State Governments. This power to issue an order having the force of law upon the persons of the United States expires under the following conditions:

- The President can declare a State of Emergency in accordance with law to rule by decree for no more than thirty days in any twelve-month period.
- By a three-fifths vote, Congress may grant a single extension of no more than thirty days in any twelve-month period.
- By a two-thirds vote, Congress may grant a second extension of no more than sixty days in any twelve-month period.
- No additional extensions may be granted.
- The President may not combine the authorization of separate laws to obtain additional days to rule by decree in any twelve-month period.

The President forfeits the office to the Vice President after ruling by decree for more than one hundred eighty days during any four-year period. The President may not return to any Federal office or employment.

A three-fifths vote of Congress is required to approve the continuation or establishment of a State of Emergency within one hundred eighty days before the Final Date of Voting.

Because Presidents Trump and Biden ruled by decree during the COVID crisis, the Anti-Elitist Constitution should regulate the scope of this power. During an emergency, the public will demand resolute action and, inevitably, neglect the finer points of Constitutional limits. This Section accommodates and shapes this powerful impulse.

The 180-day limit is a hard stop to prevent the evolution of a dictatorship and protects members of Congress from caving into threats to vote for extensions. The pressure to allocate these emergency powers is irresistible, so it is better to regulate them than to ban them and later have the ban ignored.

Section 23. Takings and Taxation Through Regulation or Statute

Excepting the judgment of a State or Federal Court finding a restraint of trade causing non-competitive pricing, the costs of Government price regulations imposed upon persons for the general welfare shall be a taking by the Government. Whenever the Government regulates the price of goods or services offered in commerce, and it is set below the unregulated price, that loss of revenue shall be classified as an accrued tax paid by the owner.

Excepting conscription for military service, whenever the Government compels the provision of goods and services and offers compensation below the unregulated price, then that loss of revenue is classified as accrued taxes paid by the owner. The owner's tax liability owed to the Government that imposed the price controls or the compulsion to provide services is reduced by the amount of accrued taxes earned. The Government may not classify these accrued taxes as revenue. The Government shall pay the taxpayer any excess accrued taxes earned over the tax liability within twelve months of the end of the fiscal year.

Rent-controlled property owners get relief. This provision doesn't prevent the Government from using price controls. It recognizes that property owners should be compensated for providing a social service, not be subject to a taking. Likewise, when Hospital

> Emergency Rooms are required to accept anyone regardless of ability to pay, the State must offer tax relief.

If the Government enacts a new law or regulation governing the use of the property to promote a public purpose, and that use diminishes the value of the property by more than one-tenth, and that law affects fewer than one-third of persons owning property within the Government's jurisdiction where the statute or regulation applies, then this shall be classified as a taking under Section 9 of Article 19.

> This Section addresses laws like the Endangered Species Act or Landmark Designations that change the use of the property after its purchase. When a small minority of persons have their property's value diminished in the name of a public good, the public should compensate the property owner like any other taking by the Government. If more than 1/3rd of people are affected, it rises to the level of a political question that voters can resolve through elections because so many people are broadly affected.

Except for the conscription of natural persons for Military Service and Jury Duty, The Government may not enact statutes or regulations that compel fewer than one-third of all non-government, natural persons acting jointly in a legal entity or severally as individuals within that Government's jurisdiction to fulfill a Government policy without just compensation.

> The government can compel people to use a trash service because it is widespread in all households and does not discriminate against a small minority of individuals. However, it cannot compel companies to provide office space for government employees because that targets a small minority of individuals, shouldering the burden of a public purpose without compensation. This principle of compulsory taking appears in the Third Amendment's prohibition of quartering troops in someone's home without their consent or compensation. It is ironic that Constitutional Scholars have not applied the rights implied in the Third Amendment [19] to other circumstances like those considered in Section 23.

All statutes granting administrative bodies discretion to enforce statutes, write regulations, issue licenses, or issue permits shall be subject to strict scrutiny for due process violations.

> Richard Epstein and Theodore Lowi warned about the excesses of the arbitrary powers vested with regulators captured by special interest groups.

Section 24. Publication of Records

All statutes and regulations issued by Governments must be published and made available to the public in an easily accessible and retrievable medium. Only portions of meetings where privileged information about a lawsuit or information that could jeopardize the physical safety of an individual was discussed shall be redacted from the minutes of any meeting.

Recorded deeds, liens, and the convicted criminal records of any persons shall be published. They may not be withheld or redacted without an order from a Court in response to a specific request by an interested party for compelling reasons of physical safety.

Section 25. Civil Service Eligibility And Labor Contract Restrictions

All Government Employee Labor Contracts must originate at the beginning and expire at the end of each fiscal year. Any law or negotiated contract in conflict with this Section shall be null and void. The Government fiscal year begins on January 1 and ends on December 31.

> Limiting labor contracts to one year prevents one administration from encumbering another with legal obligations that prevent exercising democratic control over expenditures.

Article 18.

Process for Constitutional Amendments

Section 1. Amendment Initiated by States

One lead sponsor and four co-sponsors will co-sponsor the Proposed Amendment language. These five State Legislatures must pass identical resolutions containing the same Amendment language by a six-elevenths majority. According to the most recent Census, these states include at least one-tenth of the population of citizens of the United States. No more than twelve months shall elapse between the passage of the Resolution by the first and last State. No State may propose more than one Amendment every twelve months.

The lead sponsor shall submit the Proposed Amendment to every remaining State Legislature and the Chief Justice. The Chief Justice may comment on the Proposed Amendment to the State Legislatures.
The Proposed Amendment must pass by a majority vote of the State Legislatures within four years after submission. Passage by a State counts as an approval of the Proposed Amendment. A subsequent vote by a State Legislature to rescind approval shall only be valid before the Amendment's approval by four-sevenths of State Legislatures. When four-sevenths of State Legislatures approve the Proposed Amendment, then the Proposed Amendment shall be submitted for Ratification by a Plebiscite by Section 5 at the next Federal Election no sooner than ninety days after the approval by four-sevenths of the States.

Section 2. Amendment Initiated by Congress

A five-ninth vote in Congress proposes an Amendment to this Constitution. Congress shall submit this proposed Amendment to the State Legislatures. If two-fifths of the State Legislatures do not vote to oppose the Proposed Amendment within one year of submission, the Proposed Amendment shall be submitted for a Plebiscite by Section 5 for inclusion on the following Federal Ballot following no sooner than one year after the approval by Congress.

Section 3. Constitutional Convention

One lead sponsor and four co-sponsors shall co-sponsor a Resolution for convening a Constitutional Convention that includes the first draft of a new Constitution or Amendment. These five sponsoring State Legislatures must pass identical resolutions containing the same language by a six-elevenths majority. According to the most recent Census, these States include at least one-tenth of the population of citizens of the United States.

> A small group of passionate supporters normally lead movements for significant change. Hence, the 6/11th hurdle for five states. By taking this initiative, these States gain some control over the structure of the proceedings of a Constitutional Convention. While writing an entirely new Constitution through the normal amendment process is possible, it is more likely to have to be rewritten within a Convention.

The lead sponsor shall submit the Proposed Amendment to every remaining State Legislature and the Chief Justice. Within sixty days, The Chief Justice may convey comments regarding this Resolution to every State Legislature. At most, twelve months shall elapse between the passage of the Resolution by the first and last State.

Only revisions or Amendments passed by a Constitutional Convention shall deprive a State of its equal suffrage in the Senate.

This Section protects the Senate's power. Adding the requirement that any action of the Senate must be from States representing a majority of Citizens should remove most objections to the Senate as a second legislative branch house.

Knowing that the Chief Justice will have the right to write comments means that the leaders of this initiative will likely solicit input from the Chief Justice before passing the Resolution. However, the fact that the Chief Justice gets to make comments ensures that there is a learned, respected figure shepherding the process. If the Resolution contains a first draft or outline of the proposed revisions, then the Chief Justice's comments could be more detailed. If the Resolution addresses subjects on which the Courts seek guidance, it could be a laudatory comment.

The States will convene after two-thirds of the States pass the Resolution four years after the submission of the Resolution. A vote to rescind the approval of the Proposed Resolution shall not have effect if passed after two-thirds of States have approved. When two-thirds of State legislatures approve the Resolution for a constitutional convention, the Convention shall convene at a time and place according to the Resolution.

The Proceedings of the Constitutional Convention shall terminate no later than six months after the final State approval for the Convention.

The most numerous House of each State Legislature shall send two voting Delegates to the Convention according to the following method:

A deadline is an essential requirement. It ensures that delay does not dissipate momentum for change.

Each member of the Legislature may cast one vote for one Delegate. Three-fifths of the Electoral Votes for their State are assigned to the Delegate receiving the most votes. The remaining Electoral Votes are assigned to the Delegate receiving the second most votes. Each Delegate shall select an Alternate to replace them if that Delegate cannot attend. Each Delegate and Alternate shall receive equal compensation from their State and shall not be engaged in any other employment throughout the duration of the Convention. Once appointed by the State Legislature, the Delegate cannot be removed or have a decrease in compensation unless expelled for misconduct during the proceedings by a three-fifths vote of the Delegates. The State represented by an expelled delegate may replace their Delegate.

> The Delegate is independent from their Legislature. Like the original Convention in 1787, the Delegate must act in the interests of the general good and not the parochial concerns of their State. Having two delegates per State, with one Delegate getting 3/5th and the other 2/5th of the electoral votes for that State, provides partisan diversity. This method will generate fractional electoral votes, not just whole numbers.

The initial Presiding Officer and Secretary shall be chosen according to the terms of the Resolution, and they may not vote on any proposals. The Convention Delegates shall choose the permanent Presiding Officer and Secretary. The Presiding Officer shall have the sole authority to issue reports and communicate to the public about debates and discussions during the Convention. The Presiding Officer must approve all requests for documents, information, and conversations with persons outside the Convention. Delegates and Alternates must consent to monitoring of all methods of communication.

All Delegates and Alternates are required to take an oath of secrecy. Any Delegate or Alternate that directly communicates or facilitates the transcription, eavesdropping, or recording of any content of the proceedings before the end of the Convention with any person who is not a Delegate or Alternate without the express, written permission of the Presiding Officer, shall be subjected to a vote of expulsion from the Convention and, if convicted by a Court, serve no less than five hundred days in prison. No State may bind the votes or conduct of its Delegate and Alternate by statute or with a fine.

> The Constitutional Convention in Philadelphia succeeded because there were no leaks about the debates and tradeoffs being considered. The men in 1787 did not have scores of media badgering them for leaks to be published online, as would the Delegate for

future Conventions. These sanctions are important for emphasizing the independence of the Delegate, who cannot check back for advice from the State Legislatures.

The Electoral Votes assigned to a State Delegation during the Proceedings shall be according to the number of Members of the House of Representatives from that State plus one on all questions except votes for expulsion. Delegates attending proceedings, representing one-half plus one of the Electoral Votes, constitute a Quorum for the Convention.

Unlike the 1787 Convention, under the Anti-Elitist Constitution, each State does not have equal voting strength in a Convention. The Federal Districts and Territories do not send Convention Delegates, but their voters will vote on its ratification.

The sponsors of the Resolution for the Constitutional Convention shall have the responsibility and privilege of sponsoring the venue for the Convention, submitting the first draft of a document, an agenda, and Rules for the Conduct of the Proceedings, and selecting the permanent President and Secretary as the first discussion items for debate by the Delegates.

This is the reward for the resolution initiators. They likely have the most enthusiasm, so they should have priority in setting the agenda and discussion items.

The Document supported by six-elevenths of all the Electoral Votes of the Constitutional Convention shall be submitted for Ratification by Plebiscite in accordance with Section 5 at the first Federal Election no sooner than one-hundred eighty days after approval by the Convention.

Section 4. Amendment for Bill of Individual Rights

Excepting Section 1 of Article 19, a six-elevenths vote by Congress sends the Proposed Amendment to Article 19 of the Bill of Individual Rights to the Supreme Court for Judicial Review to rule if the Amendment qualifies as an Article 19 amendment. If a two-thirds majority agrees that it does, the Elections Board submits the Amendment to

Article 19 for Ratification by Plebiscite by Section 5 at the first Federal Election no sooner than twelve months after the approval by Congress.

If the Plebiscite ratifies it, then the Amendment shall remain in force for six years from the date of ratification. The second Plebiscite will occur at the third Federal Election following the first Plebiscite. The Amendment shall expire on the date of the third Federal Election after the initial ratification unless it is ratified by Plebiscite a second time by Section 5. After the second ratification vote, the Amendment shall remain in force.

The 1787 Constitution's amendment ratification process is too onerous. The Anti-Elitist Constitution recognizes that changes in the structure of the government should face a more significant hurdle than modifications and additions to Individual Rights.

Past battles for Civil Rights often led to the Supreme Court inventing rights on the fly or Congress passing laws that violated the letter of the Constitution. Lowering the threshold for ratification makes it more likely that the courts and legislatures won't flout the text of the Constitution so readily.

Article 19, Section 1 is not an individual right but a definition of the scope of the rights protected by the Federal Government and those reserved to the States. Therefore, it requires a 2/3 vote threshold for amending the Constitution's structural elements.

Section 5. Plebiscites for Constitutional Amendments

The Final Voting date for the Plebiscites in Sections 1, 2, 3, and 4 of this Article and Article 22 shall be held on the date of a Federal Election under the auspices of the Election Board.

Excepting the Candidates for Federal Office, in the case of a Plebiscite under Section 1, 2, or 4, the ballot may only contain the Question: *Shall the Constitution of the United States be amended by the following provision {text of Proposed Amendment}?*

Excepting the Candidates for Federal Office, in the case of a Plebiscite under Section 3, the ballot may only contain the Question: *Shall this Document {text of Proposed Constitution} be approved as the New Constitution of the United States?*

The choices are *Yes* or *No*. All eligible voters will receive a copy of the proposed changes without charge.

Eligible Voter votes are converted to Electoral Votes according to the following formula:

The choice receiving a plurality of the votes in a district for a Member of the House shall be one Electoral Vote.

The choice receiving a plurality of the votes in the entire state shall receive one electoral vote.

The choice receiving a plurality of the combined votes in the Federal House District shall receive one Electoral Vote.

The Document or Amendment is Ratified if nine-seventeenth Electoral Votes are *Yes*.

> Requiring every amendment to the Constitution to win a Plebiscite with a 53% super-majority vote enshrines the notion that the power for enumerating Rights and governing those who govern the Citizenry resides with the Citizens, not their government. The Government serves as a filtering mechanism for bringing an issue to the voters for the final decision. Requiring a Plebiscite is necessary for stamping out the doctrine of Substantive Due Process. The Plebiscite elevates Citizens as the ultimate authority, deciding which rights are memorialized in the Federal Constitution. This kind of direct democracy was utilized with the Ratification of the Constitution by the States in 1787. The Anti-Elitist Constitution continues that tradition.
>
> Ratification does not rely on the popular vote. Instead, Section 5 converts popular votes into electoral votes to ensure a widespread consensus prevails for ratification.

Section 6. Restrictions For Amendments

The following parts of this Constitution can only be amended through a Constitutional Convention by Section 3 of this Article:

- Article 1
- Article 16, Section 16
- Article 18, Sections 3 and 6
- Article 19, Section 1
- Article 23

Article 19.

The Bill of Individual Rights

Section 1. Scope of Rights Protected by Federal and State Governments

All rights enumerated in this Article shall apply to the States, Territories, Federal Districts, Indigenous Sovereign Nations, and Federal Government. Individual Rights protected under this Article are reserved for restraints against the exercise of force by the Government and other persons against these enumerated rights.

Guarantees for Individual Benefits are reserved exclusively for the States.

Individual Benefit Guarantees impose a Constitutional requirement that the Government make pecuniary and non-pecuniary transfers to persons or groups to supplement their income and provide food, medical services, housing, education, and other goods and services. However, Individual Benefit Guarantees are not Rights under this Constitution.

> Making welfare benefits a right hamstrings the fiscal decision-making of a future Congress. It is better to let the States compete in offering programs to attract residents and let them experiment with tying down their Legislatures with Constitutional constraints.

The power to enumerate Civil Rights in this Constitution and State Constitutions resides with the Citizens. The rights enumerated in State Constitutions may differ between the States as determined by Citizens in their respective States. This Constitution and State Constitutions do not protect all claims for Civil Rights by individuals. The Eligible Voters can prioritize and enumerate the rights meriting protection in their Constitutions.

This Section revises the original 9th and 10th amendments. It acknowledges that just because a right isn't enumerated doesn't mean it doesn't exist. However, it also says that not all rights necessarily rise to the level of a Constitutional right worthy of court protection. This paragraph erases the substantive due process doctrine that allowed courts to discover unwritten rights.

The Federal Enforcement of a Civil Right to Protect All Citizens or Persons of the United States requires an amendment enumerating this Right within this Article to enforce a uniform National Right. Neither the Judiciary, the Executive, nor the Legislature of the States or Federal Government shall arrogate this power from the Eligible Voters.

This paragraph ends the doctrine of substantive due process, used to legislate new rights from the bench. It recognizes a whole list of unenumerated common law civil rights, but it leaves those under the control of the Citizens through their State Constitutions and Legislatures. Only amendments to Article 19 can enumerate something as a Federally protected right. The Anti-Elitist Constitution lowered the barrier to amend Article 19, making it easier to add widely practiced and accepted rights. Without the pretext of enumerated powers in the 1787 Constitution, we can dispense with the 9th and 10th Amendments in this Anti-Elitist Constitution. The Citizens shall ratify any unenumerated rights yet to be discovered, not the Courts.

Any amendment to this Article can only take effect with the inclusion of language explicitly repealing any portions of the existing Sections that conflict with the Amendment. The repeal of existing language shall be separate from the adopted Amendment. The Speaker of the House shall submit the proposed language to the Supreme Court for review. If six Permanent members of the Supreme Court do not object, then the Amendment may be submitted to the State Legislatures by Article 18, Section 4.

Section 2. Freedom of Religion

The Government shall make no law or adopt policies endorsing or discriminating against a Religion or Religious Organization or prohibit the free exercise thereof, including the repudiation of a Religion. The Government shall not discriminate in the eligibility to hold office and employment with the Government based upon the profession of belief in a Religion or affiliation with a Religious Organization. Elected Officials are free to express their convictions during the exercise of their duties. However, no Government resources may be used to proselytize religious doctrines or to compel participation in a religious ceremony.

> This Section prevents the Government from favoring and supporting religion or discriminating against religion and protects critics of religion, including atheists. There is further recognition that Congress may open its sessions with a sectarian prayer if it wishes, but it cannot use government resources to proselytize. Religion is an area where it is difficult to get precise language to cover all circumstances. Inevitably, many evolving Supreme Court doctrines will decide close cases.

The Government shall not discriminate in the provision of financial assistance and use of its property based upon the profession of belief in a Religion, affiliation with a Religious Organization, or restrictions on membership within the Religious Organization. A person who accepts an elected office, employment with, or contracting services with the Government is not entitled to accommodations or conduct in conflict with the equal application of rules regulating persons not affiliated with their Religious Organization that are necessary and proper for the consistent and uniform provision of public services.

> This paragraph revises the *Lemon v. Kurtzman* [20] case regarding the tripartite test to determine violations of the Establishment Clause. This section ensures that religions don't receive special treatment and that the Government cannot discriminate against a religion due to the doctrines and membership of their organization. The Government could not refuse to rent out Government property to a Group that doesn't permit homosexuals as members any more than the Government could rent out a facility to another group that excludes non-members who fail to pay dues from attending an event. The Government cannot be an arbiter of acceptable doctrines as a condition for using its property.

This paragraph ensures that a Muslim employed by the Government cannot demand breaks during the day to pray to Mecca or that government meetings conform to a religious calendar. However, the Government cannot prevent a Jew from wearing a kippa unless it obstructs service delivery. The Government could prevent an employee from wearing a niqab that covers her face because that undermines the uniform dress code for identifying a public employee, and covering the face prevents identification and accountability by the public when a civil servant does improper actions. This area of Constitutional law will continue to be litigated at the margins.

Unless a high school prohibits all unreserved displays on a football field, a coach can pray on the 50-yard line with his players. The school cannot discriminate against its employees' leading prayers but allows an employee to endorse a political candidate using a bullhorn on the 50-yard line. The Government must be neutral.

Religion refers to a specific body of beliefs about the behaviors of persons that are prescribed and proscribed and the reasons for holding these beliefs. Adherents of these beliefs may form *Religious Organizations* to transmit these beliefs and behaviors among their children and other adherents in communal rituals. They may also proselytize non-members by Section 3 of this Article.

This paragraph defines religion to be something more than a belief in God. A belief in a God is not required to qualify as a religion. Therefore, *In God We Trust* on coins is not discrimination in favor of religion vis a vis atheism because asserting the existence of God is a metaphysical, not a religious belief. A government-sponsored crucifix would be an endorsement of Christianity. However, hanging art in a government museum with pictures of Christian religious themes should not be considered discrimination in favor of a religion.

Section 3. Freedom of Expression Without Suppression

Citizens have the right to speak, write, publish, and disseminate information and ideas. The right to communicate information and ideas that others oppose and try to suppress is fundamental to this freedom. Any prior restraint by the Government upon the publication of information is subject to a prompt hearing by a Court on the grounds of imminent endangerment of the lives or property of Citizens, residents, and Government agents. The Government may only abridge these rights when the speaker advocates the use of physical violence or when the speaker discloses private information to aid and abet those intending to cause bodily injury, death, and destruction of property. Mental anguish and emotional distress are not grounds for abridging these rights.

The Government may regulate and prohibit the distribution and production of the audio, visual, and written depiction of sex acts, nudity, bodily trauma, and mutilation of persons or animals to persons under eighteen years. The Government may regulate the time and place of the dramatic commercial production and distribution of this content to persons over eighteen years.

> These paragraphs permit government regulation of any offensive material to persons under eighteen. These limitations regulate for-profit pornography to persons over eighteen. It would not prohibit documentaries or news containing offensive matters to persons over eighteen. The government could institute Zoning Laws, but it would not prohibit this pornography.

Excepting conditions of Section 21, the Government shall make no law that compels the speaker, writer, or publisher to offer the use of their property to other persons as a condition for the use of a communications medium regulated and licensed by the Government.

> This paragraph recognizes that freedom of the press in the internet age, when bloggers report the news, means something different than in 1787. It broadens free expression protections but recognizes situations where prior restraint upon publication may be justified. It prohibits the adoption of a *Fairness Doctrine*.

The speaker or publisher must pay reasonable attorney fees to an Elected Official for a judgment of slander or libel. The Elected Official may only collect monetary damages from a non-government person if the speaker or publisher contested the lawsuit and did not offer an acceptable apology and retraction or provide an opportunity for rebuttal to the audience for the offending act. Elected Officials may not use public funds to pay for these legal expenses.

> This paragraph weakens the New York Times v Sullivan [22] decision, making it extremely difficult for politicians to sue the media for libel and slander. It proposes a non-financial remedy if the publisher offers a forum for rebuttal to its libelous claims. It is not a new version of the Fairness Doctrine. Equal time is only required with a conviction for slander or libel.

The Government may not impose any financial burden or restraint upon Citizens exercising their freedom of expression because of threats of violence or property damage against the speaker or host.

> This paragraph responds to the scourge of ANTIFA campus activists who disrupt speakers with violence and mayhem. It prohibits government colleges from imposing exorbitant security costs upon hosts to suppress the airing of unpopular views on campus.

The right of a Citizen to write, speak, and disseminate information to an audience that was lawfully assembled and hosted by that Citizen in a physical or virtual space under their control has value only if the Government and persons do not obstruct or sabotage the ability of this audience to view, read and listen to the writer and speaker. Persons guilty of issuing or carrying out these threats of violence, property damage, sabotage, or disruption shall be guilty of a felony and liable for damages suffered by Citizens exercising their freedom of expression.

> This paragraph covers the disruption of meetings by persons who trigger fire alarms or other pranks to force an assembly to disperse. It covers people who engage in disruptive chants that drown out the speaker. It covers people who gather up student newspapers and throw them into the trash. It addresses any attempts to silence speech by forceful intervention. It excludes claims that anyone can speak out of turn to an audience if they didn't pay to assemble the audience in a venue under their control. Speaking in a public park is not protected. It covers online hacking of websites, implanting viruses, and other sabotage.

Section 4. Freedom of Association

The Government shall make no law abridging the Citizens' right of free association to admit and exclude any person from membership in organizations not engaged in commerce.

> This Section permits religious organizations, political parties, and other non-profit endeavors the greatest freedom to decide who can join their groups.

Section 5. Right to Privacy

The Government shall make no law abridging the right of consenting Citizens who have attained the age of eighteen to engage in non-commercial and non-lethal activities involving any sexual acts, rituals, games, meetings, performances, consumption of food, drink, herbs, plants, or chemical compounds of their choosing within the privacy of their homes. The Government may not prohibit persons from administering tests to other persons to detect proscribed substances to exclude users from an association or commercial enterprise.

> This Section guarantees the right to privacy in matters we expect while still leaving the Government free to outlaw prostitution and casinos by limiting these privacy protections to non-commercial activities occurring in the home. It allows for private enforcement of illicit drug use rather than reliance upon Government law enforcement.

Section 6. Protection from Government Surveillance and Intrusion

The Government shall not violate the right of persons to be secure in their bodies, private residences, papers, and effects against unreasonable searches and seizures. No warrants shall be issued but upon probable cause supported by Oath or affirmation, particularly describing the place to be searched and the persons or things to be seized. Unreasonable searches include physical entry and technical means of recording activities or retrieving information, including information about a person's location and travels, that have a reasonable expectation of privacy, whether acquired from other parties or by persons controlled by the Government.

> This paragraph covers infrared surveillance to determine if persons are inside a building, measuring sound vibrations on windows to track conversations and other methods that don't require physical entry into a building. It also covers the Government's purchase of mobile phone location tracking data to determine whether someone was at a crime scene. The Government must obtain warrants for these situations.

The Government may monitor communications over the electromagnetic spectrum without a warrant to uncover unlawful conspiracies by non-citizens, but no evidence gathered by this method without a warrant may be used as evidence in a prosecution against a Citizen.

> This paragraph covers the National Security Agency's data-gathering programs exposed by Edward Snowden. Allowing this program to continue if the evidence collected cannot be used against a Citizen is a compromise.

The Government may screen passengers and their belongings on common carriers and private vehicles traveling on public thoroughfares. The Government has the burden of proof for utilizing profiles of race or ethnic origin or other physical characteristics to engage in the non-random selection of persons for screening.

> This paragraph covers highway checkpoints where the police inspect cars, trucks, and buses. It also covers screenings at airports. If everyone is screened or randomly screened, then there are no issues. Otherwise, law enforcement must have a valid justification for profiling.

The Government may obtain recorded surveillance of public spaces by private persons by issuing warrants as evidence to prosecute specific crimes. Metered inflows and outflows of energy, water, and effluent into a residence or business may be used as evidence to establish probable cause to secure a warrant.

The widespread use of video recording at homes and businesses provides law enforcement with evidence for solving crimes. There are limitations on property rights when a private person conducts surveillance of public spaces. This paragraph clarifies the government's power to obtain private information. The second sentence covers situations where covert marijuana growing is inferred when unusual water and energy usage occurs. Also, the chemical composition of sewage discharge from a residence can be presented to a judge to obtain a warrant.

Upon issue of a warrant, the Government may gather unique identifying information from a person's body. If the Government legally collects biological information, it may conduct a search to compare evidence from a crime to this biological information to identify suspects.

Section 7. Right of Assembly, Solicitation, and Political Action

Government shall make no law abridging the right of Citizens peaceably to assemble, communicate, cooperate, or plan to petition the Government to redress grievances or to support or oppose candidates for office. The Government shall make no law infringing upon the non-commercial solicitation of a person for political action in public spaces or at their residence, except when a person has affirmatively communicated their preference for non-solicitation.

Section 8. Double Jeopardy

No person shall be subject to the same offence, to be twice put in jeopardy of life or limb. If a person can be tried for an offence to a Federal statute and a State statute pertaining to the same criminal act, then the Federal Court shall assign the jurisdiction for the alleged offense to either the State or the Federal court for a single trial.

This Section guards against prosecutors who use the laws of the State and Federal governments covering the same crime to pursue a defendant twice for the same act.

Section 9. Compensation for Government Taking of Private Property

The Government shall not take private property by easement or expropriation for a public purpose without just compensation. The Government shall pay compensation when law enforcement activities damage the private property of innocent persons.

If the Government forces the property sale to recover delinquent taxes, a judgment, and reasonable liquidation costs, the Government shall return any remaining proceeds to the owner. Private property shall include land, buildings, commercial goods, intellectual property, loans receivable, financial securities, and chattel.

A proper public purpose for the taking, easement, or compelled lease of land and buildings includes transportation, water, sewage, transmission lines for power and communications, flood control, recreation, parklands, and Government operations. The appraisal of just compensation shall be conducted by a disinterested third party selected by the Court and paid by the Government.

If the Government takes private property for the benefit of a non-government person to develop a project, then the public purpose shall be an increase in the amount of tax collections. The tax collections must exceed double the compensation for the taking during the first twenty years from the date of the taking. The valuation date shall be before any disclosure of the intent for the taking and based upon the use of the property before this disclosure.

During these twenty years, the Government shall, in addition to the original compensation for the taking, make annual payments to the original and subsequent property owners the larger of two sums: one-twentieth of the incremental amount of yearly tax collections or one-half of the original amount paid for the taking, adjusted for percentage increases in the Compensation Index.

This Section addresses the problems in the *Kelo v. City of New London* [23] case decided by the Supreme Court in 2005. For urban renewal purposes, the Government might condemn land of low value so that a developer can come in to increase the value of the land or generate jobs with income tax revenues. This clause ensures that the threshold of the improvements must be high, and the current property owners will make a nice profit. This Section prevents the Government from offering excessive tax breaks to entice a developer to build the project because the rationale for creating it is to increase Tax collections — a public purpose. Other situations arise when a lot is situated to block the assembly of adjacent lots to develop the parcels in a value-maximizing manner.

Section 10. Indictments and Protection Against Self-Incrimination

No natural person shall be held to answer for a capital, or otherwise infamous crime, unless on a presentment or indictment by a Grand Jury, except in cases arising in the armed forces, or in the Militia, when in actual service in time of War or public danger or an Administrative Law Court; nor shall be compelled in any criminal case to be a witness against themselves.

Language from the 1787 Constitution with a few modern additions.

Upon arrest, the police must advise the suspect of their right to remain silent and consult with legal defense counsel, who could receive compensation from the Government for no less than one-sixth of the estimated marginal expense of the Government's prosecution of the case. This protection shall extend to cases in Administrative Law Courts.

The Government shall punish law enforcement officials for violations of this right. However, the Court may admit any evidence obtained provided that the punishment is a material deterrent against violations of this right.

This Section incorporates language from the 1787 Constitution, Miranda protection, and Administrative Law exceptions. It weakens the exclusionary rule when law enforcement officials have meaningful penalties to deter this behavior.

Section 11. Speedy Trial By Jury and the Rights of Jurors

Excepting espionage by non-citizens, in all criminal prosecutions, the accused shall enjoy the right to a speedy and public trial. Excepting prosecution for espionage by non-citizens, in all trials, the accused shall enjoy the right to an impartial jury of the State and Territory wherein the crime shall have been committed, which district shall have been previously ascertained by law, and to be informed of the nature and cause of the accusation; to be confronted with the witnesses against them; to have compulsory process for obtaining witnesses in their favor, and to have the Assistance of Counsel for their defense. Non-public trials for espionage of a Citizen shall be adjudicated by a panel of no fewer than five Federal Judges if a jury or public trial would endanger national security.

> The Government does not prosecute many spies because the accused have the right to a public trial, and they would reveal sources and methods of espionage during the trial. Carving out this exception empowers the Government to prosecute spies while providing the accused with the right to be heard by a panel of 5 judges.

Residents of the District of Columbia and any newly formed Federal District who are Government employees or vendors of the Federal Government are ineligible to serve on Juries for Federal criminal or civil cases in the District. Adjoining States may include residents of the Federal Districts in their jury pools for State crimes.

> Excluding Government employees of Federal Districts and their vendors from serving on Juries for Federal cases ensures that there is no bias in the jury pool.

Jurors must be Citizens who have attained thirty years and not more than eighty years. Their convenience shall supersede those of the Judges, Staff of the Judicial Branch, plaintiffs, and defendants. To encourage the formation of the most representative jury pools, trials by Jury shall be scheduled at times that impose the least disruption to the ability of Jurors to earn compensation and to care for their dependents, or the Government shall provide sufficient compensation and support services to offset these disruptions. The Government may not compel any employer to pay compensation to its employees serving as Jurors. Government employees may not be paid more than one-half of their normal compensation if they take a leave of absence during jury service. Except for a voluntary waiver by a juror, sixty months must elapse from the time of a citizen's prior jury service before the Government may compel jury service for that citizen.

> The paragraph enhances the right to Trial by Jury by limiting the Judiciary's exploitation of Jurors. This paragraph puts the onus upon the Government to schedule trials in the evenings and weekends, provide childcare services, and make meaningful jury payments. If the Government must provide compensation, the Judiciary will run trials with fewer breaks and complete these trials faster than current practices. Government employees won't get full pay if they don't show up to work to serve on a jury. This paragraph prevents stacking juries with Government employees. It incentivizes the Government to accommodate its employees' work schedules when setting trial dates.

Section 12. Right of Trial By Jury

In Suits at common law, where the value in controversy shall exceed one-twentieth of the Compensation Index, the right of trial by jury shall be preserved, and no fact tried by a jury, shall be otherwise re-examined in any Court, other than according to the rules of the Common Law. Suits in Administrative Courts shall preserve the right of trial by jury according to Article 10.

Section 13. Bail, Punishment, and Asset Forfeiture

The Government shall not require excessive bail, impose excessive fines, inflict severe pain, mutilation, sleep deprivation, or solitary confinement for more than thirty days within ninety consecutive days while a suspect or prisoner is in the custody of the Government.

> Solitary confinement has been abused against prisoners and caused actual psychological harm. This Section adds sleep deprivation to the list of cruel and unusual punishments.

Except for contraband defined under a Federal or State statute, any property alleged to be used to facilitate the commission of a crime, where there is a legal interest in the property, can be forfeited to the prosecuting jurisdiction before a conviction. After a hearing with due process before a judge in a criminal court, the judge may order the transfer of the seized property to an impartial custodian appointed by the Federal Judiciary for a maximum of three-hundred sixty-five days. After a conviction, the custodian shall deliver proceeds from the sales of these assets to the Government with jurisdiction over the case to retire any outstanding Government Debt. The Government deposits the remaining proceeds into its General Fund. The Government is responsible for paying the custodian for the proper storage of seized, tangible property, and it must compensate the defendants with a legal interest in the property for any damage to the property if they are acquitted.

A penalty of death by hanging from the neck is a permitted form of punishment, but the Government can offer the condemned alternative methods of execution. Excepting a Court Martial, a penalty of death may not be executed before the fifth anniversary of the verdict.

This Section drops the term *cruel and unusual punishment*. Judges have used the term to outlaw the death penalty and to prevent local authorities from removing homeless people from public spaces. Instead, this Section offers a precise list of torture methods employed against suspects and prisoners. It prevents abuse of Asset Forfeiture by law enforcement agencies that get the proceeds of the sale of the seized property.

Death by hanging is defined as an allowable form of punishment to encourage using lethal injection or other more humane methods of execution. This Section mandates a five-year waiting period before executing a prisoner to give the condemned an opportunity to introduce new evidence to reverse a wrongful conviction.

Section 14. Slavery and Prison Labor

Excepting compulsory military service and Jury Duty, neither slavery nor involuntary servitude, except as a punishment for crime whereof the party shall have been duly convicted, shall exist within the United States or any place subject to their jurisdiction.

No person convicted of a crime may be required to provide labor for any tasks as a condition for fulfillment of or shortening the length of their sentence. The Government may only shorten the sentence when the convict earns income during their imprisonment and voluntarily offers to pay damages directly to their crime victims.

> This Section uses language from the 13th Amendment, Section 1, plus a prohibition against labor camps used by the Soviet Union. The accounts of prisoner abuse in the Gulags motivated this protection. Allowing prisoners to earn money to pay restitution to victims of their crimes is an exception.

Section 15. Due Process and Equal Protection

No Government shall collect fines or temporarily or permanently confiscate all or part of the property of any person without due process of law. No Government shall execute, imprison, or detain a natural person without due process of law. The Government may not deny the equal protection of the laws to any person within its jurisdiction.

> Instead of using *nor be deprived of life, liberty, or property*, this Section substitutes more precise wording. Recent expansive definitions of life, liberty, and property have created many unenumerated rights subject to substantive due process. This Section distinguishes between a natural person's rights and a legal person's rights.

Section 16. Discrimination and Preferences by Government

Citizens of the United States shall not be denied nor given preferences for services or employment offered by the Government based on race, color, national or ethnic origin, sex, religion, sexual orientation, or Political Party affiliation. Any person receiving payment for services or assistance from the Government must comply with this Section. If evaluations of the qualifications for employment or contracting of services do not disclose the identity characteristics of an applicant, then that creates Safe Harbor protection against any discrimination claims.

The Government may require Birthright Citizenship and prohibitions against affiliation with foreign organizations for positions in or in support of the Armed Forces, Espionage, and Security Services. Employees of the President subject to Section 8 of Article 5 are exempt from the protections of this Section. Exceptions may be considered in cases of adoption when it is in the best interests of the minor children.

> This Section prohibits Affirmative Action programs. If the Government utilizes anonymous evaluation of test scores for job applicants, then the Safe Harbor clause protects against disparate impact claims for discrimination. If the Government follows the Safe Harbor guidelines, disparate impact by race no longer justifies a presumption of prejudice. This Section makes exceptions for racial discrimination for adoption of children. This Section adds political Party affiliation to the list of proscribed categories.

Section 17. Discrimination and Preferences in Commerce

The Government and Non-Government persons engaged in commerce may not deny, abridge, or show preferences in the commerce of goods, services, or employment to Citizens of the United States on account of race, color, sex, national or ethnic origin, religion, sexual orientation, or Political Party affiliation. Religious Organizations, Political Parties, and non-commercial associations are exempt from these requirements if they are not engaged in commercial activities. If evaluations of the qualifications for employment or contracting of services do not disclose identity characteristics of an applicant, that creates Safe Harbor protection against any discrimination claims.

Section 18. Habeas Corpus

The privilege of the Writ of Habeas Corpus shall not be suspended, unless when in cases of rebellion or invasion Congress determines the public safety may require it.

> Language from the 1787 Constitution.

Section 19. Parental Authority to Direct Education

Parents or Guardians of children under seventeen are guaranteed the right to direct their children's education. This right does not confer any authority upon the Parents or Guardians to direct the operations of a Government or non-government school or instructor.

> This Section incorporates the rights established by the 1925 Supreme Court decision *Pierce v. Society of Sisters* [24]. Directing Education is not an absolute right to do what a parent pleases. However, it establishes their ranking above the Government so they can choose what is in the child's best interests. It does not give the parents the right to demand that the Government provide whatever they want.

The Government may not regulate the manner of instruction by Parents, Guardians, or educators, nor require licensing or other qualifications unless they are employees of a Government School or private persons contracting with the Government. The Government may require instructors to disclose their educational credentials and civil or criminal convictions. Any sanctions against substandard education must be based solely upon the academic achievement of the child measured on the same examinations administered to students in Government Schools of similar age.

> This paragraph thwarts the Government's use of regulations, licensing, credentials, degrees, or other means to throttle a free market in education. It protects homeschoolers and others from regulatory harassment while making them accountable to the State for providing evidence of learning.

Any examinations commissioned by the Government must be administered to all children between the ages of six and seventeen, and the content of the examinations and sanctions for substandard performance cannot discriminate based upon the education provider selected by their parents.

> Public School students will be subjected to the same exams as those who don't attend public schools.

The examinations' content is confined solely to determining the child's proficiency in reading, writing, mathematics, geography, physics, chemistry, and biology and knowledge of the history and civic institutions of their State and the United States relative to children of similar age.

> These academic subjects comprise the necessary basics for productive civic participation. Ideological indoctrination will inevitably creep into the History test, but it is less harmful than sitting through an academic year of indoctrination in the classroom.

Except for the child's age, no personal information of the child who took the test is disclosed to the persons grading the examinations. These results are strictly confidential and can only be disclosed to the Parent or Guardian and the Government authority enforcing any sanctions against deficient performance, with the Parent or Guardian's consent.

> The teachers won't have access to these results without parental consent. Anonymous grading of the tests ensures that the Government cannot bias the grading. This paragraph does not grant permission for the Federal Government to receive the individual test results.

The Government must apply any sanctions for deficient performance on the examinations uniformly to all persons directing the instruction of any child without regard to their education provider or employer. No Government may discriminate in its offer of services, benefits, or employment to any person on account of their education providers.

> This equal treatment clause makes it tricky for the Government to punish students who do not attend public schools. How could the State punish parents and teachers of public school students? The reality is that today, the Public Schools do not enforce performance requirements on their employees with any significant consequences like terminations or pay cuts. The Government cannot give preference for admissions to State Universities based on attendance in public schools to discriminate against students who did not attend public schools.

Compulsory instruction requirements cease upon attaining seventeen years of age, and children who have attained this age may direct their education.

Section 20. Occupational Licensing Protections

The Government shall have the burden of proving that occupational licensing requirements enacted are the least onerous method of protecting persons from physical injury and financial losses due to fraud or incompetence. Only the Government may approve, suspend, or deny a license. The Government may solicit advice from an Association of Practitioners, but the Government cannot require payments to or membership in this Association of Practitioners to issue a license.

> The Government has the burden of justifying its licensing. This paragraph outlaws requirements solely intended to restrain entry into the market and preserve a monopoly position. The Government cannot delegate power to private sector interests. The Government may charge license fees and then use that revenue to pay the Bar Association or Medical Association consulting costs to evaluate a practitioner's fitness. However, a government official will always be responsible for sanctions against a practitioner.

Age, Citizenship, residency, examination fees, and absence of prior criminal or civil convictions are the only requirements for taking these examinations. Except for an inactive status license, license fees cannot be contingent upon the licensee's income.

> This paragraph opens licenses to persons who haven't attained a college degree. The Government can only assess attributes required to perform the tasks of the profession.

No State may restrict interstate commerce and obstruct the solicitation, purchase, and receipt of goods and services by their Citizens from vendors who are not domiciled or licensed in the State. However, a State may require that a state-licensed attorney represent clients in that State's Courtrooms.

> This paragraph opens competition for insurance that currently is only sold and marketed to a state's residents by persons licensed in that State. While attorneys are required to pass the State's Bar to represent a client in Court Proceedings, a State cannot

exclude persons who did not pass the State's Bar from rendering legal advice for payment if they are not representing that client in a Court proceeding and for example, preparing a Living Trust, giving advice on Family Law, and preparing a contract. This paragraph would end the scam,[25] preventing eyeglasses sale without a prescription.

Professional licensing in complex and dangerous practices where practitioners could cause serious bodily harm or severe property damage exceeding one-fourth of the Compensation Index per incident can be subject to the requirement of an apprenticeship and an evaluation of expertise by practitioners in the field, but in no case shall these requirements be arbitrary or unrelated to the prevention of injury or have the effect of restricting competition by competent practitioners.

Every test for a professional license cannot be evaluated solely by a written examination. Pilots and physicians require training and apprenticeships beyond written examinations. However, preventing qualified German physicians from practicing medicine until they undergo residency training in the US is an example of what this Section is trying to stop. Requiring licenses for K-12 teachers is covered in Section 19, where student examinations uncover deficiencies. If a private school or school district wants to develop a test for hiring their staff, that's permissible. However, that's not the same as a license to teach.

If the Federal Government adopts an occupational licensing requirement, then no State may require a person with a Federal-issued License to obtain a State-issued license for a similar occupation.

Federal licenses for physicians would be helpful to avoid the hodgepodge of 50 different State regulators.

Except for interstate commerce between persons residing in different states, the Federal Government may not prevent the practice of an occupation in a State by requiring a federal-issued license. Exceptions require a three-fifths vote of Congress.

Section 21. Information Network Companies, Network Privacy

For this Section, Information is content transmitted over the electromagnetic spectrum that a person receives in visual, audio, or other sensory forms. An Information Network is a media system that utilizes the electromagnetic spectrum to connect nodes that transmit and receive information.

> This definition includes landlines, cellular phone networks, internet, and satellites.

Although the Government shall not treat an Information Network Company as the publisher or speaker of any information that is created by its Network Producers and not employed by the Information Network Company, the Information Network Company shall assume responsibility for detecting and minimizing violations of laws by its users. A Safe Harbor requirement for an Information Network Company to enjoy this treatment is that they allow any content not prohibited by Federal law and are impartial in their payment of revenue to producers, issuance of warnings, or restrictions of accessibility of producer content hosted on their network. Otherwise, the Government shall treat them as the publishers or speakers of content produced by their network producers.

> The Information Network Companies will be unable to apply politically motivated bias to exclude content while claiming the non-publisher shield.

Regarding the payment of tort claims arising from a judgment of slander, libel, or violations of intellectual property rights against its Network Producers, it shall not be a co-defendant when the Government does not treat the Information Network Company as the speaker or publisher. However, it shall indemnify the plaintiffs for any deficiency in restitution by the defendant.

> This paragraph does not treat Information Network Companies as publishers or speakers, but they still retain some limited liability

> for any abuses by their users. It forces content providers to carry liability insurance to ensure they don't encumber the Info Net Companies with deficient judgments.

Information Network Company users possess an ownership interest in any information they transmit as a condition for using the network. The Information Network Company must obtain consent and pay minimum monthly compensation to any users in exchange for collecting and distributing this private information. The minimum monthly compensation shall be the Compensation Index divided by six thousand.

> This paragraph establishes a user's property rights to their information and compels payment by the company to use this information. It ends Terms of Service Agreements with unrestricted use of browsing history to be sold to advertisers in exchange for free use of the service. Now these companies will essentially be forced to charge a minimum subscription fee to offset the monthly minimum. Linking subscription payments to a credit card or bank account will eliminate the problem of bots and fake accounts. Requiring consent from the users also eliminates the incredible power exercised by Google, Facebook, and others who collect private information without the knowledge of their users.
>
> It eliminates the current legal framework allowing Facebook, Twitter, and YouTube to engage in viewpoint discrimination against unpaid users of their services.

The Federal Government has jurisdiction over claims of violations by an Information Network Company. The prevailing party in any lawsuit may recover reasonable attorney fees and any damages awarded. Congress shall have the power to enforce this Section through appropriate legislation and to block foreign Information Network Companies that do not comply.

> This paragraph modifies Section 230 of the Communications Decency Act of 1996 that applies to interactive computer services. This section uses the term *Information Network Company* to define computer services and telecommunications broadly.

Section 22. Marriage

A Marriage is a voluntary, joint, and several partnership of only two natural persons sanctioned by the laws of the Government. A foreign government may recognize marriages with more than two persons, but the Government recognizes only one spouse under the jurisdiction of the United States.

> Because people married abroad may not conform to all the conditions listed below, we can recognize those marriages if they are limited to only two persons. You can marry your cousin or sibling in another country (not allowed in the US), but the US won't recognize polygamy (allowed in Muslim countries). Someone cannot claim to be married to their first wife one day and then turn around and claim that their second wife is their official wife another day. First, they must prove that the first one died or that they divorced. Someone can live with multiple wives, but the Government will only recognize one as their official wife.

Marriages originating under the jurisdiction of the United States must meet the following conditions for recognition: At the inception of the marriage, the parties must be fully informed, consenting persons, attained sixteen years, and not be consanguineous through parental descent, or as a sibling or first cousin. Neither person may be married to another person.

To ensure that both persons are fully informed, the Government may require the following disclosures for issuing a Marriage License: health, fertility, and paternity information, financial records, and records of prior criminal convictions, marriages, and divorces. Except for marriage license fees, the Government may not require additional restrictions.

> Anyone can have same-sex and opposite-sex partnerships. Sixteen years and older is the only restriction. The State could require an STD test or other background checks to inform the other party, ensuring they decide with complete information. This Section outlaws recognition of marriages between three or more persons. Otherwise, people could abuse the marriage contract to substitute

for a business partnership or corporation subject to additional taxation. The phrase no additional restrictions may be imposed means that gay marriage and interracial marriages are protected.

Section 23. Combatants In War Against The United States

Persons engaged in acts of physical violence, sabotage of transportation, water, power, information storage, and communication systems, or other warfare against the United States who are not affiliated with nations that are signatories to and adherents of Conventions governing the laws of war shall be classified as enemy combatants. Excepting Citizens of the United States, enemy combatants shall be under the jurisdiction of the Military Justice System. No later than six years after imprisonment, an Enemy Combatant has the right to an appeal and review by the Federal Courts, Special Courts, or Tribunals established by law to adjudicate whether the Enemy Combatant shall be given a prison sentence or released.

This Section deals with the prisoners held at Guantanamo Bay during the War on Terror. The Government argued that the Geneva Convention didn't cover them. Because the Government didn't have these prisoners in US Territory under Federal Court jurisdiction, these prisoners fell into a gray area where they could be held indefinitely without recourse. This Section provides some recourse to protect against abuse.

Article 20.

Classification of Federal Officials and Personnel

This Article clarifies the confusion in the current Constitution about who is an officer of the Government. It distinguishes Elected Officials from Principal and Inferior Officers and Employees from Officers to delineate who is eligible for Civil Service protections.

Congress gets to regulate the President's ability to fire and demote military officers because the President could abuse this power to do whatever he wishes with the military. However, the President can clean the slate and fire all Principal and Inferior Officers in Departments. At-Will Staff represent the President's further discretion in placing persons in non-officer positions loyal to the President's agenda. However, At-Will employees won't be eligible for Civil Service protection due to their temporary nature.

This Section does not outlaw strikes by Government employees, but strikers lose Civil Service protection. That is the tradeoff for receiving Civil Service protection. Also, once an employee reveals a partisan affiliation by accepting an appointment as At-Will Staff or an Officer, then they forever forfeit the ability to receive Civil Service protection.

Civil Service Protection is granted on the theory that it protects nonpartisan professionals who serve under different partisan leadership without bias. Once that veil is pierced, however, the employee loses this protection.

Section 1. Persons Compensated For Labor Services

The Federal Government employs persons compensated for Labor Services by the Federal Government, or they are vendors who are not employees of the Federal Government. The positions described in the following sections are those of federal government employees.

States may not tax the portion of income of Federal Government employees paid by the Federal Government.

> The Federal Government and taxpayers will save money because the Government can offer lower gross salaries to its employees for the same net, after-tax compensation. This benefit is in consideration of excluding Federal employees from partisan activities. Nevertheless, Federal employees will pay State income tax on investment earnings and must pay property and wealth taxes.

Section 2. Elected Officials

The President, Vice President, and House of Representatives Members are Elected Federal Government Officials.

Section 3. Officers of the Federal Government

Except for elected officials, an officer of the federal government occupies any executive, judicial, military, or legislative office created by this Constitution or by law. With an appointment by the President, the Vice President may exercise the powers of an executive officer while retaining the privileges of an Elected Official. Excepting Secretaries on a Presidential Slate, the Vice President, and At-Will Staff, the Senate may approve or reject all other officers nominated by the President.

Section 4. Principal and Inferior Officers Appointed by President

The Secretaries of Departments, Judges, Adjudicators, Justices, Chief Justice, Ambassadors, and Board Members appointed by the President are Principal Officers occupying Principal Offices.

Congress may enact laws designating no fewer than five hundred commissioned officers of the military branch whose commission is subject to a denial or approval by the Senate, but not to exceed two thousand commissioned officers. Commissioned Officers subject to Senate review are Principal Officers, and their subordinates are Inferior Officers.

Persons appointed to Principal and Inferior Offices are not eligible for Civil Service protections. Except for Secretaries of Departments, the Government may dismiss all non-military officers without cause. Congress may enact laws governing the President's dismissal or demotion of military officers.

Section 5. Other Principal and Inferior Officers

The Governor General and Ministers are Principal Executive Officers elected by Members of the House of Representatives. They exercise their office's executive powers while retaining the privileges of Elected Officials. The Speaker and Vice Speaker are Principal Officers of the House of Representatives.

Board Members appointed by the Governor General are Principal Officers. The Executive Director appointed by the Board is a Principal Officer. The Sergeant At Arms appointed by the Speaker is an Inferior Officer. Inferior Officers are appointed by the Governor General or by the Ministers to offices created by law.

Persons employed by Members of the House of Representatives are at-will staff ineligible for Civil Service protection.

Section 6. Employees With Civil Service Protection

Except as otherwise provided in this Constitution, Congress may enact Civil Service laws governing the hiring, dismissal, and demotion of grade or diminished compensation of non-military employees of the Federal Government who are not principal or inferior officers. Any employee participating in a coordinated scheme of stoppage, absence, or obstruction of normal work routines shall forfeit Civil Service protection. Any Civil Service employee who accepts an At-Will Staff appointment or appointment to a Principal or Inferior Office shall forfeit all rights to Civil Service protection if they return as an employee of the Government.

Any employee displaced from their position by the appointment of At-Will Staff shall preserve their grade and compensation as an employee within that Department, subordinate to the At-Will Staff.

Article 21.

Transition After Ratification

Section 1. Excepting Articles and Sections enumerated below, this Constitution shall take immediate effect upon Ratification.

Section 2. Articles 5, 6, and 7 shall take effect for the first Federal Election following Ratification.

Section 3. Article 4 shall take effect when the Elections and Census Boards are operational.

Section 4. Excepting Sections 1 and 7 of Article 16, Article 16 shall take full effect no later than six years following Ratification.

Section 5. The Federal Reserve shall dispose of all assets prohibited by Article 13, Section 2 no later than three years following Ratification. Otherwise, all Board Members shall be dismissed from office.

Section 6. The selection of the President according to Article 2, Section 16 by majority vote shall take effect at the first election for President after the Elections and Census Boards are operational.

Section 7. Regarding Social Security and Medicare, enforcing Article 16, Sections 13 and 14 shall take effect no later than eight years following Ratification.

Section 8. The Census and Elections Boards shall obtain all records necessary to establish the Federal Census Database and the Federal Voter Registration List. States must share their information, but the Federal Government shall compensate the States for expenses incurred. State Officials refusing to cooperate will be subject to fines no less than one-tenth of the Compensation Index and imprisonment for no less than thirty days.

Section 9. The Census and Elections Boards shall obtain all records necessary to establish the Federal Census Database and the Federal Voter Registration List from Federal Departments, Ministries, Boards, and Agencies possessing this information. The President is responsible for the enforcement of this Section upon Government personnel.

Section 10. Until the Elections and Census Boards are operational, States must conduct their Federal Elections per Article 2. State Legislatures shall redraw boundaries for Districts of the House of Representatives that remain in effect until the Elections and Census Boards are operational.

Section 11. Ten years after ratification of this Constitution, all laws and regulations of the United States Federal Government in effect before ratification shall be repealed unless re-enacted by Congress after ratification of this Constitution.

Section 12. The Personal Treasury Accounts in Article 16, Section 15 shall be established no later than the first January 1 following the six-year anniversary of the ratification of this Constitution for all natural persons alive on the prior day, December 31, who have contributed Social Security taxes and who have not attained fifty-five years of age. The account balances shall be calculated by the Secretary of the Treasury according to an account holder's prior payroll tax contributions, any interest earnings, and minus any distributions over the life of the account holder. The account balance will be the percentage of the account holder's share of the aggregate amount of Special Obligation Debt calculated for the January 1 start date. Persons aged fifty-five and older on the December 31 implementation date shall continue to be eligible for the life annuity benefit of the existing Social Security program and shall not be eligible for a Personal Treasury Account.

Article 22.

Plebiscites Following Adoption of Constitution

These Plebiscites use the Electoral Vote method of Article 18, Section 5. Instead of requiring a six-eleventh super-majority, they only need a simple majority to adopt the proposed amendments. These issues are so controversial that it makes sense to bypass the legislative filters of Article 18 and go straight to the voters for a final resolution. Electoral Votes are counted instead of popular votes to mitigate against the geographical concentration of partisan control. Counting Electoral Votes by House District, instead of just at large by State, makes approval by a popular minority vote highly unusual.

Section 1. Plebiscites To Enact Laws

With a two-thirds vote of Congress, a Plebiscite to enact a statute may be placed on the Federal Ballot no sooner than one hundred eighty days before the Final Voting Date.

Section 2. Abortion Plebiscite

At the second Federal Election following the Ratification of this Constitution, the Elections Board shall hold a Plebiscite by Article 18, Section 5 on the first Tuesday of November following the first Monday to decide the propositions concerning the rights of a mother and an unborn child. The proposition receiving the most Electoral votes is ratified as an Amendment to Article 19 of this Constitution:

> This issue has infected electoral politics and the judiciary for too long. It is time for the voters to resolve it because the representatives have ducked responsibility.

Proposition 1.

A woman has an unalienable right to control her body and terminate a pregnancy at any time before birth, without hindrance, and at the time of her choosing.

Proposition 2.

A woman who is pregnant may terminate the pregnancy without restrictions any time before the twelfth week after conception. After twelve weeks, the laws of each State shall regulate the grounds for termination of the pregnancy for any woman who has attained fifteen years. If the woman signs a Statement of Involuntary Pregnancy no later than fifteen weeks after conception, the State assumes custody of the child if the mother surrenders custody within one year of birth. The State must pay for any diminished compensation and medical costs incurred to involuntarily continue the pregnancy after the mother surrenders custody of the child. The State pays damages to the mother or her heirs if the mother dies or suffers permanent physical impairment because of the birth of the child. A State is only obligated to provide these remedies for women who were full-time residents of the State for more than nine of the twelve months before the child's birth date.

If a State fails to fully compensate any mother or her heirs within twelve months of surrendering custody of her child, then that State will be liable for treble damages and any attorney fees paid by the victim pursuing their claims for compensation.

> The Pro-Life lobby would want the language *The life of a child begins at the moment of conception, and the intentional termination of that life constitutes murder.*
>
> Others might modify that language to include exceptions for rape, incest, and endangering the life of the mother. However, those exceptions rely upon the mother's or her doctor's testimony, and those are loopholes that are not enforceable.

> The second proposition surrenders the absolutist protection at conception and moves the goalposts to twelve weeks before any restrictions occur. But then financial responsibility for the mother and child is introduced as a condition of regulating her decision about carrying a baby to term. These are fair requirements that most Americans would agree with. This alternative to an unrestricted right to an abortion would make this a very close election.

Section 3. Plebiscite for Right to Self Defense

At the second Federal Election following the Ratification of this Constitution, the Elections Board shall hold a Plebiscite by Article 18, Section 5, on the first Tuesday of November following the first Monday to decide the propositions concerning the right to self-defense. If the Proposition receives a majority of the Electoral votes, then it shall be ratified as an amendment to Article 19 of this Constitution:

Proposition:

Through neglect or lack of capacity, the Government cannot always guarantee the protection of its Citizens' lives and property against attacks by other People.

> Hearkens to the experience of Blacks in the South where whites wanted to suppress their right to own guns. We see police forces in India stand by observing Hindu mobs massacre Muslims. The fact that police may not be available to offer protection when it is needed motivates the right to self-defense. However, if you can't buy bullets or practice on a shooting range, it doesn't do any good to own a gun. This proposition incorporates a cost-benefit analysis so that the States suffer consequences when exercising the power to regulate guns for self-defense beyond federal law.

Therefore, Citizens, without a conviction for a crime causing injury to persons or property, who have attained eighteen years, possess the Right of Self Defense of their bodies and property by using weapons commonly employed for the self-defense of the police officers of their State, Federal District, or Territory. Any law that prohibits ownership or promulgates discriminatory regulation, taxation, license fees, insurance, and other impediments to the acquisition and transportation of these weapons, their supporting equipment, storage, or practice in their safe use shall be an infringement upon this Right of Self Defense.

Any Government that infringes this Right of Self Defense assumes responsibility for payment of all damages for any loss and destruction of property, injuries, ongoing medical care, and death to victims of criminal acts on their property, place of business, or private transportation. This responsibility and liability extend to those who were denied the Right of Self Defense and those in that person's custody or care. The Government has the burden of proving that its laws and regulations do not infringe upon this right of self-defense.

If a Government fails to fully compensate any victim, their insurer, assignee, or heirs within twelve months of the commission of these acts, then that Government will be liable for treble damages and any attorney fees paid by the victim pursuing their compensation claims.

> This proposition doesn't prevent anti-gun regulations. It just inserts a cost-benefit analysis upon any State imposing them. It limits the kinds of weapons allowed. The scope of the need is not to repel an army but rather to defend against criminals. Possessing weapons to equip an independent militia that could threaten the State's police powers is not a protected use of self-defense. Imposing a cost to the State is limited to acts committed in homes or places of business where it is less controversial that the use of a gun should be permitted. The proposition does not protect a right to concealed carry, just Self-Defense in the home or business.
>
> Also, in cases where the Government (e.g., Portland, OR) makes it a criminal offense to kill someone attacking and destroying property, the Government shall be liable for covering the costs of the destruction if it fails to quell the rioters. Essentially, the Government has a cost-benefit analysis to allow rioters to rampage at will.

Article 23.

DEFINITIONS

State Legislature shall mean the most numerous House if the State has more than one Legislative Body. The Legislatures of the States are composed of representatives elected by Eligible Voters of that State. Any provision of a State Constitution or State law in conflict with this definition of the Legislature for purposes of this Constitution shall have no effect. These State Legislatures may not delegate any power to appoint Senators, approve Proposed Amendments, or any other responsibilities this Constitution or Federal Law assigns.

Department is an executive body under the authority of the President.

Secretary is the Executive in the President's *Cabinet* with authority over the Department.

Ministry is an executive body under the authority of the Governor General.

Minister is the Executive under the Governor General with authority over the Ministry

The per-capita basis is the number of Citizens in a State divided by the total Citizen population of all States in the most recent Census accounting multiplied by the Federal Government's total expenditures for a State.

The State shall refer to the Government of a State and include the Legislative, Executive, and Judicial Branches and any political subdivisions of the State that exercise the authority to impose taxes, enact laws and regulations, adjudicate lawsuits, and apply force in its exercise of power.

Safe Harbor is a policy that provides protection against prosecution for a penalty or liability claim.

Government, used without modification, shall refer to the Federal Districts, Federal Territories, Indigenous Sovereign Nations, Federal and State governments, and their political subdivisions collectively.

Congress refers to the House of Representatives and the Senate.

A *Person* can be either a natural person or a legal person. A *Natural Person* is a human being; no animal can be accorded the legal rights of a person. A *Legal Person* is an association of natural persons or other legal persons derived from associations of natural persons. It is formed and authorized to operate according to law, and it is governed by its charter to act as a single person under the law.

Due Process requires that the Government provide the accused with notice of an offense, an opportunity to be heard, and an impartial tribunal.

The *Compensation Index* equals the sum of the pecuniary and non-pecuniary compensation of a Member of the House of Representatives during the previous fiscal year.

The sum of years of tenure for each Court and each Board member determines the denominator used to calculate majority and super-majority percentages. The sum of years of tenure of members voting aye or nay yields the numerator for votes on questions by a Court and a Board. Dividing the numerator by the denominator yields the *Tenure Percentage Vote.*

Under this Constitution and the laws of Governments, the classification by sex of a female or woman and a male or man shall be according to biological criteria related to the chromosomes, gametes, genitalia, and reproductive organs unique to females and to males that can be consistently recognized by inspection or biological testing at the time of birth.

www.ingramcontent.com/pod-product-compliance
Lightning Source LLC
Chambersburg PA
CBHW031537260326
41914CB00032B/1841/J

* 9 7 9 8 9 9 1 2 8 7 6 1 6 *